Transport Justice

Transport Justice develops a new paradigm for transportation planning based on principles of justice. Author Karel Martens starts from the observation that for the last fifty years the focus of transportation planning and policy has been on the performance of the transport system and ways to improve it, without much attention being paid to the persons actually using – or failing to use – that transport system.

There are far-reaching consequences of this approach, with some enjoying the fruits of the improvements in the transport system, while others have experienced a substantial deterioration in their situation. The growing body of academic evidence on the resulting disparities in mobility and accessibility, have been paralleled by increasingly vocal calls for policy changes to address the inequities that have developed over time. Drawing on philosophies of social justice, *Transport Justice* argues that governments have the fundamental duty of providing virtually every person with adequate transportation and thus of mitigating the social disparities that have been created over the past decades.

Critical reading for transport planners and students of transportation planning, this book develops a new approach to transportation planning that takes people as its starting point, and justice as its end.

Karel Martens is Associate Professor at the Faculty of Architecture and Town Planning, Technion – Israel Institute of Technology (Haifa, Israel) and at the Institute for Management Research, Radboud University (Nijmegen, the Netherlands). He also holds the Leona Chanin Career Development Chair at the Technion.

Transport Justice
Designing Fair Transportation Systems

Karel Martens

Routledge
Taylor & Francis Group

NEW YORK AND LONDON

First published 2017
by Routledge
711 Third Avenue, New York, NY 10017

and by Routledge
2 Park Square, Milton Park, Abingdon, Oxon OX14 4RN

Routledge is an imprint of the Taylor & Francis Group, an informa business

Library of Congress Cataloging in Publication Data
Names: Martens, Karel, 1967- author.
Title: Transport justice : designing fair transportation systems / Karel Martens.
Description: New York, NY : Routledge, 2016.
Identifiers: LCCN 2016001298| ISBN 9780415638319 (hardback) | ISBN 9780415638326 (pbk.) | ISBN 9781315746852 (ebook)
Subjects: LCSH: Transportation--Planning--Moral and ethical aspects. | Transportation and state--Moral and ethical aspects. | Social justice. | Equality.
Classification: LCC HE193 .M365 2016 | DDC 174/.9388--dc23
LC record available at http://lccn.loc.gov/2016001298

ISBN: 9780415638319 (hbk)
ISBN: 9780415638326 (pbk)
ISBN: 9781315746852 (ebk)

Typeset in Sabon
by Saxon Graphics Ltd, Derby

For my mother, Joke Martens-Hereijgers, who taught me that fairness can be practiced

For my father, Cees Martens, who nurtured my passion for transport (and buses in particular)

Contents

x *Contents*

Illustrations

Figures

Tables

Boxes

Preface

Amidst a conservative political atmosphere across much of the developed world, justice is back on their agendas, at least those of civil society organizations and the general public. Social movements across the globe are involved in struggles against often brutal forms of social, environmental and spatial injustices, which often directly threaten persons' lives or livelihoods.

Against this background, the injustices in the domain of transportation hardly ever attract attention. They are typically not a matter of life and death and, as a result, are seldom visible to the public eye. Yet the importance of transportation, and the possible impacts of a lack of transportation, can hardly be overestimated. Transportation is a fundamental requirement to participate in the labor market, obtain health care, enjoy education, or meet family and friends. It is a basic prerequisite for a life of meaning and value. Injustices in the domain of transportation should thus not be ignored, even if their impacts do not make it to newspaper headlines.

Moreover, transportation systems are to a large extent the outcome of intentional design. Governments at all levels, in developed and developing countries alike, have a leading role in the design of these systems. The design is typically guided by concerns over economic growth and economic efficiency. Yet, more than any other actor, governments as the representative of all persons in their jurisdictions have the moral obligation to act as guardians of the interests of all persons. Their actions should thus avoid pertinent injustices, while promoting justice where practically feasible. The design of transportation systems cannot be an exception to this rule. Governments fail and an injustice is done whenever the design of transportation systems ignores the plight of persons lacking adequate transport services.

This book presents an alternative approach to the design of transportation systems, an approach that takes principles of justice as its starting point. The resulting proposal may seem radical at first. But it should be recalled that when women's voting rights or basic education were proposed in the nineteenth century, their proponents were also depicted as radicals. Yet more than a century later it is hard to imagine that reasonable people ever opposed these ideas, let alone imagine a world without these basic rights. It has been my ambition with this book to strengthen and support the proponents who call for transportation justice, whether they are radical advocates, hard-working civil servants, visionary politicians, or others. It is my hope that, through their work, transportation justice will be seen as something obvious in the future, even though its shape may be fundamentally different from the one laid down in this book.

I first thought to write this book at least ten years ago, when I was working among a delightful group of young researchers at Tel Aviv University's Environmental Simulation Laboratory, including Erez Hatna, Karin Talmor, Eyal Hurvitz, Amir Porat, and Eitan Maza. It must have been the buzz in this group that inspired me to take up the challenge. A generous research grant from the Volvo Research and Educational Foundations, which I received in the early stages of my research, gave me the confidence that I was embarking on an exciting journey.

Many people have inspired and stimulated me along the way to persist in my endeavors. These include Itzhak Benenson, who has made me see the relevance and value of simulations and agent-based modeling and who has never refrained from questioning my justice perspective. He also deserves praise for continuing the efforts to provide empirical evidence for my claims, through detailed studies of accessibility patterns, most recently in conjunction with Yodan Rofe. Yodan has been a source of inspiration, by showing through personal example that civil servants can change seemingly unshakeable governance practices.

The members of the Environmental Justice Committee of the Transportation Research Board have provided a welcoming home for the past eight years. While my approach has not always been fully in tune with the North American perspective, shaped as it is by justified concerns over race, I have always enjoyed a supportive atmosphere to share and discuss my ideas with the 'EJ' community. I especially want to mention Glenn Robinson, Aaron Golub, David Aimen, Anne Morrison, and Marc Brenman for the great company they offered during my visits to Washington DC. Aaron and Glenn deserve special mention, as we have jointly developed some of the ideas presented in this book.

A warm thank you also goes out to all the members of the EU COST-Action on Transport Equity Analysis. The multiple workshops and short scientific missions have provided fertile opportunities to further develop and test my ideas. Special thanks go out to members of the core group and others with whom I have exchanged thoughts on many occasions: Floridea Di Ciommo, Karen Lucas, Ariane Dupont-Kieffer, Yoram Shiftan, Pierluigi Coppola, Elisabete Arsenio, Bat-hen Nahmias-Biran, and Anestis Papanikolaou.

I also want to express appreciation to my students who have taken up some of the questions on transport and justice and, by doing so, have challenged me and deepened my knowledge of the issue. A special note of gratitude goes to those students whose work has particularly inspired me: Andreas Rooijakkers, Sonam Plomp, Jeroen Bastiaanssen, Sari Wolters, Jurriën Thijssen, and Koen Vonk. Jeroen and Sonam deserve additional praise. As junior researchers, they have not only contributed to the book through the analyses they have conducted of the Utrecht and Amsterdam regions, they have also been a source of sometimes critical inspiration over the past two years. The Amsterdam case study would also not have been possible without Dirk Bussche of Goudappel Coffeng, who was not only generous enough to share data on potential mobility and accessibility in the region, but also showed genuine interest in my endeavors.

Clearly, I could not have written this book without the support of my colleagues at the Department of Geography, Planning and Environment at Radboud University. A special word of thanks for all those who accepted a perhaps somewhat erratic colleague working in the library and behind closed doors on 'his book': Rob van der Heijden, Erwin van der Krabben, Peter Ache, Sander Meijerink, Linda Carton, Ary Samsura, Huub Ploegmakers, Lothar Smith, Roos Pijpers, my PhD students Sara Levy, Jasper Beekmans, Geert Tasseron, and Kasper Kerkman, and many more. I have also warmly welcomed the regular 'nudge' from Barrie Needham to persist in my endeavor. Arnoud Lagendijk deserves special mention, as he was willing to proof-read a draft version of the book. His comments have been especially helpful to set the stage for the argument of the book in the first two chapters. A special word of appreciation also goes to Bart van Leeuwen and Olivier Kramsch, 'brothers in arms' in the struggle for justice, and to Huib Ernste, with whom I had the pleasure of organizing a Von Humboldt lecture series on Spatial Justice. This series gave me the opportunity to discuss my work with distinguished scholars such as Susan Fainstein, Don Mitchell, Robert Cervero, John Urry, Harvey Jacobs, and Michael Merry.

Carolien deserves a special mention, for reasons she will hopefully have forgotten.

But none of this would have been possible without the support, patience and understanding from the home front. Tamy not only continues to introduce me to new and unexpected perspectives on life, she has also been a perceptive and compassionate sparring partner to explore the soundness of some of the arguments in the book. My warm and loving gratitude also go out to my children Jonatan, Nathalie and Noa, who continuously prove that there is more to life than studying and writing. Over the past years, Tamy and the children have courageously endured my passion for transport and justice and have given me the time and space to develop my ideas to bring this book to a good end. I can only hope that I have not neglected my duties as a spouse and a father during this period. There can be no justice in the public domain without laying its foundations in the private sphere.

Karel Martens
Nijmegen/Tel Aviv, August 2015

Part I
Introduction

1 Introduction

Point of departure: Los Angeles

Edward Soja opens his book *Seeking Spatial Justice* with what he calls "a remarkable moment in American urban history" (Soja 2010, p. vii). In October 1996, in a courtroom in downtown Los Angeles, a lawsuit brought against the Los Angeles Metropolitan Transit Authority (MTA) by a coalition of grassroots organizations was resolved in an unprecedented consent decree. It was decided that, for at least the next ten years, the MTA would have to give their highest budget priority to improving the bus system that was (and still is) primarily serving the transit-dependent urban poor. According to the decision, the transit authority was required to purchase new buses accessible to wheelchair users, reduce overcrowding on buses, freeze fare structures, enhance bus security, reduce bus stop crime, and provide special services to facilitate accessibility to jobs, education, and health centers. As Soja states, "if followed to the letter, these requirements would soak up almost the entire operating budget of the MTA, making it impossible to continue its ambitious plans at that time to build an extensive fixed rail network" (Soja 2010, pp. vii-viii).

The direct cause that sparked the lawsuit was a proposal of MTA in early 1994 to raise the bus fare from $1.10 to $1.35, eliminate the monthly passes used by many poor bus riders, and cut service on several bus lines. In response to this proposal, the Labor/Community Strategy Center, a community organization and think-tank addressing concerns at the intersection of ecology, civil rights, and workers' and immigrants' rights, mobilized bus riders to demonstrate at a public hearing. In spite of this protest, the MTA board approved the original proposal in June 1994. The final spark for the lawsuit occurred just seven days later, when the MTA board voted to spend an additional $123 million on the next phase of an extensive rail program that was primarily serving the affluent suburban population of the larger Los Angeles metropolitan area (Grengs 2002).

Following this highly controversial MTA decision, the Labor/ Community Strategy Center formed the Bus Riders Union, which was initially composed of 1,500 dues-paying members, mostly low-income bus riders. The Bus Riders Union built a mass base by conducting recruitment campaigns directly on the buses. In parallel, the movement brought on board a range of other organizations, including Justice for Janitors, the Filipino Workers Center, and the Korean Immigrant Workers Advocates. This broad coalition eventually filed the lawsuit against the MTA on behalf of 350,000 bus riders (Grengs 2002).

In the lawsuit the grassroots coalition drew on various arguments. They argued, first and foremost, that the decision of MTA to give priority to the development of an extensive rail network constituted a racist practice. In a parallel to the famous legal case about racial practices in education (the Brown vs. Board of Education case, dating back to 1954), it was argued that poor ethnic minorities living in urban centers were being denied their rights by the existence of "two separate but unequal systems" in the provision of mass transit, arguably a vital urban service particularly for the poor (Soja 2010, p. viii). While the transportation needs of poor and ethnic minority populations were never entirely ignored by transportation planners, either in Los Angeles or elsewhere, the coalition of grassroots organizations argued powerfully that these needs "were systematically subordinated to the needs and expectations of those living well above the poverty line" (Soja 2010, p. x). Indeed, as the coalition showed, although 94 percent of MTA's customers were bus riders, the MTA was spending 70 percent of its budget on the 6 percent of its ridership that were rail passengers (Grengs 2002).

The coalition also explicitly linked their cause to the environmental justice movement, which emerged in the USA in the 1970s and 1980s and emphasized the role of space in the injustices befalling poor and ethnic minorities due to environmentally polluting facilities and practices. Drawing on the arguments championed by this movement, the coalition argued that the MTA practices constituted a form of discrimination based on place of residence, claiming that where one lived should not have negative repercussions on important aspects of daily life as well as personal health (Soja 2010, p. viii). Furthermore, the coalition revealed the vast disparities in subsidies going to different types of public transport service, showing how each trip by rail, predominantly used by white and affluent travelers, was subsidized at a rate of more than $21, while the figure was a little over $1 per bus trip, used primarily by the urban poor (Soja 2010, pp. xiv–xv; see also Grengs 2002).

The lawsuit was an exceptionally successful case of grassroots activism, not least because the resulting decree was radically progressive in character, as Soja underlines: "Giving such priority to the needs of the inner-city and largely minority working poor was a stunning reversal of the conventional workings of urban government and planning, as service provision almost always favored wealthier residents even in the name of alleviating poverty" (Soja 2010, p. viii). Indeed, in its essence the decree implied the transfer of billions of dollars from a plan that disproportionately

right investments

favored affluent suburbanites to a plan that worked more to the benefit of the poor, ethnic minorities and transit-dependent populations.

Seeking transportation justice

The Los Angeles lawsuit powerfully exposes the inherently political decisions that constitute the very essence of transportation planning and policy. Transportation planning is inevitably political because interventions in the transportation system always affect different persons in different ways. However, in the everyday practices of transportation planning across the world, their political character often disappears into the background (with some notable exceptions, such as Cleveland's experiences with equity planning in the 1970s; see Krumholz 1982). Typically, mostly well-intentioned planners and engineers follow professionally accepted procedures to analyze the state of the transportation system and to develop solutions to alleged problems such as road congestion, air pollution, increasing costs, or poor service levels. The way in which these solutions work out for different persons, and the often systematic way in which they affect different persons, are routinely ignored in the practice of transportation planning. It was only because of the blatant disparities in the Los Angeles case, between the urban poor and the suburban rich and between a neglected bus service and a flagship rail project, that the inevitably political nature of transportation planning could be so clearly exposed.

The Los Angeles case thus powerfully illustrates the inevitable political choices and trade-offs that have to be made in transportation planning and policy. Let me highlight three crucial domains of choice, all intricately related to differences between persons: place of residence, level of income, and abilities and skills.

residence income abilities

The first issue that emerges from the Los Angeles case is the role of place. The grassroots coalitions argued that place of residence should not determine a person's quality of life. Yet transportation systems, by their very nature, are bounded in space. They provide service to some jurisdictions and thus to some persons, while hardly providing benefits to other jurisdictions or other persons. It is by no means clear how transportation planning should take this inevitable spatial dimension into account. Should transportation planning seek to provide the same level of service to all persons, irrespective of their place of residence? In other words, should a largely comparable transportation system be provided over an entire metropolitan area or region? And, if so, does this imply that transportation facilities should be heavily subsidized in peri-urban and rural peripheries, where there are fewer persons to shoulder the costs of transportation facilities? Or is it legitimate to provide higher levels of service in urban centers, while providing less service on the periphery, thereby avoiding the necessity of cross-subsidization between areas? And how should 'service' be defined in a spatially diverse context? Should it be defined in terms of kilometers of road space per inhabitant, in terms of travel speeds on the transportation network, or in any other way? Should all persons be provided with the same range of choice between different transportation services, irrespective of residential location? Is it at all legitimate to expand the transportation choices in some areas while reducing the level of choice in other areas? These questions clearly played a role in Los Angeles, where sparse but highly subsidized, high quality rail services were provided to suburban residents, while basic bus services were delivered to urban residents living in relatively high-concentration areas. What, if anything, could warrant such apparent spatial disparities in financial support and service quality? And, if the Los Angeles disparities are not warranted, what other kinds of differences between areas could be justified?

The second key issue that emerges from the Los Angeles case relates to the pricing of transportation services. Since incomes vary strongly between persons in virtually every society, the pricing of transportation services will affect persons in different ways. Since pricing policies also strongly shape who can and will use what kind of transportation service, and thus who can and cannot access destinations and thus activities, the issue is fundamental to transportation planning. Multiple questions emerge here. Should transportation infrastructures and services be seen as a regular private good to be sold against market prices? In other words, should all travelers pay the full costs of their journeys? Or are there valid reasons to subsidize travel? If so, what makes transportation infrastructures and services different from other services, like restaurants, cinemas or health clubs? And if it is justified to subsidize travel, should all travel receive a subsidy or should subsidies be targeted to particular groups? Which groups would that be? Is it justified to subsidize public transport services, while requiring car users to pay the full price of travel? Can a subsidy on transportation fuel or even car ownership be warranted? If so, under what circumstances? Should transportation budgets be distributed evenly over the population? Clearly, the Los Angeles decree has hardly provided a satisfactory answer to any of these questions. The decree did not challenge the large subsidies for rail travel, while it did accept a small fare increase for the bus services. Moreover, no explicit argument was given justifying the continuation of these disparities. The questions thus remain out in the open.

Finally, while less prominently featuring in the Los Angeles case, persons differ fundamentally in their abilities to use various modes of transportation. For instance, in developed countries over one percent of the population suffers from various forms of visual impairments, which often inhibit persons from driving or cycling independently. Likewise, public transport services are often not accessible to persons using a wheelchair or experiencing particular types of travel-related impairments. But also more subtle exclusionary mechanisms may be at play, as when concerns about traffic safety prevent persons and particularly women from cycling, or when concerns about personal safety inhibit persons, for instance older persons or children, from using particular public transport services at particular times of the day. Clearly, any mode of transportation assumes particular skills and abilities and every transportation mode, even walking, is thus likely to exclude some people while bringing advantage to others. These differences in persons' abilities to use transportation modes turn transportation planning into a profoundly political exercise, as it implies that difficult trade-offs have to be made. Should transportation planning give priority to investment in the most inclusive transportation modes as opposed to transportation modes that exclude a substantial share of the population? Or should transportation planning seek to design and deliver a system that can offer the cheapest service to most people, according to the famous dictum 'the greatest good for the greatest numbers'? If important transportation modes cannot be used by all persons, because of differences in persons' abilities, what kind of differences in service level between various transportation modes are acceptable? What would justify these differences, apart from technical considerations?

These difficult trade-offs are not unique to the Los Angeles case, the USA, or even large cities in the 'developed' world. They are likely to play a key role anywhere in the practice of transportation planning, whether in large cities or small towns, at the local level or at the national scale, in the Global North or the Global South. It is only because transportation planning is typically presented as the technical exercise of providing a well-functioning transportation system to society that these trade-offs often fail to reach the public eye or enter the public debate. But governments, as elected bodies that have been endowed with the primary responsibility for the operation, maintenance and development of the transportation system, cannot simply ignore these difficult choices when they present their transportation plans. It may be expected from well-functioning governments that they openly engage in these difficult trade-offs and explicitly justify the choices they make. And such a justification is not possible without reverting to notions of justice and fairness. Like any other form of public planning, transportation planning is thus inevitably a normative activity. It follows that the core question of this book is not *whether* transportation planning should be based on principles of justice, but on *which* principles of justice it should be based.

It is my ambition with this book to answer this question. I aim to contribute to the search for transportation justice by developing explicit principles of justice for transportation planning, drawing on both philosophies of justice and the particularities of transportation. Formulated in more ambitious terms, my aim is to develop a new paradigm, or comprehensive theory, for transportation planning, based on principles of justice.

What kind of theory?

The aim of this book is to develop a theory of fairness in the domain of transportation. This ambition requires further specification as to what type of theory I intend to develop. For this purpose, it is useful to draw on the classical distinction between procedural and substantive theories on the one hand, and empirical versus normative theories on the other (Yiftachel 1989).

The distinction between procedural and substantive theories of planning was pioneered by Faludi (1973). He argued that it was of essential importance for the discipline of (urban) planning to make a systematic distinction between both types of theories, terming them theories *of* planning and theories *in* planning, respectively. Procedural theories relate to the process and methods of decision-making, whereas substantive theories pertain to the (interdisciplinary) knowledge relevant to the content of planning, that is, relevant to the understanding of land use dynamics (Yiftachel 1989). The distinction between empirical and prescriptive theories was introduced implicitly by a number of authors and made explicit by Yiftachel (1989). Empirical or explanatory theories seek to understand the 'real world' as it is out there; in other words, they seek to understand and explain how the world *is*. Prescriptive theories, in turn, provide abstract and general guidance on how the world *should be;* in others words, they provide guidance for action and intervention. By juxtaposing these two distinctions, four types of theories can be distinguished (Figure 1.1).

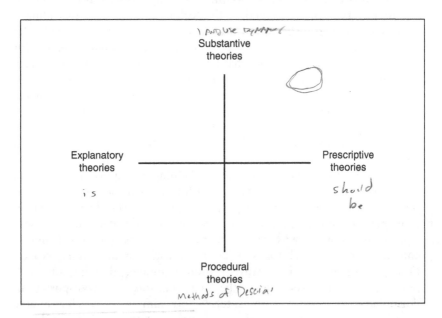

Figure 1.1 Four types of theories.
Source: Yiftachel 1989.

The theory to be developed in this book is both substantive and prescriptive in nature (i.e., it belongs to the top-right quadrant in Figure 1.1). The focus on fairness and justice inevitably puts it firmly in the domain of prescriptive theories. The aim is to develop a theory that is helpful in the normative assessment of the transportation system. The theory is substantive in nature because it seeks to define what is a fair transportation system. Based on this definition, I will then develop an abstract set of principles of justice for transportation planning. The principles are to help practitioners analyze the state of a transportation system and identify interventions that move the system closer to the fair ideal. The theory hardly addresses the process of decision-making and thus does not define in any detailed manner how transportation planners and others should arrive at decisions in a fair way. If fairness is defined as "a just distribution justly arrived at" (Harvey 1973), the theory in the book thus falls short of providing a full account of fairness. It will first and foremost seek to define what constitutes a fair transportation system, leaving the reader to obtain inspiration regarding the fairness of decision-making processes from the abundance of theories on, for instance, deliberative democracy and communicative planning (e.g. Dryzek 1990; Healey 1995; Innes and Booher 2004). The theory developed in the book thus contrasts with most prescriptive planning theories developed over the last decades, which have focused on the process rather than the content of planning. At the same time, the ambition to develop a substantive normative theory also proves to have its limitations, as I will conclude in Chapter 7. These limitations can only be surmounted by complementing a substantive approach with a procedural one. Yet the substantive approach remains a pivotal component of the theory developed here, as it sets boundaries on the role of a procedural approach (see Daniels 1996 and Daniels 2008 for a comparable approach to the domain of health and health care). I will therefore devote most of my effort to developing the substantive component of the theory.

Who could use the theory?

The ambition I have with this book reaches further than merely the development of a theory. The aim is to develop a substantive theory that is relevant for practice, in line with O'Neill's claim that "fruitful work in ethics or politics must be practical. It must address the needs of agents who have yet to act, who are working out what to do, not the needs of spectators who are looking for ways of assessing or appraising what has already been done" (O'Neill 2000, p. 7). Indeed, my aim is to develop a theory that is not only useful for spectators, seeking to assess and criticize the state of affairs, but also for practitioners and decision-makers who have to make day-to-day decisions regarding interventions in the transportation system, as well as for advocates searching for transportation justice in their advocacy efforts.

The focus on substance rather than process or procedures may lead to the interpretation that the theory developed in the book fits the rational–comprehensive paradigm to planning; that it provides guidance to the almighty central actor who, in his (not her) wisdom, can determine which interventions are necessary in the transport-land use system. The book is not intended that way. Quite the contrary: it is meant for different audiences.

It may indeed serve as a source of inspiration for government officials and decision-makers who currently hold the final responsibility for transportation planning. For them, the approach developed here can be perceived as a comprehensive guidebook on how to conduct 'good' or 'proper' transportation planning. However, the book is also meant as a source of inspiration for non-governmental organizations and citizen groups that seek to influence the process and outcomes of current practices of transportation planning. For them, the book provides an ideal type of what good transportation planning could look like; it provides them with a comprehensive alternative to mainstream approaches. As such, it can be used as a vehicle for change: a tool in the hands of those that seek to make transportation planning more sensitive to social needs. No actor can single-handedly determine transport policy in a vacuum; actors will have to negotiate interventions in the transportation system with a wide range of others. A clear understanding of what fair transportation planning may look like is a key input for moving the outcomes of this decision-making process towards the ideal.

While I argue that the approach developed in this book is comprehensive in nature, it is by no means a blueprint. Even if the prescriptive theory developed in the book were to be implemented in a comprehensive way by transportation planning authorities, it would not in any deterministic way stipulate what actions those authorities should engage in. In this sense, the theory developed here is not a dogma. First, it is not a dogma because it limits itself to framing the societal debate around transport problems in a new way. Within this frame, there is substantial room for interpretation and debate between involved stakeholders. Second, it is not a dogma because the approach is an unfinished project. It will require refinement and adjustments, based on further elaborations of its foundations, and explorations of the possible consequences of the approach, as well as applications in actual planning practice.

Box 1.1 On accessibility

The notion of accessibility will be central throughout the book, so a brief elaboration of the notion is in place. In a classical paper, Hansen (1959) has defined accessibility as the potential of opportunities for interaction with locations dispersed over space.

More precisely, Hansen states that accessibility captures "the spatial distribution of activities about a point, adjusted for the ability and the desire of people ... to overcome spatial separation" (Hansen 1959, p. 73). Hansen thus underscores that the notion of accessibility relates to the possibilities for interaction.

Scholars often make a distinction between person accessibility and place accessibility. While the terms are often used interchangeably and both notions are often simply referred to as accessibility, it is important to clarify the difference between them (see Pirie 1979; Kwan 1999; Miller 2007 for more elaborate discussions). Person accessibility is an attribute of a person: a person has accessibility (or not) to a certain set of locations. Place accessibility, in turn, is an attribute of an (activity) location: a location is accessible (or inaccessible) for a certain set of people or from a certain set of other locations. Person and location accessibility are thus each other's mirror image (Figure 1.2). A justice perspective on transportation planning directs the attention to persons, as justice requires the fair treatment of persons, not of places. The notion of person accessibility also stresses the ability of a person to act, which is in line with the emphasis on a person's agency as a basic component of virtually all philosophies of justice. Hence, in the remainder of this book I will focus on person accessibility, i.e. on accessibility as experienced by persons. For reasons of readability only, I will simply use the term accessibility rather than person accessibility throughout the book.

The conceptualization of accessibility as a potentiality underscores that accessibility can vary in 'size', 'amount' or 'volume'. In other words, persons can experience high or low levels of accessibility. Hansen's definition stresses that the accessibility level experienced by a person depends on the context and the person. The context captures both the "spatial distribution of activities" as mentioned by Hansen, and the transportation systems that (potentially) connect a person to these activities. These transportation systems encompass the variety of infrastructures and transportation services that enable persons to travel through space, such as roads, public transport services, bus stops, bicycle paths, gasoline stations, traffic lights, parking places, and so on. These systems directly affect the "ability of a person to overcome spatial separation". But that ability is as much affected by a multitude of attributes of a person, ranging from a person's income to a person's gender, from a person's access to vehicles to a person's knowledge of the transportation systems, from a person's place of residence to a person's household composition, and from a person's physical abilities to a person's knowledge of the available activities. Persons will differ widely in their attributes and are thus likely to differ widely in their actually experienced levels of accessibility. Kaufman and colleagues (2004) stress that a person's ability to overcome spatial separation depends on their appropriation of possibilities for movement. That is, the ability to overcome spatial separation is not merely a pre-given and passive attribute of a person, but needs to be actively fostered by that person through actually engaging in the act of traveling. A person's accessibility increases, that is to say, as a person builds up experience in using transportation systems to access activities distributed over space.

The context, consisting of the spatial distribution of activities and the available transportation systems, delineates the maximum set of opportunities or maximum level of accessibility persons can obtain. Since the ability to overcome space is dependent on resources in the most general sense of the word, a maximum can only be determined based on a general, predefined, ability to overcome distance, as defined in e.g. time, costs, cognitive requirements, discomfort or fear. The level of accessibility as experienced by real persons will, in the ideal case, be identical to that maximum, but will typically be lower due to limitations in a person's ability to overcome distance. For instance, a wealthy, time-rich person who is able to access all transportation systems may well experience the highest possible level of accessibility. But any person that experiences some resource limitation, in terms of e.g. money, time, physical abilities or cognitive skills, will experience a lower level of accessibility. The ability of a person to overcome spatial separation thus determines the subset of opportunities that are actually available to a person.

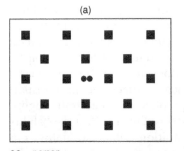 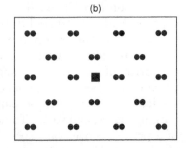

●● = person
■ = activity location

Figure 1.2 Person accessibility (a) versus place accessibility (b). The borders of each diagram indicate the area that can be travelled within, for instance, a certain time budget, money budget or time-and-money budget.
Source: Dijst 1995, p. 28.

Clearly, much more can be said about accessibility and I will do so throughout the book. For now it suffices to stress a number of key points: accessibility captures a potential for interaction; accessibility can be measured in terms of its volume or quantity; and a person's accessibility depends on both context (transportation systems and land use patterns) and personal attributes (such as vehicle ownership, income level, abilities).

The outline of the book

The aim of this book is to develop principles of justice for transportation planning. I will start in Chapter 2 with a critical exploration of the principles of justice underlying the traditional approach to transportation planning. I will conclude that this approach falls short of providing a convincing set of justice principles to underpin transportation planning. This conclusion provides the backdrop for what follows in the remainder of the book.

The second part of the book will be devoted to philosophical explorations. I will draw on only a small selection of the abundance of theories and approaches to social justice developed over the past thousands of years. I will first briefly outline what to expect from a theory of justice in the domain of transportation (Chapter 3). I will then draw on Michael Walzer's *Spheres of Justice* (Walzer 1983) to present an argument outlining why justice in transportation deserves a treatment separate from other domains of government intervention (Chapter 4). I will argue that the importance of transportation does not derive from the potentiality for movement it enables, but from the accessibility to destinations it confers on persons, a position that is increasingly supported by researchers and practitioners in the domain of transportation (see Box 1.1 for a brief explanation of the notion of accessibility). Taken together, these two chapters provide the solid foundation from which to explore the possible principles for transportation planning.

In Chapter 5, I take up John Rawls' famous theory of justice. Rawls' magnum opus *A Theory of Justice*, published in 1971, is widely seen as a landmark in Western thought on the subject of social justice. Perhaps against expectations, I will show that Rawls' powerful line of reasoning cannot deliver principles of justice for transportation or transportation planning. Yet it is possible to derive a number of important concepts from his rich theory of social justice, which will be merged into the explorations that follow.

Chapter 6 contains the theoretical heart of the book. It draws on yet another theory of justice: Ronald Dworkin's theory on equality of resources (Dworkin 2000). Dworkin's approach, elaborated in his *Sovereign Virtue*, makes resource scarcity an intrinsic element of reasoning about justice and fairness. He does so through the development of a complex auction scheme as a methodological device to reason about justice. In Dworkin's auction, fundamentally equal persons bid for goods and purchase insurance against various forms of bad luck, such as impairments. Based on the auction scheme, Dworkin is able to delineate what members of society owe to each other under different circumstances. I will extend the auction scheme to the domain of transportation by developing a set of hypothetical scenarios in which persons can insure themselves against various forms of transport-related bad luck. This will ultimately result in the definition of a set of justice principles for the transportation domain. The—perhaps somewhat lengthy—argument in this chapter will lead to a conclusion that is intuitively appealing: a fair transportation system provides all persons with a sufficient level of accessibility under most, but not all, circumstances.

The next chapter is devoted to further developing the notion of sufficiency (Chapter 7). The aim of the chapter is to develop an approach through which stakeholders could reach an agreement about what counts as sufficient accessibility and what as insufficient accessibility. Drawing loosely on the work of Amartya Sen and Norman Daniels, I will develop an approach containing a substantial and a procedural component, with the former setting boundaries for the latter. The chapter ends with a demarcation of the duties that persons have vis-à-vis each other in cases of sufficient and insufficient accessibility.

The philosophical explorations provide the basis for the last part of the book, in which I present a practical approach to transportation planning based on principles of justice. Chapter 8 is the heart of this part of the book. It starts with a discussion of a number of key issues, such as the measurement of accessibility and mobility, the development of fairness indicators, and approaches to the assessment of transportation interventions. Based on these discussions, the chapter presents the 'rules' of transportation planning based on principles of justice. These rules are formulated in such a way that stakeholders committed to seeking transportation justice could follow them in their everyday practice.

Chapter 9 is devoted to a case study, illustrating how the rules or steps of transportation planning based on principles of justice could be applied in actual practice. Featuring as this case study is the metropolitan region of Amsterdam, the Netherlands, a region which has also been discussed by Susan Fainstein in her book *The Just City*. The case study shows that the approach to transportation planning developed in this book leads to a fundamentally different assessment of the transportation problems in the Amsterdam region than is common in policy documents or societal debates. Indeed, in line with expectations, the approach redirects the political and intellectual attention away from the functioning of the transportation system and related concerns about congestion, towards a systematic assessment of accessibility patterns and the situation of persons experiencing sub-standard levels of accessibility.

The book ends with some final observations (Chapter 10). First, I turn to the financing of the transportation system, as a fair financing system is a prerequisite for transportation planning based on principles of justice. Based on the philosophical explorations in the book, I will design a radically different financing scheme from those seen in countries around the world, along the way shedding a refreshing light on debates about the legitimate ways to use the tax proceeds collected primarily from car drivers. I will then explore whether congestion, as the main concern of traditional transportation planning, is still a problem from the perspective of transportation planning based on principles of justice and under what conditions it could still be addressed. I will end the book with a brief reflection on the radical changes needed if the search for transportation justice is taken seriously.

References

Daniels, N. (1996). *Justice and Justification*. Cambridge, Cambridge University Press.

Daniels, N. (2008). *Just Health : meeting health needs fairly*. Cambridge, Cambridge University Press.

Dijst, M. (1995). *Het elliptisch leven: actieruimte als integrale maat voor bereik en mobiliteit*. Utrecht/Delft, Koninklijk Nederlands Aardrijkskundig Genootschap/ Faculteit Bouwkunde Technische Universiteit Delft.

Dryzek, J.S. (1990). *Discursive Democracy: politics, policy, and political science*. Cambridge, Cambridge University Press.

Dworkin, R. (2000). *Sovereign Virtue: the theory and practice of equality*. Cambridge, MA/London, Harvard University Press.

Faludi, A. (1973). *A Reader in Planning Theory*. Oxford, Pergamon Press.

Grengs, J. (2002). Community-based planning as a source of political change: the transit equity movement of Los Angeles' Bus Riders Union. *Journal of the American Planning Association*, 68(2): 165–178.

Hansen, W.G. (1959). How accessibility shapes land use. *Journal of the American Institute of Planners*, 25: 73–76.

Harvey, D. (1973). *Social Justice and the City*. Bungay, Edward Arnold Publishers.

Healey, P. (1995). Discourses of integration: making frameworks for democratic urban planning. In: Healey, P. (ed.). *Managing Cities: the new urban context*. Chichester/New York, John Wiley and Sons: 251–272.

Innes, J.E. and D.E. Booher (2004). Reframing public participation: strategies for the 21st century. *Planning Theory & Practice*, 5(4): 419–436.

Kaufmann, V., M.M. Bergman and D. Joye (2004). Motility: mobility as capital. *International Journal of Urban and Regional Research*, 28(4): 745–756.

Krumholz, N. (1982). A retrospective view of equity planning Cleveland 1969–1979. *Journal of the American Planning Association*, 48(2): 163–174.

Kwan, M.-P. (1999). Gender and individual access to urban opportunities: a study using space-time measures. *Professional Geographer*, 51(2): 210–227.

Miller, H.J. (2007). Place-Based versus People-Based Geographic Information Science. *Geography Compass*, 1(3): 503–535.

O'Neill, O. (2000). *Bounds of Justice*. Cambridge, Cambridge University Press.

Pirie, G.H. (1979). Measuring accessibility: a review and proposal. *Environment and Planning A*, 11: 299–312.

Rawls, J. (1971). *A Theory of Justice*. Cambridge, MA, Harvard University Press.

Soja, E.W. (2010). *Seeking Spatial Justice*. Minneapolis, University of Minnesota Press.

Walzer, M. (1983). *Spheres of Justice: a defense of pluralism and equality*. New York, Basic Books.

Yiftachel, O. (1989). Towards a new typology of urban planning theories. *Environment and Planning B: Planning and Design*, 16(1): 23–39.

2 Fairness in Traditional Transportation Planning

Introduction

In this chapter, I will expose the principles of justice underlying the traditional approach to transportation planning. My purpose is to show that this approach fails to provide a convincing account of justice in the domain of transportation and thus fails to provide convincing arguments for settling the difficult trade-offs that are inevitable in transportation planning. This conclusion then presents the rationale for the explorations that follow in the remainder of this book.

I acknowledge that the traditional approach has been challenged for a number of reasons and that other approaches have emerged as a result. This includes what I have called 'transportation planning for sustainability' and 'transportation planning for accessibility' (see Martens 2014). *Wiener?* However, these alternatives have not yet developed into a comprehensive approach consisting of a complete set of formal and informal rules on how to conduct transportation planning. For this reason, I limit myself in this chapter to the traditional approach. In Box 2.1, I briefly reflect on these two alternatives to traditional transportation planning.

The chapter is organized as follows. I start with a brief account of an institutional approach to transportation planning. In line with this approach, the practice of transportation planning is seen as an informal institution encompassing rules that give guidance to professionals on how to conduct 'proper' transportation planning. I then turn to traditional transportation planning. I start with a brief introduction, then outline the rules of traditional transportation planning, and subsequently explore which (implicit) notions of justice are embodied in this approach to transportation planning. I end with a conclusion regarding the shortcomings of the traditional approach in adequately and systematically addressing concerns of justice.

Box 2.1 Traditional transportation planning and its alternatives

The traditional approach to transportation planning is clearly not the only possible way to plan for movement and accessibility. Over the past decades, the traditional approach has been criticized on a number of grounds. This has led to the emergence of two, partly overlapping, alternatives: transportation planning for sustainability and transportation planning for accessibility. Let me briefly summarize the basic tenets of these approaches (for a more elaborate account, see Martens 2014).

Transportation planning for sustainability has emerged in response to the growing awareness of the enormous environmental impacts of an approach that uncritically seeks to cater for the projected demand for (car-based) travel. In response, transportation planning for sustainability seeks to limit the impact of the transport sector on the environment, predominantly through a reduction in (the forecasted increase in) car-based travel. For this reason, the approach has also been termed 'predict-and-prevent' to underscore the shift away from 'predict-and-provide' as embodied in traditional transportation planning (Owens 1995). Much of the relevant literature discusses and assesses the potential of various policy strategies to reduce car travel, without explicitly developing a comprehensive approach to transportation planning.

Transportation planning for sustainability's concern with the environment has far-reaching implications from the perspective of justice. This is so because addressing the environmental impacts requires a better understanding of car travel as the main 'culprit'. It also demands an assessment of transportation interventions in terms of their contribution to attract car drivers to other transportation modes, to a reduction in vehicle miles travelled, or to a reduction in the environmental externalities caused by car-based travel. Thus, paradoxically, the ambition to reduce car use inevitably leads to a focus on car use. As a result, the approach will tend to support transportation interventions that serve the travel patterns of (former) car users rather than those of car-less households. Transportation planning for sustainability is thus likely to perpetuate and strengthen existing disparities in potential mobility and accessibility between persons with and without access to a car, rather than reduce them. From the perspective of justice, then, the consequences of transportation planning for sustainability do not seem to deviate much from traditional transportation planning.

Transportation planning for accessibility provides a more promising alternative from the perspective of justice. It places people at the heart of transportation planning by emphasizing that the prime goal of transportation systems is to provide persons with access to destinations. This basic tenet implies that the approach could potentially address the observed disparities in accessibility levels. Yet, while the accessibility literature abounds with studies describing, analyzing and sometimes criticizing the unequal landscapes of accessibilities, it provides little guidance for a systematic normative assessment of these landscapes. The approach has so far fallen short of developing an explicit justice framework for transportation planning that could replace the traditional approach.

Interestingly, most advances have been made in practice, notably in the UK. Here, an approach to accessibility planning has been developed in response to concerns about the contribution of transportation systems to the exclusion of vulnerable population groups from mainstream society. The approach was path-breaking in nature, as it explicitly required local authorities to assess accessibility to key destinations in their locality and to propose and implement measures to improve accessibility in case of unmet mobility needs (Lucas 2012). The related policy documents use wordings like 'accessibility deficits' and define minimum thresholds for accessibility, often expressed in terms of a maximum distance or travel time to the nearest destination (e.g. school, grocery shop, doctor). These wordings imply an explicit acknowledgment of the existence of not merely inequalities, but actual injustices, in the realm of accessibility. This suggests that the UK approach provides valuable ingredients for an approach to transportation planning that is based on principles of justice. At the same time, however, the UK approach has failed to provide an overall framework for transportation planning. First, accessibility planning has been framed as a local responsibility, implicitly suggesting that accessibility is not a relevant goal of transportation planning at the national level. This implies that large-scale investments in transportation infrastructure and services, which strongly shape accessibility patterns in the long-term and are in part responsible for the persistence of injustices in accessibility observed at the local level, fall outside the scope of accessibility planning. Second, even on the local level, accessibility planning has developed into an add-on, addressing concerns of vulnerable population groups, rather than an integrative approach shaping investments in the entire transportation system at the local level. For these reasons, the UK approach to accessibility planning, while containing valuable elements, should be seen as an auxiliary instrument to address the special needs of weak population groups, rather than as an approach that could provide the justice underpinnings of transportation planning for accessibility.

> The aim of this book is exactly to develop such an overarching framework. If successful, the book will thus contribute to the further development of transportation planning for accessibility. To formulate it somewhat differently: transportation planning based on principles of justice *is* transportation planning for a fair distribution of accessibility.

Transportation planning as an institution

The critical analysis of the traditional approach to transportation planning draws loosely on institutional theory. In this body of thought, institutions have been conceptualized as the "formal or informal ... humanly devised constraints that structure political, economic and social interactions" (North 1990, p. 3), or as "the prescriptions that humans use to organize all forms of repetitive and structured interactions including those within families, neighborhoods, markets, firms, sports leagues, churches, private associations, and governments at all scales" (Ostrom 2009, p. 3). It may be clear that a wide variety of institutions, ranging from laws and regulations to informal conventions, shape the decision-making regarding interventions in the transportation system. These institutions include, for instance, rules defining the roles and responsibilities of various governmental and non-governmental bodies in developing, maintaining and managing transportation systems, rules regarding democratic decision-making and citizen involvement, and rules delineating the right of appeal and financial compensation.

This book is not about all these different types of institutions that together describe the practice of transportation planning. Rather, the focus is on a relatively narrow set of rules that prescribe how decisions regarding interventions in the transportation system are to be *prepared* (Cervero, Neil *et al.* 2001). More precisely, as stated in Chapter 1, I am interested in the substance and not in the process of preparation. The focus is, in other words, on what could be termed the analytical, professional or 'technical' part of the transportation planning process, which feeds the political process that ultimately results in decisions to (not) intervene in transportation systems. These 'preparation' rules relate to the type of analyses that should be carried out to determine the character and scope of transportation 'problems' worthy of policy attention, the type of solutions that may be considered to address these problems, the way possible solutions are to be assessed and evaluated, and, ultimately, the type of information to be provided to different stakeholders involved in the, inevitably political, decision-making process. These various analytical steps tend to be carried out by professionals with training and expertise in transportation planning and related fields.

The 'prescriptions' that guide this important part of the practice of transportation planning can be formal and informal in nature. Formal rules are enshrined in laws and regulations. Deviations from these rules are often sanctioned, for instance when a government withholds financial contributions to an infrastructure project if particular rules are not followed. The requirement to carry out an environmental impact assessment is a typical example of such a formal rule (Wood 2003). Another example is the use of a particular type of appraisal methodology, which has become a formal element of transportation planning for major infrastructure investments in a range of countries (Hayashi and Morisugi 2000; Martens 2006). The informal rules refer to the 'shared practices' of the community of transportation planners (broadly defined). These rules also function as prescriptions, as they, too, can embody sanctions, for example in a refusal to accept arguments from, or to cooperate with, an organization that does not follow the informal rules. For instance, in some countries, applying a particular type of transport model has become a dominant element of the practice of transportation planning, without any formal obligation to do so (see e.g. Hensher and Button 2000; de Jong, Daly *et al.* 2007). Transportation planning agencies that do not follow this practice run the risk of being ignored or continuously challenged for not employing the shared practices of 'good' transportation planning.

Fairness can be implicitly or explicitly addressed in the formal and informal prescriptions that organize the practice of transportation planning. They can be explicit, if rules require agencies involved in, or responsible for, transportation planning to address and evaluate the impacts of transportation interventions on different population groups or communities (e.g. Title VI requirements in the US; see e.g. Sanchez, Brenman *et al.* 2008; Martens, Golub *et al.* 2011; Golub and Martens 2014). They can also be implicit, for instance if the informal rules guiding transportation planning embody a particular definition of fairness and the resulting practices lead to interventions in the transportation system that adhere to this definition.

This chapter critically reflects on the—often implicit—principles of justice that are embedded in the traditional approach to transportation planning. This approach has been enormously influential across most of the world and therefore deserves explicit attention. I acknowledge that my account of the approach is an archetype of a wide variety of actual practices that can be observed across the world (see for instance Litman 2013). Yet the fundamental elements of the approach still shape the international practice of transportation planning and for that reason deserve explicit attention.

Background of traditional transportation planning

The fundamentals of traditional transportation planning were developed in the USA during the 1950s, when area-wide transportation studies were carried out in Chicago, Detroit, Pittsburgh, and other metropolitan areas in the USA (Cervero, Neil *et al.* 2001; Black 2003; Kane and Del Mistro 2003; Mees 2010). These studies were in an important way a response to the congestion that began to appear "on a paralyzing scale" in USA cities after World War II (Black 2003, p. 217). From its inception, then, transportation planning was framed as an activity to tackle the problem of congestion—a focus which remains dominant till today in virtually all industrialized countries (Levine 2013). This focus on speed may not come as a surprise, given the wide-spread agreement among transportation planners that "[t]ime is a much-valued, irretrievable resource" (Cervero, Neil *et al.* 2001, p. 15874). Hence the observation and expectation of Cervero and colleagues that "planning for speedy movement has always been, and will always be, central to transportation planning" (ibid.). In line with the emphasis on speed, traditional transportation planning has generally been defined as the field of governance intervention that aims to ensure the effective and efficient movement of people and goods (Shiftan, Button *et al.* 2007; Cervero, Neil *et al.* 2001).

Rules of traditional transportation planning

The prescriptions guiding the practice of traditional transportation planning are well-known and have been described in a number of text books (e.g. Lane, Powell *et al.* 1971; Black 2003). The rules can be briefly summarized as follows. The first step of 'proper' transportation planning practice is the forecasting of future demand for travel—often mistakenly referred to as 'travel needs' (e.g. Hartgen 2003; Owens 1995, p. 44). The standard tool to identify this demand is the well-known four-step travel-demand forecasting model. On the input side, this model requires data on the size and spatial distribution of the population and economic activity in the future. These data are used for a series of sequential mathematical steps, which lead to the output of the model: detailed forecasts of future trips on major road links and transit lines in a metropolitan area (Cervero, Neil *et al.* 2001). These data on travel on each transport link are then used to assess the future performance of the existing transportation system, to identify transport links in the region that lack sufficient capacity, and to forecast the impact of possible transport investments on the performance of the system. The performance of the system is typically measured in terms of level-of-service, congested roadway miles, or the number of vehicle hours lost (Black 2003, p. 304). The assessment of the performance of the transportation system and its composite links results in the identification of solutions that are most suited to avoid congestion on the major links of the system, with the ultimate aim to maintain free-flow traffic across the entire system. In the ideal situation the programming and construction of capital improvements like new highways or railway extensions is subsequently based on the outputs of this four-step model and aim to guarantee that congestion is avoided altogether.

The identification of solutions to maintain free-flowing traffic across the entire transportation network would only be the final result of transportation planning in a world of unlimited resources. In the real world it is not possible to upgrade all links that experience some level of

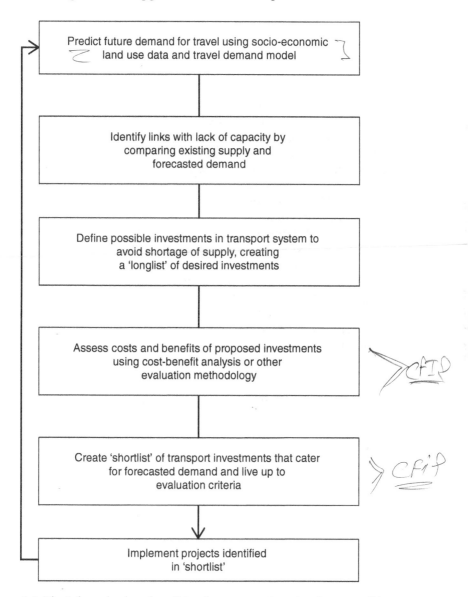

Figure 2.1 The informal rules of traditional transportation planning prescribing how to conduct 'proper' transportation planning.

CBAs

congestion, if only because of a lack of funds. Hence the necessary step following the modeling efforts encompasses a way to prioritize possible investments. While various evaluation frameworks have been applied over the past decades (Browne and Ryan 2011), one has emerged as the dominant tool in most industrialized societies: social cost-benefit analysis (Willis, Garrod *et al.* 1998; Bristow and Nellthorp 2000). Cost-benefit analysis (CBA) generates data on the economic efficiency of a transport project, which can be defined as the maximization of the net contribution of the project to the national income. The typical cost-benefit analysis of transportation projects takes into account only a part of the social benefits and social costs. Typical benefits included are travel time savings and reductions in motoring costs and, increasingly, improvements in road safety. On the other side of the equation, initially only investment and maintenance costs were included. However, the growing concern about the environmental impacts of the transport sector in general, and road building in particular, has resulted in a broadening of the approach in many countries over the past two decades. Currently, many countries incorporate a number of environmental impacts in cost-benefit analysis, most notably air and noise pollution.

The assessment of costs and benefits of proposed solutions usually results in a set of indicators for each project: cost-benefit ratio (C/B ratio), net present value (NPV), and internal rate of return (IRR). Typically, projects with a certain score on one or more of these indicators are considered worthwhile investments from a macro-economic perspective and are supposed to be implemented, provided sufficient funds are available.

Note that in a number of countries, some of these steps have actually been enshrined in laws and regulations, giving (components of) traditional transportation planning a firm footing in practice (Bristow and Nellthorp 2000).

The two faces of fairness in traditional transportation planning

So far we have been looking at the familiar story of traditional transportation planning. What underlying notions of fairness can be discerned in this approach? Textbook discussions of traditional transportation planning tend to ignore this question. But the approach is based implicitly on quite powerful principles of fairness, which have far-reaching distributive consequences.

Let me start, perhaps against the intuition of the reader, with the egalitarian tendencies that are embodied in the traditional approach. Traditional transportation planning developed from the practice of highway planning in the USA (Weiner 2008). Early highway planning in the USA concentrated on developing a network of high quality roads connecting various parts of the nation. A comparable approach was taken in European countries after the Second World War. The approach to highway planning reflected the modernist ambitions prevalent in other domains of civil engineering, such as water resource, electricity and sanitary engineering, which aimed at providing a basic service to an entire population by gradually expanding the system to all parts of a nation (Graham and Marvin 2001). The aim of highway planning was comparable: providing a system of roads of comparable quality across a nation, irrespective of the costs or benefits of connecting particular geographical areas to the network. The early days of traditional transportation planning thus clearly reflect egalitarian tendencies. Indeed, in those days, when resource restrictions played a smaller role than nowadays in decisions regarding infrastructure investments (see Black 2003, p. 214) and the use of cost-benefit analysis was much less common, substantial road building efforts occurred in peripheral areas across developed nations, reflecting the practical workings of the principle of equality in highway planning.

These egalitarian tendencies can also be discerned in the informal rules of traditional transportation planning as it gradually replaced highway planning. One of the key steps in the approach is the identification of links in the transport network which lack capacity to serve the expected demand (the second step of the informal rules). A lack of capacity, whether measured in terms of level-of-service, congested roadway miles, or the number of vehicle hours lost, is seen as the prime transportation problem to be solved by planning (see e.g. Black 2003; Mees 2010). The modernist ambition of the engineering disciplines to provide every citizen with a comparable service level is reflected in this ambition to guarantee identical level-of-service across the transportation network. Indeed, in terms of fairness, traditional transportation planning hides a powerful distributive yardstick: in an ideal world without resource restrictions, everybody is to receive unhindered travel speed on the transportation network of her choice. That is, car drivers are to receive free flowing travel speeds on the road network, irrespective of a person's characteristics like residential location, income, race or gender. While less pronounced, the informal rules of traditional transportation planning suggest a comparable standard regarding public transport: public transport users are to receive uncongested services, defined as services providing sufficient capacity to cater for demand, likewise irrespective of residential location, income, race or gender. The distributive principle behind traditional transportation planning is thus equality. I will qualify this statement below. But for now, it is important to stress the point: traditional transportation planning is seeking for equality in the transportation domain. More precisely, traditional transportation planning seeks to provide every citizen with uncongested travel on the main links of the available transport networks. Given the powerful force of the notion of equality, this may explain some of the appeal of traditional transportation planning, even though the goal of equality was hardly ever explicitly acknowledged in theory or practice.

The above analysis presents the progressive face of traditional transportation planning. There is, however, also a second, regressive, face to traditional transportation planning. This second reading starts from the users of the transportation system, rather than from the quality of that system. The principle of equality quickly evaporates on this second reading.

Let me first turn to the users who can make use of the road system, as traditional transportation planning was developed first and foremost as an approach to guide the expansion of the road system and address the increasing levels of road congestion. Clearly, the principle of equal speeds across the network is of relevance for the users of the road system. But it seems also reasonable to assume that the users of the road system are even more interested in the question of how they can use speed on the network effectively for their own purposes. More precisely, users are likely to be more concerned about potential mobility and accessibility provided by the road system than in speed per se. Potential mobility is commonly understood as the ease with which a person can move through space (e.g. Sager 2005; see Chapters 4 and 8 for a more elaborate discussion). It depends not only on the speed on links of the network, but as much on the density of the network. Given identical speeds on all network links, a sparse network offers a much lower level of potential mobility than a highly dense network. More precisely, if all links would provide an identical speed, then the level of potential mobility is determined entirely by network density: the higher the number of links, the higher the level of potential mobility (ignoring delays at junctions) (see Black 2003, p. 259). Equality in network speed, as emphasized by traditional transportation planning, can thus coincide with *in*equalities in potential mobility. These inequalities, in turn, may translate into substantial disparities in revealed mobility (i.e. in the number of trips), which may subsequently be reproduced through the workings of traditional transportation planning (see below).

The same analysis holds for accessibility. Accessibility was defined loosely in Chapter 1 as the potential for interaction with locations dispersed over space (see Box 1.1; more on accessibility in Chapters 4 and 8). Equality in speed is even more likely to lead to *in*equalities in accessibility between different users of the road system, as accessibility is not only determined by speed on the transport network and by the network structure, but also by land use patterns. Since land use patterns are by their very nature characterized by center and periphery (Puu 2005), providing equal travel speeds on a road network across a population dispersed over a geographical area will inevitably lead to structural inequalities in accessibility across that area. Furthermore, as in the case of potential mobility, these inequalities in accessibility may subsequently be perpetuated if transportation planners work according to the informal rules of traditional transportation planning (see below).

This analysis holds even more profoundly once we no longer narrow down the analysis to persons who are able to use the road system, but instead turn our attention to all potential users of the entire transportation system. The practice of *separately* assessing the quality of the road system and public transportation system (and largely ignoring the infrastructure supporting cycling and walking; see Koglin and Rye 2014), as is common practice in traditional transportation planning, has pervasive consequences in terms of fairness across the entire transportation system. This is so for two interrelated reasons. First, as noted in Chapter 1, all existing transportation systems exclude some persons from their use, because of physical, legal or financial reasons. Thus, we may assume that some persons are excluded from using the road system, while others are excluded from riding on (parts of) the public transportation system. Second, the principle of congestion-free travel on the road and public transport networks does not translate into identical speeds on both networks, let alone into the provision of identical levels of potential mobility or accessibility by both networks. This is so because the networks will tend to have fundamentally different characteristics in terms of network structure, even if all links in both networks are uncongested. These differences between both transportation modes will almost inevitably translate into *inequalities* between persons in terms of all three indicators: speed, potential mobility and accessibility. The rules of traditional transportation planning are thus likely to systematically produce, reproduce and reinforce inequalities between persons with access to different transportation systems, as will be discussed below.

Transportation planners' early preoccupation with free flow on the (road) network, rather than potential mobility or accessibility, is probably a remnant from the field's roots in other engineering disciplines. For instance, in water or electricity systems it is irrelevant where a particular element, like a water molecule, would 'travel' to. The main issue is guaranteeing that each link of the network has enough capacity to cater for the demand as manifested across the network, so that an unhindered flow in the entire network is guaranteed. Detours caused by a sparse network are not relevant from the perspective of a water molecule, nor from the perspective of the end user of water. For the functioning of these technological systems, unhindered flow was indeed an adequate and sufficient indicator for the system's performance and for the provision of an equal level-of-service to all persons connected to the network. It was but a small step to take this approach and, first, apply it to each transportation system separately (road versus public transport), and, second, translate the notion of unhindered flow into speed on the transport network, even though this implied ignoring the fact that network structure is of key importance from the perspective of the 'units' circulating in transportation systems, i.e. from the perspective of persons using the transportation system, as it shapes both potential mobility and accessibility as experienced by the users.

It should be acknowledged that inequalities between persons in terms of speed, potential mobility and accessibility do not necessarily constitute injustices. It requires systematic normative argumentation to draw this conclusion (see Chapters 5 to 7). But the analysis does underline the importance of a careful selection of the proper dimension of justice in the transportation domain. Sen and others have argued that the debate over social justice in any domain is in an important sense a debate about the proper dimension of analysis (Sen 1980). Traditional transportation planning provides an implicit answer to this (virtually non-existent) debate in the domain of transportation: the key dimension is the performance of the transportation system. Inevitably, if the attention is directed to a different dimension, what are equalities in the first instance will turn into inequalities in the second. While it seems reasonable to assume that persons have a stronger interest in potential mobility or accessibility than in travel speeds on the network, this claim clearly requires a more profound justification. This important challenge of selecting the appropriate dimension for a justice analysis will be taken up more elaborately in Chapter 4.

The non-egalitarian tendencies enshrined in the fairness principles underlying traditional transportation planning are further perpetuated by the workings of two informal rules of the traditional approach: the rule requiring the forecasting of future travel demand (the first rule in Figure 2.1) and the rule requiring the systematic assessment of costs and benefits of proposed transportation investments (the fourth rule in Figure 2.1).

The first informal rule of traditional transportation planning requires that the planning process starts with the forecasting of future demand for travel. This forecasting exercise derives future demand for travel from existing travel patterns (Martens and Hurvitz 2011). The implicit assumption behind the employed travel demand models is that travel flows are a result of free choice, i.e. that travelers "have freely chosen one possibility over all others, which in turn suggests that the observed pattern of trips represents the best possible set of actions that individuals could have taken given their preferences and the spatial structure of the city" (Sheppard 1995, p. 112). However, as the vast body of literature on spatial mismatch, women and transport, and transport-related social exclusion shows, current travel demand is as much the result of constraint as it is of choice. These constraints include not only household budgets (time and money), but also households' access to different transportation modes and the availability of transport services in its broadest sense (roads, parking facilities, public transport services, bicycle paths, pavements, pedestrian crossings, and so on). These constraints will be reflected in the existing travel patterns of households, with households experiencing larger constraints to movement revealing lower levels of travel, ceteris paribus. Travel models that use existing travel patterns as the basis for forecasting will, implicitly, reproduce these differences. That is, such models will predict a strong growth in travel among population segments experiencing relatively limited constraints on travel, while showing little growth among population groups restrained in traveling. By ignoring the fact that current travel patterns are a reflection of the way in which transport resources have been distributed in the past, transport models thus create an inherent feedback loop. Since transport models were introduced at a moment in time when roads were already being constructed and car ownership and use were rapidly increasing, the models inevitably resulted in extrapolation of increases in car use in the future. These extrapolations, in turn, led to predictions of a lack of capacity on the existing road system in the future. Together with the egalitarian principle of uncongested travel, these predictions subsequently favored policies that catered to this growth through improved services for car owners (typically, extensions of the road system). These improved services, in turn, resulted in higher trip rates or longer trip distances among car owners, certainly if they included new roads and thus substantial improvements in potential mobility through the network effect. From here on the circle started all over again (Figure 2.2) (see also Owens 1995). If transport models had been introduced at a time that public transport ridership was expanding at a rapid pace, the models would have reproduced this trend in their forecasts and transportation planning would probably have generated proposals for the (near perpetual) improvement of the public transportation system.

The focus on travel demand is thus more than a necessary step in the technical exercise of prediction. It actually suggests an implicit assumption that demand constitutes the just principle upon which the distribution of new transport facilities is to be based. The consequence is that traditional transportation planning, with its emphasis on the proper functioning of the transportation system, is likely to reinforce the existing disparities in trip patterns between population groups differing in terms of their access to modes of transport and especially to the motorcar.

From a social justice perspective, the fourth informal rule of traditional transportation planning is also of key importance. This rule prescribes that transportation planners carry out an assessment of costs and benefits of proposed transportation investments. Social justice considerations have traditionally played a role in the development of the methodology of cost-benefit analysis, most notably in the monetary valuation of travel time savings. Since time savings typically account for the vast majority of benefits generated by a transport investment, the way in which the monetary value of these savings is calculated is of the utmost importance. In virtually all countries using CBA, the value of travel time savings is linked to wage rates, so the key question is which wage level to use in the calculation. The theoretical foundations underlying CBA suggest the use of market-based values and differentiating the value of travel time savings according to differences in income levels of groups of travelers. The possible consequences of such an approach were recognized as early as the 1960s (Mackie, Fowkes *et al.* 2003). If market-based values were to be used, transport investments that primarily benefit higher income groups would score substantially better in cost-benefit analyses than alternatives that would serve poor population groups, all else being equal. In order to address this bias, the so-called 'equity value of travel time' was introduced in many countries (Hayashi and Morisugi 2000). The equity value of time is based on an average income level and is used for all travel time savings, independent of the income level of the traveler that benefits from the time saving. Note that in many countries differential values of time are still used for trips with different travel motives, creating a bias for trips with a high economic value.

While the use of equity values is certainly to the benefit of weaker groups in society, the focus on these values hides another, even more powerful, distributional mechanism at work in cost-benefit analysis. This mechanism relates to the link between the total number of trips and the total benefits generated by a transport improvement. The more trips are forecasted for a specific link for a certain year in the future, the more travel time savings can be earned by improving that link, and the higher the total benefits related to that improvement. This principle works to the advantage of stronger population groups with high levels of car ownership, as they are characterized by substantially higher trip rates than weaker population groups with low levels of car ownership (see above). For instance, the improvement of a link between a well-to-do suburb and a large retail area will virtually always perform better in a cost-benefit analysis than an improvement in the transport link between a disadvantaged neighborhood and the same retail area. This is especially important, as the capacity of a transport link cannot be increased in a gradual way, but only in discrete portions (typically, an additional traffic lane). The application of cost-benefit analysis is thus likely to lead to a systematic bias in investment priorities, especially in societies with a strong spatial segregation of population groups by income, as this spatial segregation is likely to be replicated, at least to some extent, in their use of particular infrastructures (Hodge 1995).

The analysis above suggests that the principle of equality of uncongested movement thus goes hand in hand with the principle of demand for travel or demand for mobility, defined here as the actual movement of a person in terms of distances covered. On a closer inspection it can even be said that the principle of equality is nothing other than the principle of demand in disguise. By striving for uncongested travel on the various transportation networks, traditional transportation planning has to take demand as its starting point. Only by catering for demand is it possible to deliver equality in terms of speed within a network. This is, obviously, in line with other engineering disciplines, in which extrapolation of expected demand is key to the design of well-functioning networks. Clearly, the practice of transportation planning has revealed that catering for demand has not been able to deliver uncongested travel on the network. But more important from my perspective is the observation that the principle of demand, rather than the principle of equality, is the pervasive distributive principle underlying traditional transportation planning (see also Mees 2010, p. 30).

Let me summarize, then, the regressive face of traditional transportation planning. The principle of equality implicitly enshrined in traditional transportation planning translates into pervasive inequalities between persons in terms of travel speed, potential mobility, accessibility and, ultimately, revealed mobility. The traditional approach is blind to these differences in potential mobility and accessibility and unconditionally accepts the differences in revealed mobility as a representation of choice. Because of this, the approach is likely to strengthen these inequalities, while purportedly seeking to provide identical level-of-service in terms of congestion-free travel for all users of the transportation system. The informal rules of traditional transportation planning thus result in a vicious circle, which at best maintains existing differences in all dimensions and at worst leads to a continuous growth in inequalities in terms of travel speed, potential mobility, accessibility and revealed mobility, between persons with access to, and persons excluded from, the dominant car-road system. Figure 2.2 provides a graphic representation of these tendencies enshrined in the rules of traditional transportation planning.

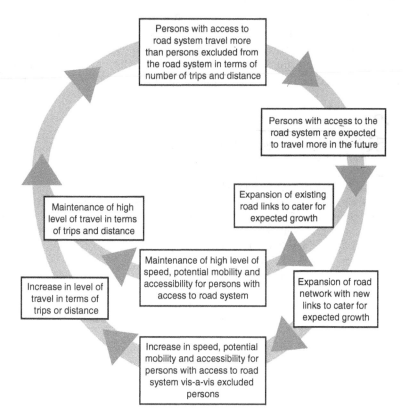

Figure 2.2 The vicious circle embodied in traditional transportation planning.
Source: Adapted from Martens 2006.

Conclusion

The practice of transportation planning is clearly highly diverse and in continuous flux. Yet the central elements of the traditional approach to transportation planning as presented in this chapter are still apparent in much of the practice across the world. The exploration of the implicit principles of fairness embodied in the approach is thus of the utmost importance. The results of the exploration are sobering at best: from the perspective of justice, the traditional approach to transportation planning is highly problematic.

A first reading of traditional transportation planning suggests that the approach is based on the powerful principle of equality. Indeed, the traditional approach aims to provide uncongested movement for all. A more critical reading, however, quickly reveals that equality can only be achieved by planning according to demand. As a consequence, traditional transportation planning generates vast disparities in terms of travel speeds, potential mobility, accessibility and, ultimately, revealed mobility. As underscored by the vast strands of literature on transport-related social exclusion, spatial mismatch and women and transport, these disparities go hand in hand with real hardships among persons lacking access to the dominant means of transportation. It requires systematic normative reasoning to determine whether these disparities actually constitute injustices. That challenge will be taken up in the second part of the book.

References

Black, W.R. (2003). *Transportation: a geographical analysis*. New York, The Guilford Press.

Bristow, A.L. and J. Nellthorp (2000). Transport project appraisal in the European Union. *Transport Policy*, 7(1): 51–60.

Browne, D. and L. Ryan (2011). Comparative analysis of evaluation techniques for transport policies. *Environmental Impact Assessment Review*, 31(3): 226–233.

Cervero, R., J.S. Neil and B.B. Paul (2001). Transportation Planning. In *International Encyclopedia of the Social & Behavioral Sciences*. Oxford, Pergamon: 15873–15878.

de Jong, G., A. Daly, M. Pieters, *et al.* (2007). Uncertainty in traffic forecasts: literature review and new results for The Netherlands. *Transportation*, 34(4): 375–395.

Golub, A. and K. Martens (2014). Using principles of justice to assess the modal equity of regional transportation plans. *Journal of Transport Geography*, 41(0): 10–20.

Graham, S. and S. Marvin (2001). *Splintering Urbanism: networked infrastructures, technological mobilities and the urban condition*. London/New York, Routledge.

Handy, S. (2005). Planning for accessibility: in theory and in practice. In: D.M. Levinson and K.J. Krizek (eds), *Access to Destinations*. Amsterdam, Elsevier, 131–147.

Hartgen, D.T. (2003). Guidelines for highway needs studies. *Transportation Quarterly*, 57(2): 57–79.

Hayashi, Y. and H. Morisugi (2000). International comparison of background concept and methodology of transportation project appraisal. *Transport Policy*, 7(1): 73–88.

Hensher, D.A. and K.J. Button (eds) (2000). *Handbook of Transport Modelling*. Oxford, Pergamon.

Hodge, D.C. (1995). My fair share: equity issues in urban transportation. In: Susan Hanson (ed.), *The Geography of Urban Transportation*. New York/ London, The Guilford Press.

Kane, L. and R. Del Mistro (2003). Changes in transport planning policy: Changes in transport planning methodology? *Transportation*, 30(2): 113–131.

Koglin, T. and T. Rye (2014). The marginalisation of bicycling in Modernist urban transport planning. *Journal of Transport and Health*, 1(4): 214–222.

Lane, R., T.J. Powell and P.P. Smith (1971). *Analytical Transport Planning*. London, Gerald Duckworth and Company.

Levine, J. (2013). Urban transportation and social equity: transportation-planning paradigms that impede policy reform. In: N. Carmon and S.S. Fainstein (eds), *Policy, Planning, and People: promoting justice in urban development*, University of Pennsylvania Press: 141–160.

Litman, T. (2013). The new transportation planning paradigm. *ITE Journal*, 83(6): 20–28.

Mackie, P.J., A.S. Fowkes, M. Wardman, G. Whelan, J. Nellthorp and J. Bates (2003). Value of travel time savings in the UK: Summary Report. Leeds, Institute for Transport Studies, University of Leeds/John Bates Services.

Martens, K. (2006). Basing transport planning on principles of social justice. *Berkeley Planning Journal*, 19: 1–17.

Martens, K. (2014). *Traditional transportation planning and its alternatives*. Paper presented at the AESOP Conference, 9–12 July 2014, Utrecht.

Martens, K. and E. Hurvitz (2011). Distributive impacts of demand-based modelling. *Transportmetrica*, 7(3): 181–200.

Martens, K., A. Golub and G. Robinson (2011). *A fair distribution of transportation benefits: interpreting Title VI for transportation investment programs*. Paper presented at the 90th Annual Conference of the Transportation Research Board, 23–27 January 2011, Washington DC, USA.

Mees, P. (2010). *Transport for Suburbia: beyond the automobile age*. London/ Washington DC, Earthscan.

North, D.C. (1990). *Institutions, Institutional Change and Economic Performance*. Cambridge, Cambridge University Press.

Ostrom, E. (2009). *Understanding Institutional Diversity*. Princeton, Princeton University Press.

Owens, S. (1995). From 'predict and provide' to 'predict and prevent'? Pricing and planning in transport policy. *Transport Policy*, 2(1): 43–49.

Puu, T. (2005). On the genesis of hexagonal shapes. *Networks & Spatial Economics*, 5(1): 5–20.

Sager, T. (2005). Footloose and forecast-free: hypermobility and the planning of society. *European Journal of Spatial Development*, 17: 1–23.

Sanchez, T., M. Brenman, J. Ma, *et al.* (2008). *Right to Transportation: moving to equity*. American Planning Association.

Sen, A. (1980). Equality of what? *The Tanner Lectures on Human Values, Vol. I.* Salt Lake City, University of Utah Press: 195–220.

Sheppard, E. (1995). Modeling and predicting aggregate flows. In: S. Hanson (ed.) *The Geography of Urban Transportation*. New York/London, The Guilford Press: 100–128.

Shiftan, Y., K.J. Button and P. Nijkamp (eds) (2007). *Transportation Planning*. Cheltenham, Edward Elgar.

Weiner, E. (2008). *Urban Transportation Planning in the United States: history, policy and practice*. Washington DC, Springer.

Willis, K.G., G.D. Garrod and D.R. Harvey (1998). A review of cost-benefit analysis as applied to the evaluation of new road proposals in the UK. *Transportation Research Part D: Transport and Environment*, 3(3): 141–156.

Wood, C. (2003). *Environmental Impact Assessment: a comparative review*. Harlow, Pearson Education.

Part II
Philosophical Explorations

3 Setting the Stage

TRAVEL seeks Annihilate Space

Introduction

It would be an understatement to claim that transportation has not been the favorite subject matter of philosophers of social justice over the past centuries. Indeed, no philosopher has explicitly and systematically addressed justice in the domain of transportation. At best, scholars of social justice have touched upon transportation on the sidelines, as an example to develop a broader, typically unrelated, argument (see, for instance, Michelman 1973, p. 980; Walzer 1983, p. 115; Sen 1983, p. 160; Sadurski 1985, p. 161; Braybrooke 1987, pp. 18–19; Elster 1992, pp. 59–61; Miller 1999, p. 7).

The lack of attention for transportation goes hand in hand with a more elementary trait of philosophies of social justice: they are fundamentally a-spatial in character (Pirie 1983). Theories of social justice routinely ignore the inherently spatial dimension of the human condition. They fail to acknowledge that ignoring space in fact implies the introduction of a strongly simplifying assumption, which, if brought into play, could have profound implications for theorizing about social justice. Indeed, this is precisely what the emerging body of literature on spatial justice seeks to highlight and explore (e.g. Dikec 2001; Dikec 2009; Soja 2009; Marcuse 2009). The a-spatial character of social justice theories means, almost by implication, that transportation can go unobserved, because transportation is the direct opposite of space: space necessitates travel and travel, in a fundamental way, seeks to annihilate space (Harvey 1990).

The explorations of justice in the domain of transportation can therefore never be simply a matter of 'applying' theories of social justice to transportation. The explorations will always require the extension of a theory to account for the fundamental spatiality of human life. Yet this does not imply that the extremely rich body of theories of social justice cannot serve as a source of inspiration. Indeed they can and I will draw on a number of these theories in the chapters that follow.

The current chapter aims to set the stage for those that follow. Drawing heavily on an argument developed by Amartya Sen (2006), I will define what I expect from a theory of justice for the domain of transportation.

As I will argue, there is no need to develop a complete, transcendental, theory of justice in order to derive fairness principles for transportation planning. I will end the chapter with a brief outline of the argument as it will unfold in the four subsequent chapters.

What do we want from a theory of justice for the domain of transportation?

In Chapter 1, I argued that a proper understanding of fairness is necessary as a basis for transportation planning. The goal of the subsequent chapters is to learn from theories of justice what fairness in the domain of transportation could mean. But before tackling this challenge, it is important to specify more precisely what I expect these theories of justice to deliver.

Sen has taken up this question in a more general sense in his paper titled 'What do we want from a theory of justice?' (Sen 2006). Sen argues that the most influential contemporary theories of justice have taken a transcendental approach in seeking to answer the question: What is a just society? The aim of such theories is to identify perfectly just arrangements. Sen contrasts this with a comparative approach, where the focus is on ranking alternative societal arrangements in terms of being 'less just' or 'more just' than other arrangements, without defining the perfectly just 'end state'. The most well-known transcendental theory is John Rawls' theory of justice, which will be discussed in Chapter 5. Sen argues that comparison is of crucial practical importance in order to advance justice in a society. Comparison of different 'states' of society is necessary in order to determine whether a particular state is more just than another. Sen's claim is that transcendental theories are neither sufficient nor necessary as a basis for comparative assessment.

Transcendental theories on their own are not sufficient, according to Sen, because they create a grand partition between the just and the unjust. This grand partitioning would leave most societies on the side of the unjust, even after the implementation of large-scale reforms. As a result, transcendental theories can only propose "a radical jump to a perfectly just world" (Sen 2006, p. 218). The specification of the 'right' or 'completely just' social arrangement, even if understood as the best social arrangement, does not say much about the grading of two non-best alternatives. This is especially so because any transcendental theory of justice will be characterized by multiple dimensions of justice, complicating the assessment of any advancement towards the 'right' social arrangement. For instance, in the context of Rawls' theory of justice, it is by no means clear how an improvement in the protection of liberties could be weighed against an increase in the income and wealth of the least-advantaged groups. Transcendental theories could be extended to include such weighing, but, Sen argues, such extensions "lie well beyond the specific exercise of the identification of transcendence, and are indeed the basic ingredients of a 'comparative' rather than a 'transcendental' approach to justice" (ibid., p. 220).

Sen argues that transcendental theories are also not necessary to rank any two alternatives in terms of justice. He argues against the (implicit) claim of proponents of transcendental theories of justice that the possibility of comparison implies the possibility of identifying the very best option. Sen argues that a sequence of pairwise comparisons does not invariably have to lead to the identification of the very best. He argues that such a 'natural endpoint' of comparison is only possible when a perfect, i.e. complete and transitive, ordering of all alternatives is possible. There may be a number of reasons why this may not be achieved, including judgmental unresolvability between disparate considerations (such as liberties versus income and wealth) or unbridgeable gaps of information. Yet, Sen argues, such "incompleteness would not prevent comparative judgments of justice in a great many cases, where there might be fair agreement on particular pairwise rankings, about how to enhance justice and reduce injustice" (ibid., pp. 225–226).

Sen suggests that it may be possible to reach agreement on ranking of various alternatives without having to rely on a transcendental theory of justice. He proposes to employ the notion of impartiality as developed by Adam Smith (2010 [1759]) as a vehicle to achieve such rankings. The impartial spectators proposed by Smith are imagined observers who are not themselves parties to the societal decisions that are to be taken. They actually need not be members of the particular society at all. Their impartiality derives precisely from the fact that they are not affected by the decision; they are disinterested (distant) observers. The advantage of the procedure of impartiality is that it can be applied to assess different courses of action, without having to rely on a transcendental theory.

Comparison versus completeness

Clearly, Sen's observations about transcendental approaches to justice are also of relevance for the domain of transportation. Transportation planning, like any domain of government intervention, is inevitably an exercise of comparison, of comparing various policy options against each other. Would it be possible to reach fair agreement on particular pairwise rankings of transportation interventions without having to rely on a transcendental theory of justice for the domain of transportation?

The power of Sen's argument seems to depend strongly on the examples he provides. Few would disagree that widespread hunger, slavery, or rampant illiteracy constitute an injustice, inarguably if they involve children. A transcendental theory of justice hardly seems necessary in these cases in order to compare and rank alternatives in terms of justice. But such agreement is clearly more difficult to reach when injustices are less apparent. For instance, it is less clear whether the lack of shops with fresh fruit and vegetables in certain neighborhoods in the US and UK (so-called 'food deserts') constitute an injustice or merely an unfortunate consequence of largely 'just' housing and retail markets. In such cases, it will be much more difficult to reach fair agreement/on grounds of justice (rather than on grounds of reducing public health expenditures) whether actions are needed at all, let alone on pairwise ranking of possible alternative policy interventions. In these cases, a clearer delineation of justice in the domain of food or health may be warranted. The example suggests that a comparable situation may emerge in the domain of transportation. Here, too, it may often be difficult to reach a fair agreement based on impartial pairwise comparison of policy options. The lack of debate about fairness in the domain of transportation in many countries may well be related to the fact that it is by no means clear whether existing inequalities in that domain actually constitute injustices.

The second weakness of the comparative approach lies in the fact that alternatives can seldom be compared in only one dimension. Clearly, virtually every policy action brings with it costs in terms of time, money, or restrictions on persons' actions. Inevitably, the comparative approach requires a weighing of possible alternatives in all relevant dimensions, and it is highly likely that different persons will reach different conclusions. Thus, while most will easily agree that any policy that reduces hunger, slavery or illiteracy is to be preferred over policy options that do nothing to address these phenomena, opinions may rapidly diverge once the related obligations and sacrifices for each alternative are specified. Clearly, the proliferation of opinions is even more likely for inequalities with less clear impacts in terms of human suffering, such as differences in accessibility to employment or health care.

Thus Sen's claim that a comparative approach to justice may be sufficient to advance justice in society seems at best to hold only under a particular condition, namely that of a substantial distance between the current state of a society and any possible ideal state. This condition is represented in a graphic way in Figure 3.1. The current state of society is depicted as a point on the left-hand side of each diagram. Possible transcendental positions, on which people who seek to reach a fair agreement may implicitly or intuitively draw, are depicted by the points in the shaded area on the right-hand side of each diagram, with the shaded area representing the range of possible transcendental positions. If we implement policy alternative x we end up at the 'position' in the figure indicated by box X. If we implement policy alternative y we end up at the 'position' in the figure indicated by box Y. When the distance between the current state and possible ideal states is large, as is the case in the left-hand diagram, it is relatively easy to rank the policy alternatives x and y, since alternative x clearly brings the society closer to the ideal, irrespective of the transcendental position one is embracing. However, the situation changes as steps are

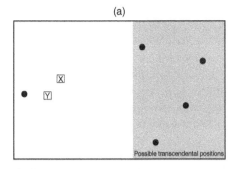 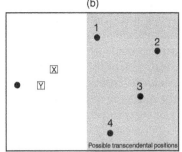

Figure 3.1 Transcendental versus comparative approaches to social justice under conditions of (a) large and (b) small disparities between the current situation and possible (implicit) transcendental positions.

made towards justice and the current state advances towards each of the transcendental positions. Then, a comparison of policies x and y based on the distance to different (implicit) transcendental positions is more likely to lead to a different ranking of x and y. In the example depicted in the right-hand side of Figure 3.1, x is preferred over y if one upholds, perhaps only intuitively, one of the three transcendental positions 1, 2 or 3, while y is preferred over x if one draws on ideal position 4. Clearly, reaching fair agreement merely on comparison of alternatives without exploring the validity of the underlying transcendental positions becomes more problematic as societies move (as some have) towards a possible ideal. The difficulty only increases if we take note of the multiple dimensions that need to be taken into account in comparing the alternatives.

Does this imply that a full-fledged transcendental theory, identifying the 'right' or 'best' social arrangement, is a necessary (albeit not sufficient) prerequisite for comparing alternatives in the case of less blatant injustices? Not necessarily. What we expect from a theory of justice under such a condition is an attempt to delineate the *range* of possible ideal positions, so that fair agreement about the ranking of policy interventions becomes again possible. That theory does not have to achieve 'completeness', i.e. define precisely what is a just state of affairs. It should merely deliver arguments strong enough to convince reasonable persons that particular, perhaps hitherto widely defended, positions fall outside the range of possible ideal positions. In terms of Figure 3.1, what is needed is a theory that provides arguments sufficiently powerful to exclude at least position 4 from the set of (implicit) transcendental positions, so that it is again possible to rank interventions x and y. Clearly, whatever can be said of the (lack of) progress in philosophies of social justice, and however incomplete many theories of social justice may be, philosophical scholarship over the past centuries has succeeded in reducing the range of possible transcendental positions. For instance, there is now wide agreement among philosophers that each and every person is of intrinsic value and should always be perceived as an end and never (only) as a means. This is not to suggest that it is possible to define the 'right' social arrangement in a step-by-step process by reducing the range of possible ideal positions with every step. Clearly, eliminating transcendental positions from the range of possibilities will become harder and harder the more narrow the remaining range of possibilities. Indeed, identifying a single transcendental position may prove to be ultimately elusive, as Sen has powerfully argued.

This argument is obviously in need of further development, but I will leave this for another occasion. What can be concluded here is that there is a middle ground between Sen's comparative approach and a transcendental approach to social justice. This is encouraging, as the development of a full-fledged transcendental theory has proven to be illusory (see e.g. Sandel's powerful criticism of Rawls' theory of justice; Sandel 1982). The incompleteness of such a 'middle-ground theory of justice' should not be perceived as a problem, because "a theory that makes systematic room for incompleteness [can] allow[s] one to arrive at possibly quite strong judgments" (Sen 2006, p. 223). Indeed, for our practical purposes, an incomplete theory of justice in transportation may well be sufficient and we thus need not be too concerned if we do not succeed in developing a complete transcendental theory.

To summarize, the goal of subsequent chapters is not to develop a complete, transcendental, theory of justice for the domain of transportation. The goal is to limit the range of possible ideal positions, so that it is possible to develop an approach to ranking policy interventions in the transportation system (and, possibly, interventions in land use patterns and service delivery) on grounds of justice. This will be sufficient to achieve our goal: to define a set of robust principles of justice on which transportation planning should be based.

Towards a theory of justice for the transportation domain

The argument developed in this chapter has resulted in a refinement of the goal of the second part of this book. Its aim is not to develop a complete, transcendental, theory of justice in transportation, but to reduce the range of possible transcendental positions for the domain of transportation.

In the following chapters I will take up this challenge by drawing on a range of theories of social justice. I deliberately take inspiration from a range of theories, because different theories can provide important components for a larger argument. As may be clear from the previous section, I do not uphold the position that the answer to practical questions of justice requires a comprehensive, transcendental, theory of justice. Rather, I stipulate the opposite: the tendency to hold on to one, preferred, comprehensive theory of justice often stands in the way of systematic reasoning about fairness in a particular domain of life. The tendency, among philosophers and others, to reject particular theories because they contain 'flaws' or because their application to particular, sometimes highly unrealistic, cases leads to counter-intuitive results, is hardly fruitful in the search for answers to questions of practical relevance. Theories, no matter how comprehensive, can always be refuted based on a particular case. But justice is too important to remain within the realm of academic debate. Real questions of justice, regarding the distribution of real goods, regarding power and domination, oppression and autonomy, are too important to be left unresolved because no comprehensive framework can be designed to solve them once and for all. Comprehensive theories of justice should be perceived as powerful tools to engage with and to help resolve practical questions of justice. Not because these theories can be simply applied to a particular question of fairness, but because they provide a powerful line of reasoning that can help shed light on the question of justice at hand. The failure of a theory to provide a fully satisfactory answer should be perceived neither as a reason for refuting the theory, nor as a sign of an intractable question of justice. Rather, every theory of social justice should be assessed in terms of the extent to which it succeeds in reducing the plethora of (implicit) transcendental positions to a range that allows for a practical ranking of policy options.

This, then, is the aim of the second part of this book: to narrow down the range of (implicit) transcendental positions regarding fairness in the domain of transportation. In order to do so, I will take up a number of theories and analyze what light they can shed on the question of fairness in the domain of transportation. The aim is not to juxtapose these theories, but to explore how the distinct lines of reasoning that emerge from them can, *taken together*, reduce the range of transcendental positions. In even more practical terms, the book will succeed in its goal if it can eliminate from the range of possible positions the traditional approach to transportation planning as presented and critically discussed in Chapter 2.

In the chapters that follow, I will draw on three major philosophies of social justice to develop the outline of the argument: Walzer's spheres of justice (Chapter 4), Rawls' theory of justice (Chapter 5), and Dworkin's theory of equality of resources (Chapter 6). How can I draw on such diverse theories of justice? To justify this, I need to give a brief overview of the main line of the argument as it will be developed in the coming chapters.

I start in the following chapter with an exploration of Walzer's theory of distributive spheres. From his theory I take the argument that theories of social justice should not deal with the basic structure of society or with abstract goods, as argued by Rawls, but rather with the wide range of goods that are actually produced in society and subsequently shared, divided and exchanged in specific ways between the members of that society. Among this wide variety of 'real' goods some stand out because they have what Walzer calls a 'distinct social meaning'. He argues that the distribution of goods with such a distinct social meaning should not be determined by market exchange. These goods deserve a distinct 'sphere', which basically means that the distribution of the goods is to be guided by explicit distributive principles. As I will argue in Chapter 4, accessibility is a good of prominent importance for persons and as such deserves a separate sphere.

In the following step of the argument, I accept Walzer's point of view that one single theory of justice cannot give direction to the fair distribution of all goods with a distinct social meaning. Indeed, each good may require a different principle of distribution. I reject, however, Walzer's claim that the proper distributive principle can be identified by analyzing the shared understandings of members of society regarding the social meaning of a particular good. Rather, I claim, it is necessary to invoke analytical theories of social justice, such as those developed by Rawls and Dworkin, in order to derive and justify fair principles of distribution for each sphere. Obviously, I will limit myself to the transportation sphere when invoking analytical theories of justice. Yet the analytical approach proposed here could also be followed for other spheres, although it may be necessary to employ a different set of theories or lines of reasoning for each sphere.

In Chapter 5 I explore whether it is possible to derive distributive principles for the transportation domain from Rawls' influential theory of justice. This exploration leads to the conclusion that Rawls' theory cannot provide parameters with regard to the fair distribution of accessibility. Possible extensions of his theory all run into the so-called problem of interpersonal comparison, which inevitably involves complex value judgments. A theory of justice can only be successful in providing a solid footing for a fair distribution of goods if it succeeds in avoiding, at least as much as possible, such value judgments. Through a very careful design, Rawls has largely succeeded in doing so in his theory of justice. The incorporation of accessibility into Rawls' theory would fundamentally weaken this powerful characteristic of his framework. This is a disappointing conclusion, but it also underscores the earlier observation that a complete, transcendental, theory of social justice may be an impossibility. This conclusion further supports the path suggested above: to develop principles for the fair distribution of 'real' goods based on analytical philosophy and to refrain from developing a 'grand theory of social justice'. If successful, such a sphere-by-sphere approach would push the problem of interpersonal comparison to the boundaries between the spheres, while either limiting the range of possible fair distributions within each sphere or, ideally, generating a convincing argument for one particular set of principles for the distribution of each good.

In Chapter 6 I turn to Dworkin to follow the path of analytical philosophy to develop principles for the fair distribution of accessibility. Dworkin's theory of equality of resources has two advantages for my purposes. First, while not explicitly posited by Dworkin, his line of reasoning can be extended to different goods and thus to different 'spheres of justice', without requiring the development of a grand, overarching theory of social justice. As I will show, such an extension of his theory is also possible for the domain of transportation and the distribution of accessibility. Second, and in contrast with some other approaches to social justice, Dworkin's theory links fairness in distribution directly to the cost of delivering the desired distribution. By doing so, principles of fairness are not developed in an idealized situation without resource constraints, but directly take into account the inevitable sacrifices involved in delivering a fair distribution.

Dworkin links fairness and resource scarcity through the notion of a hypothetical insurance scheme. I will follow this path and explore whether members of society would be willing to purchase insurance to avoid a lack of accessibility should various forms of brute bad luck strike, such as travel-related impairments or a low income. The analysis leads to the conclusion that prudent persons would typically want to purchase an insurance scheme that guarantees them a sufficient level of accessibility if bad luck strikes, but also that the insurance schemes may work out differently over space. Furthermore, it shows that the mere existence of an insurance scheme for accessibility would lead to different dynamics in land use and housing markets, which would change urban structure and accessibility patterns.

In the final chapter of this part of the book, I will further explore the notion of sufficient accessibility. These explorations will be rooted first and foremost in the transportation domain itself. But I will also draw loosely on theories of justice, most notably on the capability approach developed by Sen and Nussbaum.

Taken together, these philosophical explorations will provide the basis for the last part of the book, in which I will present a practical approach to transportation planning based on principles of justice.

References

Braybrooke, D. (1987). *Meeting Needs*. Princeton, NJ, Princeton University Press.

Dikec, M. (2001). Justice and the spatial imagination. *Environment and Planning A*, 33(10): 1785–1806.

Dikec, M. (2009). Justice and the spatial imagination. In: P. Marcuse, J. Connolly, J. Novy *et al.* (eds) (2011), *Searching for the Just City: debates in urban theory and practice*. London, Routledge.

Elster, J. (1992). *Local Justice: how institutions allocate scarce goods and necessary burdens*. Cambridge, Cambridge University Press.

Harvey, D. (1990). *The Condition of Postmodernity: an enquiry into the origins of cultural change*. Malden, MA/Oxford, Blackwell.

Marcuse, P. (2009). Spatial Justice: derivative but causal of social injustice. *Justice Spatiale | Spatial Justice*, 1.

Michelman, F.I. (1973). In pursuit of constitutional welfare rights: one view of Rawls' theory of justice. *University of Pennsylvania Law Review*, 121: 962–1019.

Miller, D. (1999). *Principles of Social Justice*. Cambridge, MA/London, Harvard University Press.

Pirie, G.H. (1983). On spatial justice. *Environment and Planning A*, 15(4): 465–473.

Sadurski, W. (1985). *Giving Desert its Due: social justice and legal theory*. Dordrecht, D. Reidel Publishing Company.

Sandel, M. (1982). *Liberalism and the Limits of Justice*. Cambridge, Cambridge University Press.

Sen, A. (1983). Poor, relatively speaking. *Oxford Economic Papers*, 35(2): 153–169.

Sen, A. (2006). What do we want from a theory of justice? *The Journal of Philosophy*, 103(5): 215–238.

Soja, E. (2009). The city and spatial justice. *Justice Spatiale | Spatial Justice*, 1.

Walzer, M. (1983). *Spheres of Justice: a defense of pluralism and equality*, New York, Basic Books.

4 The Social Meaning of Transportation

Introduction

The development of a theory of justice for the domain of transportation requires, as I have argued at the end of the previous chapter, a two-step process. First, it involves a justification for setting the good of transportation apart from other, regular, goods produced by members of society. Second, it requires the systematic development of principles of justice that can guide the distribution of the transport good. In this chapter, I take up the first challenge. The chapter will start with a brief account of Walzer's theory of justice. This will set the stage for an exploration of the social meaning of the transport good in the subsequent section. That exploration will result in a conclusion that is in line with the large body of literature that has developed over the past decades: the distinct social meaning of the transport good lies in the *accessibility* it confers to persons. I will then develop an argument for why the distribution of accessibility should be set apart from the distribution of other, regular, goods. Finally, I will argue that Walzer's approach cannot deliver well-founded principles of justice for the distribution of accessibility. This conclusion demarcates the starting point for Chapters 5 and 6, in which I will draw on Rawls' and Dworkin's theories of justice to develop principles of justice for the fair distribution of accessibility.

A brief account of Walzer's *Spheres of Justice*

The theoretical starting point for the proposed justice approach to transport is Walzer's *Spheres of Justice* (Walzer 1983; Walzer 1995). In line with most other contemporary scholars (but see Young 1990), Walzer takes a distributive approach to social justice by asking the question how benefits and burdens are and should be distributed over members of society. However, unlike other scholars of social justice such as Rawls (1971), he does not focus on the distribution of abstract goods. Rather, he views society as a distributive community in which people produce a *wide variety of goods* that are subsequently shared, divided and exchanged in specific ways. These goods, according to Walzer, can neither be reduced to a set of abstract goods, nor be idiosyncratically valued. Goods are, by definition, social goods; their meaning is socially constructed (Walzer 1983, p. 7). Goods can have different meanings in different societies; the same 'thing' may be valued in one place, while it is hardly valued or even disvalued in another. Likewise, goods with a comparable 'market value' may differ fundamentally from a distributive perspective, because they differ in terms of the social meaning that members of a particular society attach to them. Precisely because of the differences in the social meaning of goods, Walzer argues, there can be no single criterion in virtue of which all goods are to be made available to members of society. Commonly defended criteria like free exchange, need or desert cannot determine the distribution of *all* goods available in society. Furthermore, distributive criteria and arrangements are intrinsic not to the good-in-itself but to the social good: "If we understand what it is, what it means to those for whom it is a good, we understand how, by whom, and for what reasons it ought to be distributed" (ibid., p. 9). The social meaning of a good is therefore of crucial importance in Walzer's approach. It is the basis for determining what constitutes a fair distribution: "All distributions are just or unjust relative to the social meanings of the goods at stake" (ibid., p. 9).

Based on this 'theory of goods', Walzer then develops the concept of 'distributive spheres'. Distributive spheres are the prerogative of goods that have a *distinct* social meaning in a particular society that sets them apart from regular goods. While regular goods, like necklaces or cutlery, may also have a social meaning, they can be distributed through the market and their distribution can be determined through the principle of free exchange. Goods to which a particular society ascribes a distinct social meaning, by contrast, are to be taken out of the sphere of free exchange. Typical examples in modern Western societies are health and education. These and comparable goods, Walzer argues, 'deserve' their own distributive sphere.

For Walzer, a distributive sphere is characterized by two basic features. First, it requires that the distribution of a particular good be guided by a distributive principle other than free exchange. As discussed, these principles can differ—ranging from equality to need—but are to match the social meaning of the good in a particular society (Trappenburg 2000). Second, a distributive sphere should guarantee that the distribution of the particular good is autonomous from the way in which other goods are distributed. According to Walzer, injustice occurs if spheres are not autonomous. In that case, the distribution of one good or one set of goods can become dominant and determine the distributions in all, or many, spheres of distribution. Typically, according to Walzer, money and power are the goods to claim dominance, and much of the political debates, like those in the fields of basic education or health services, are about limiting their domination. Ultimately, autonomy guarantees what Walzer terms 'complex equality': a situation in which inequalities *within* spheres may exist, but in which the autonomy of distributive spheres will guarantee that inequalities will not necessarily *sum up across* different goods or spheres.

Walzer's approach is certainly not without problems (see below, and see e.g. Dworkin 1983a; Teuber 1984; Fabre 2007). Its strength lies in the theoretical foundation it provides for the political reality in modern societies. In modern societies, government intervention is not concerned with the distribution of abstract primary goods, such as those distinguished by Rawls (1971), but with the distribution of a wide variety of real, tangible, goods. Prominent among these are income, education, health care, and housing. Principles of justice play a central role in the distribution of each of these goods, although these principles may differ between societies.

The importance of Walzer's theory of justice, and its core concept of spheres, lies in the fact that it can provide a theoretical foundation for a distributive approach to transport. From Walzer's perspective, a distributive approach to a particular good is called for if that good has a distinct social meaning: "When meanings are distinct, distributions *must* be autonomous" (Walzer 1983, p. 10—emphasis KM). If this condition holds for the transport good, i.e. if the transport good has a socially distinct meaning, than a distributive approach to transport can be justified.

Walzer's theory of justice thus raises three key questions for the field of transport. The first concerns the social meaning of the transport good. Only if a clear social meaning can be ascribed to the transport good, is it fruitful to enter a discussion about the relevance of a separate transport sphere. The second, and perhaps principal, question is whether the social meaning ascribed to the transport good is distinct enough to draw boundaries around the good and set it apart from other goods and create a separate 'transport sphere'. Then, if the answer to this second query is positive, the third question is how the transport good should be distributed, i.e. which distributive principle is appropriate to guide the allocation of the transport good. In this chapter, I will address the first two questions. The third, crucial, question will be taken up in Chapters 5 through 7.

Defining the social meaning of transportation

The first question raised by Walzer's approach concerns the social meaning of what has thus far been referred to as 'the transport good'. Obviously, and in line with the critique of Dworkin (1983a), the demarcation of *the* social meaning of the transport good is not a simple one. Opinions may differ widely between and within societies, depending on people's backgrounds, perspectives and personal lives. Hence the discussion below is not a final answer, but an attempt to demarcate a social meaning that might be widely shared in modern societies.

First, when people relate to transport, it is about the possibilities it offers to travel to places, to access people and opportunities, or to experience the freedom to escape one's locality (see e.g. the contributions in Bergman and Sager 2008). The social meaning of the transport good therefore seems to lie in the benefits related to transport, rather than in the burdens that transportation generates. Even in academic discourse, the burdens related to transport, such as greenhouse gas emissions, are defined as negative *externalities*, emphasizing that they are not a core part of the transport good. This suggests that the distribution of the transport good should first and foremost be guided by the benefits that are related to it, rather than based on the burdens it may generate.

This is a fundamental point, because much of the debate on transport and equity has focused precisely on the distribution of transport-related burdens (e.g. Feitelson 2002; Forkenbrock and Schweitzer 1999; Schweitzer and Valenzuela 2004). Walzer's approach does not suggest that the distribution of these burdens is not a matter of justice. In line with his theory, it can actually be argued that in current (Western) societies, a healthy environment is a good with a distinct social meaning that deserves to be set apart from other goods. Walzer's approach thus suggests that the distribution of the transport-related environmental burdens should be related to environmental burdens from other sources and that their distribution should be jointly considered. The principle guiding the distribution of the total set of environmental burdens should subsequently be derived from the social meaning ascribed to a healthy environment. Note that the desired distributions in the 'environment sphere' may well have implications for the possible distributions in the 'transport sphere'. We will briefly return to this issue in the concluding chapter of this book. For now, it suffices to conclude that Walzer's emphasis on the social meaning of a good as the basis for its distribution suggests that the benefits of transport should be the starting point for the debate about the distribution of the transport good.

Second, it may be clear that the transport good as such does not exist. The good—however conceptualized—is a combination of objects like cars and bicycles; artifacts like roads and railways; services like public transport lines, car repair services and guarded parking facilities; and less tangible goods like driving licenses, traffic regulations or route guidance systems. In this sense, the transport good is comparable to a good like basic education, explicitly discussed by Walzer in his book. Like transport, basic education is not a concrete good that is transferred from one person to another. Basic education as a social good is the outcome of the combination of a multitude of tangible and less tangible goods: class rooms, teachers, school books, teaching materials, learning methods, and so on. These goods combine to form the good which Walzer refers to as 'mediated education': the systematic transfer of knowledge and skills to pupils and students. It is this good, rather than the different parts constituting it, which, according to Walzer, should be set apart in a separate sphere and distributed in a way compatible with the social meaning of the good in a particular society (Walzer 1983, pp. 197–226).

Following this line of reasoning, the distributive question in transport does not relate to the individual objects, artifacts and so on that constitute the 'transport good', as the social meaning of each of these parts stems from the social meaning of the overarching 'transport good'. Following Walzer, it is the social meaning of the overarching good that should provide the compass for the distribution of the good over members over society. The allocation of the composite parts—individual objects, artifacts, services and other goods—should be derived from this, not the other way around. This is, again, a fundamental point, as much of the literature and policy debates on distributive justice in transport have focused on precisely the composite parts, such as road and gasoline taxes (Altshuler 1979); transit investments and subsidies (Cervero 1981; Hodge 1988; Garrett and Taylor 1999); infrastructure investments (Lucy 1988; Bröcker, Korzhenevych *et al.* 2010); road user charges (Smeed *et al.* 1964; Richardson 1974; Ecola and Light 2009); and transit services (Rucker 1984; Murray and Davis 2001; Wu and Hine 2003).

For Western societies, and increasingly so for non-Western societies, and in line with much of the transport literature, two distinct meanings of the overarching transport good can be distinguished: potential mobility and accessibility (e.g. Garb and Levine 2002; Vigar 1999).

Potential mobility refers to the ease with which a person can move through space (e.g. Sager 2005; see also Chapter 2). Note that I explicitly distinguish between mobility and potential mobility, or movement and potentiality of movement, terms that are often used interchangeably in the literature (Kaufmann 2002, pp. 13–14). An increase in mobility implies that a person travels over longer distances, more frequently, or both, in a particular period of time. By contrast, an increase in potential mobility only implies an increase in a person's capacity to overcome distance in space—it does not imply the actual realization of this capacity (Sager 2005, pp. 3–4). Accessibility has a meaning quite distinct from potential mobility. As discussed in Chapter 1, it refers to the potential of opportunities for interaction (Hansen 1959; see Box 1.1). Like potential mobility it captures a capacity: an increase in accessibility implies an increase in a person's capacity to access places. Like potential mobility, it does not imply the actual 'consumption' of accessibility.

Both the concepts of potential mobility and of accessibility are directly related to important values in Western societies. The conceptualization of the transport good as potential mobility can be linked to notions such as freedom of movement and freedom of choice. (Potential) mobility is often even equated with freedom of movement (e.g. Cresswell 2006), although the latter refers to a right rather than to a capacity varying in strength. Freedom of choice and potential mobility are strongly intertwined—with a high level of potential mobility implying a high level of choice in terms of employment opportunities, health care services, leisure facilities, and so forth. Mobility is also closely linked to widely cherished values such as open-mindedness, discovery, experience and adventure (Kaufmann 2002), and to notions like escape and autonomy (Zeitler 1999; Lomasky 1997). Perhaps most importantly, high (potential) mobility is linked to the ambition to break the tether of physical friction—a desire enshrined in Western society and exemplified in the expansion of the Roman empire, the geographical discoveries of the fifteenth and sixteenth centuries, and the search for speed since the industrial revolution (Couclelis 1996; Harvey 1990; Sager 2005).

The concept of accessibility also has deep roots in Western value systems. Accessibility indicates ability, i.e. the ability to accomplish a broad range of actions, by linking to places and people that are set apart in space and time (Talen 2001). As such, accessibility is also linked to freedom of choice, with higher levels of accessibility indicating higher levels of choice and hence a higher potential for personal fulfillment and satisfaction. Yet, at the same time, accessibility also stresses that choice and freedom of movement are limited: a person has accessibility to certain places but not to others, a person has the ability to accomplish certain actions but not others. Accessibility, precisely because it links transport to land use, stresses the fact that space creates a friction, a barrier between origin and desired destination. Moreover, the notion of accessibility presupposes knowledge about destinations, thus eliminating connotations of adventure, discovery or even new experience, so closely intertwined with potential mobility. Accessibility as a concept is thus at odds with key values of Western society like autonomy and freedom, by underscoring the place-boundedness of people, bound as they are to an 'origin' and a given set of destinations, linked together by a known set of links. In this sense, accessibility contrasts starkly with potential mobility, which stresses freedom rather than limitations, endlessness rather than place-boundedness, and autonomy rather dependence.

These explorations underline that the identification of the social meaning of a good is not a straightforward matter. Indeed, Walzer stresses that "conception and creation [of goods] are social processes" (Walzer 1983, p. 7). The social meaning of a good is thus the result of a sometimes lengthy process of social construction, in which certain associations related to a particular good become uncontested and taken for granted. As Lessig underscores, individuals or particular groups in a particular society may point at, or uphold, latent or subversive meanings, which may obstruct the emergence of a hegemonic shared understanding (Lessig 1995). Indeed, the ongoing debate in the domain of transportation between the proponents of (potential) mobility versus the proponents of accessibility underscores that the social meaning of the transport good is contested in current societies, at least within academia and increasingly so among government officials (e.g. Cervero 1996; Vigar 1999; Handy 2005; Preston and Rajé 2007). This may come as no surprise. First, given the firm roots of the notion of potential mobility in Western culture and the lengthy process of social construction, it is only reasonable that the notion does not easily give way to an alternative social meaning. Second, as Lessig emphasizes, social meanings are not merely passive containers reflecting how people perceive particular goods. They "are also tools—means to an end", which can actively shape people's perceptions (Lessig 1995, p. 956). Thus, powerful actors may deliberately seek to shape the process of social construction to maintain or create a social meaning that works to their advantage. Clearly, upholding (potential) mobility as the dominant conceptualization of the transport good serves multiple interests (Schiefelbusch 2010).

In spite of the still-dominant conceptualization of the transport good as potential mobility, I argue that ultimately accessibility best reflects the social meaning of the transport good in Western societies. The equation, in popular discourse, of potential mobility with notions like freedom, adventure and choice is based on a fundamentally flawed understanding of the spatial condition. True, for a given person in a given space-time setting, a higher level of potential mobility always implies more choice, more experience, more possibilities for adventure, and, ultimately, more freedom. However, this conceptualization is clearly flawed in a comparative perspective. Because space is neither a uniform nor a static entity, households with comparable levels of potential mobility may well differ fundamentally in the level of choice and the level of freedom they experience (Figure 4.1). Hence, in a comparative perspective, potential mobility cannot be equated directly with key values like choice, experience or freedom. This, in turn, suggests that it would be incorrect to equate the transport good with potential mobility. By contrast, the notion of accessibility correlates closely with these underlying values, with higher

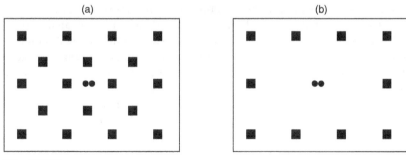

●● = person
■ = activity location

Figure 4.1 Potential mobility and choice level. The person in diagram (a) has the same level of potential mobility as the person in diagram (b), as indicated by the identical size of the diagram. However, person (a) clearly has a substantially higher level of choice than person (b).
Source: Adapted from Dijst 1995, p. 29.

levels of accessibility representing choice, possibilities for experience, and freedom. I therefore argue that accessibility rather than potential mobility best captures the social meaning of transportation in current Western societies. This conceptualization is in line with the increasing number of studies into the distribution of accessibility over different population groups (e.g. Kawabata and Shen 2007; Hess 2005; Benenson, Martens *et al.* 2010), building on much earlier work in this direction (e.g. Wachs and Kumagai 1973; Schaeffer and Sclar 1975; Black and Conroy 1977), and the rising attention for accessibility in transportation planning, as highlighted by an increasing number of publications (see, for instance, Cervero, Neil *et al.* 2001; Levine and Garb 2002; Bertolini, le Clercq *et al.* 2005; and many others). As may be clear to the reader, by arguing in favor of accessibility as the proper conceptualization of the transport good, I am de facto contributing to the ongoing process of *re*constructing the social meaning of the good.

Accessibility as a separate sphere

Now that the social meaning of the transport good is more clearly demarcated, the question needs to be answered whether the good, defined as accessibility, should be singled out and a separate sphere created to guarantee a certain level of autonomy in the distribution of accessibility. Two lines of argument can assist in answering this question. The first focuses on the value of the transport good in current societies, while the second explores the way in which the transport good defined as accessibility is currently distributed over members of society.

No one would dispute that the social meaning of transport has changed tremendously over the past two centuries (e.g. Knowles 2006), and, in its wake, the value of the transport good. In traditional societies, transport was primarily a matter of walking, with necessities of life located within walking distance of most homes (Mumford 1961). Only a small segment of society could afford regular travel by horse or horse-drawn carriages. The near-universal ability to walk—with the exception of small infants and persons with impairments—implied that accessibility, at least to everyday destinations, was possible for all, although in many cities regulations and social codes de facto curtailed accessibility levels for e.g. women or lower classes (Muellner 2002; Braidotti 1994). Thus, while accessibility levels will have differed between people, depending on the exact residential location of a person within the city (walls) and vis-à-vis key land uses like the central market place, the dominance of walking guaranteed sufficient accessibility levels for virtually all and relatively small differences in these levels, at least to everyday destinations.

The introduction of motorized transport for movement of people, but especially the rise of private, individualized, motorized transport, changed the situation fundamentally (e.g. Illich 1974). The widespread availability of the motorcar, triggered by vast investments in the road system, implied a fundamental shift in the meaning of transport. The dominance of the motorcar resulted in a vast dispersal of urban functions over space, eliminating walking as a feasible alternative for most trips. As a result, motorized transport changed rapidly from a luxury into a necessity. Few people in industrialized societies are now able to manage their daily lives without individualized or collective motorized transport. Mobility has become a structuring dimension of social life (Kaufmann, Bergman *et al.* 2004; Urry 2000).

The rise of motorized transport has thus reshaped the social meaning of the transport good. Once, transport was hardly perceived as a good, but rather taken for granted as a natural extension of life itself. Now, the ability to travel through space has become so important for everyday lives that it can be considered an asset. Kaufmann, Bergman *et al.* (2004) even consider potential mobility—or motility as they term it—a form of capital, that can form links with, and be exchanged for, other forms of capital, whether economic, cultural or social. The availability or unavailability of transport, in other words, shapes people's life opportunities. It is this interrelationship that shapes the social meaning of transport in today's industrialized societies and underscores that accessibility is the appropriate conceptualization of the social meaning of the transport good.

The second line of argument that can provide ammunition for the qualification of transport as a separate distributive sphere, relates to the way in which the transport good is currently distributed over members of society. Over the past decades, a substantial body of evidence has been collected describing and explaining the substantial disparities in accessibility found in developed societies. The evidence can be derived from various strands of literature, including the spatial mismatch literature, studies on transport and gender, and the more recent body of work on transport and social exclusion. Taken together, these strands of research draw a picture of how a lack of accessibility limits the possibilities for personal accumulation of economic and social capital, to paraphrase the words of Kaufmann, Bergman *et al.* (2004). The spatial mismatch literature, for instance, has generated substantial evidence that the concentration of low income groups in central cities, the decentralization of low wage jobs, and the lack of investment in new public transport facilities, have in combination led to a sharp decline in job access among the urban poor (e.g. Ihlanfeldt 1993; Ong and Miller 2005). The literature on women and transport provides insight into the mobility problems experienced by women combining multiple tasks, especially if they do not own and operate a car (e.g. Blumenberg 2004). The social exclusion literature draws a qualitative picture of the everyday transport dilemmas faced by deprived population groups: the decisions to forgo a doctor's appointment, a meeting with family and friends, a job interview, or even a full-fledged job opportunity due to lack of adequate transport means. By doing so, this literature also highlights the intricate relationship between a lack of accessibility and the wider process of social exclusion (e.g. Cass, Shove *et al.* 2005; Hine and Mitchell 2001; Lucas 2004; Lucas 2012).

Taken together, I argue that a strong case can be made for the establishment of a separate distributional sphere. Transport has developed from a taken-for-granted and hardly disputed good, into a highly desirable good, an indispensable resource shaping one's life path, and a good whose availability is the subject of public debate. Furthermore, as shown in Chapter 2, the traditional approach to transportation planning allows the distribution of accessibility to be strongly shaped by the distribution of income, resulting in substantial hardships and even social exclusion due to a lack of accessibility among a considerable part of the population. The large body of evidence, only briefly summarized here, seems strong enough to draw boundaries around the transport good and set it apart from other goods. In the words of Walzer, the transport good has a sufficiently 'distinct' social meaning to create a separate sphere within which the distribution of the transport good, defined as accessibility, is to be governed.

The identification of accessibility as the good that best captures the social meaning of transport has clear implications for the conceptualization of that separate sphere. It suggests that this sphere does not coincide with the traditional demarcation of transportation as a field of government intervention, because the distribution of accessibility is also strongly shaped by other fields of policy intervention, most notably land use planning and service delivery policies. Note that the good of accessibility does not differ in this respect from a good like 'health', as the distribution of the latter, too, is not only determined by health care in a narrow sense, but also by, for instance, government programs that provide proper sanitation and avoid epidemics (Daniels 2008). The broadly defined *accessibility sphere* does encompass a range of traditional policy domains that, in the ideal situation, would operate in coordination to deliver a fair distribution of accessibility over members of society. This is, again, nothing new, because for many years academics and practitioners have argued strongly in favor of the integration of transportation planning and land use planning (see e.g. Cervero 1996; Curtis and Scheurer 2010; te Brömmelstroet and Bertolini 2010).

Conclusions

In this chapter, a first step has been taken towards the development of a theory of justice for the domain of transportation. Based on Walzer's theory of justice, accessibility has been identified as the proper conceptualization of the transport good and arguments have been provided for why accessibility, as a good with a distinct social meaning, deserves a separate sphere of justice. The next challenge is to identify the appropriate principles of justice to guide the distribution of accessibility. Before taking up that challenge in the next two chapters, it is important here to underscore why working along the lines of Walzer's theory of justice alone would not lead to an appropriate set of principles of fairness. Basically, there are three reasons for this.

First, Walzer's proposal for the identification of the principles of justice for each sphere is weak at best. Walzer argues that the principles for distribution are internal to each sphere and are to be extracted from a proper 'reading' of the shared understanding of the good. This approach thus assumes a world of common meanings. But, as Teuber argues, a modern society "may have nothing quite like a collective consciousness and, in so far as it does, the collective sensibility may be so thin that it cannot constitute a world of common meanings rich enough to provide the kind of guidance Walzer's view requires" (Teuber 1984, p. 120). The discussion about the latent social meaning of the transport good only underscores this point.

Second, even if a society would be characterized by widely shared understandings, we can have no certainty that these common meanings actually provide an appropriate basis from which to derive principles of fairness. Throughout history, dominant groups have attempted, and often succeeded, to impose their worldview on others. Sometimes, indeed, such perspectives become so powerful that they are taken for granted as 'natural' or 'inevitable'. Drawing on such shared understandings would be equal to accepting the world view of the dominant group and the distributive principles they uphold. This may even occur in fairly enlightened societies, as illustrated by the fact that many of the great philosophers of ancient Greece failed to denounce the practices of slavery and infringement of women's rights in their own society. Young (1990) refers to these processes as domination and oppression and considers them the most pervasive forms of injustice in societies. In other words, while it may be possible in a fairly homogenous society to 'abstract' distributive principles from shared meanings, it is by no means certain that these principles do not reproduce the sometimes hidden forms of domination and oppression that structure society. Relying on the shared understandings in society is hardly an appropriate approach to deriving principles of justice for a particular sphere (see Dworkin 1983a; Dworkin 1983b; Elster 1992; Sandel 1982).

Third, even if it were possible to arrive at 'robust' distributive principles from the social meaning of a particular good, Walzer's theory still falls short of providing any guidelines regarding the share of assets that should be made available to achieve the fair distribution of that good. Clearly, a fair distribution of goods within a separate sphere can often only be achieved if these goods are produced in the first place. This certainly holds for goods like education, health, or accessibility. If these goods are taken out of the domain of free exchange, their production will inevitably require a substantial transfer of funds between members of society. Thus the identification of principles of fairness cannot merely be based on the shared understandings in society within a sphere, but will need to take into account the related costs to society for upholding such principles of justice.

Put differently, Walzer's ambition to set borders around spheres has overstretched the independence of these spheres. Walzer has defined these borders merely from the perspective of the recipients of the goods. But as the production of most goods with a distinct social meaning requires substantial means, the spheres in which goods are being distributed cannot have closed borders, but need to be 'semi-permeable' at least, to allow an influx of resources from the sphere of money. Walzer does not address this inevitable interrelationship between the dimensions of production and distribution of a particular good. The costs involved in producing a social good may well set borders on the possibilities for a fair distribution, thereby shaping the principles of fairness for the distribution of the good. Indeed, as I will show in Chapter 6, the costs of providing accessibility strongly shape the principles guiding the distribution of accessibility over members of society.

What, then, are the building blocks for a theory of justice in transportation that can be derived from Walzer's approach? First, I follow Walzer in his argument that justice should address the distribution of a wide range of tangible goods and that no single principle of justice can sensibly guide the distribution of all these goods. This perspective is not only attractive because it is in tune with the actual institutions of modern societies. It is also of practical importance, because it enables the development of principles of justice that are based as much on moral reasoning and philosophies of justice as on the particularities of an actual social good. This is especially important for the good of accessibility, because of the pervasive role space plays in its possible distributions. Second, I take from Walzer the argument that (potentially) dominant goods like money and power should not distort the distribution within a sphere. This latter point will be taken up in detail in the final chapter of this book, when I discuss fair ways of financing the transportation system.

I will now turn to Rawls' famous theory of justice in order to explore to what extent this theory can provide the theoretical basis for delineating the principles for a fair distribution of accessibility. As I will show, Rawls' theory can be relevant in a limited range of situations, but it cannot provide the solid foundation for a workable set of fairness principles for the transportation domain.

References

Altshuler, A. (1979). *The Urban Transportation System*. Cambridge, MA, MIT Press.

Benenson, I., K. Martens and Y. Rofe (2010). Measuring the gap between car and transit accessibility: estimating access using a high-resolution transit network geographic information system. *Transportation Research Record: Journal of the Transportation Research Board*, (2144): 28–35.

Bergman, S. and T. Sager (eds) (2008). *The Ethics of Mobilities: rethinking place, exclusion, freedom and environment.* Aldershot/Burlington, Ashgate.

Bertolini, L., F. le Clercq and L. Kapoen (2005). Sustainable accessibility: a conceptual framework to integrate transport and land use plan-making. Two test-applications in the Netherlands and a reflection on the way forward. *Transport Policy*, 12(3): 207–220.

Black, J. and M. Conroy (1977). Accessibility measures and the social evaluation of urban structure. *Environment and Planning A*, 9: 1013–1031.

Blumenberg, E.A. (2004). Engendering effective planning: spatial mismatch, low-income women, and transportation policy. *Journal of the American Planning Association*, 70(3): 269–281.

Braidotti, R. (1994). *Nomadic Subjects: embodiment and sexual difference in contemporary feminist theory.* New York, Columbia University Press.

Bröcker, J., A. Korzhenevych and C. Schürmann (2010). Assessing spatial equity and efficiency impacts of transport infrastructure projects. *Transportation Research Part B: Methodological*, 44(7): 795–811.

Cass, N., E. Shove and J. Urry (2005). Social exclusion, mobility and access. *Sociological Review*, 53(3): 539–555.

Cervero, R. (1981). Efficiency and equity impacts of current transit fare policies. *Transportation Research Record: Journal of the Transportation Research Board*, 799: 7–15.

Cervero, R. (1996). Paradigm shift: from automobility to accessibility planning. Berkeley, University of California. *Urban Futures*, 22: 9–20.

Cervero, R., J.S. Neil and B.B. Paul (2001). Transportation Planning. *International Encyclopedia of the Social & Behavioral Sciences.* Oxford, Pergamon, pp. 15873–15878.

Couclelis, H. (1996). The death of distance. *Environment and Planning B: Planning & Design*, 23(4): 387–389.

Cresswell, T. (2006). The right to mobility: the production of mobility in the courtroom. *Antipode*, 38(4): 735–754.

Curtis, C. and J. Scheurer (2010). Planning for sustainable accessibility: Developing tools to aid discussion and decision-making. *Progress in Planning*, 74(2): 53–106.

Daniels, N. (2008). *Just Health: meeting health needs fairly.* Cambridge, Cambridge University Press.

Dijst, M. (1995). *Het elliptisch leven: actieruimte als integrale maat voor bereik en mobiliteit.* Utrecht/Delft, Koninklijk Nederlands Aardrijkskundig Genootschap/ Faculteit Bouwkunde Technische Universiteit Delft.

Dworkin, R. (1983a). To each his own. *The New York Review of Books*, 30(6).

Dworkin, R. (1983b). Reply to Michael Walzer. *The New York Review of Books*, 30(12).

Ecola, L. and T. Light (2009). *Equity and Congestion Pricing: A Review of the Evidence.* Santa Monica, CA, Rand Corporation.

Elster, J. (1992). *Local Justice: how institutions allocate scarce goods and necessary burdens.* Cambridge, Cambridge University Press.

Fabre, C. (2007). *Justice in a Changing World.* Cambridge, Polity Press.

Feitelson, E. (2002). Introducing environmental equity dimensions into the sustainable transport discourse: issues and pitfalls. *Transportation Research Part D: Transport and Environment*, 7(2): 99–118.

Forkenbrock, D.J. and L.A. Schweitzer (1999). Environmental justice in transportation planning. *Journal of the American Planning Association*, 65(1): 96–111.

Garb, Y. and J. Levine (2002). Congestion pricing's conditional promise: promotion of accessibility or mobility? *Transport Policy*, 9(3): 179–188.

Garrett, M. and B. Taylor (1999). Reconsidering social equity in public transit. *Berkeley Planning Journal*, 13: 6–27.

Handy, S. (2005). Planning for accessibility: In theory and in practice. In: D.M. Levinson and K.J. Krizek (eds), *Access to Destinations*. Amsterdam, Elsevier, 131–147.

Hansen, W.G. (1959). How accessibility shapes land use. *Journal of the American Institute of Planners*, 25: 73–76.

Harvey, D. (1990). *The Condition of Postmodernity: an enquiry into the origins of cultural change*. Malden, MA/Oxford, Blackwell.

Hess, D.B. (2005). Access to employment for adults in poverty in the Buffalo–Niagara region. *Urban Studies*, 42(7): 1177–1200.

Hine, J.P. and F. Mitchell (2001). Better for everyone? Travel experiences and transport exclusion. *Urban Studies*, 38(2): 319.

Hodge, D.C. (1988). Fiscal equity in urban mass transit systems: a geographical analysis. *Annals of the Association of American Geographers*, 78: 288–306.

Ihlanfeldt, K. (1993). Intra-urban job accessibility and hispanic youth employment rates. *Journal of Urban Economics*, 33(2): 254–271.

Illich, I. (1974). *Energy and Equity*. London, Marion Boyars.

Kaufmann, V. (2002). *Re-thinking Mobility: contemporary sociology*. Aldershot/London, Ashgate.

Kaufmann, V., M.M. Bergman and D. Joye (2004). Motility: mobility as capital. *International Journal of Urban and Regional Research*, 28(4): 745–756.

Kawabata, M. and Q. Shen (2007). Commuting inequality between cars and public transit: the case of the San Francisco Bay Area, 1990-2000. *Urban Studies*, 44(9): 1759–1780.

Knowles, R.D. (2006). Transport shaping space: differential collapse in time-space. *Journal of Transport Geography*, 14(6): 407–425.

Lessig, L. (1995). The regulation of social meaning. *The University of Chicago Law Review*, 62(3): 943–1045.

Levine, J. and Y. Garb (2002). Congestion pricing's conditional promise: promotion of accessibility or mobility? *Transport Policy*, 9(3): 179–188.

Lomasky, L.E. (1997). Autonomy and automobility. *The Independent Review*, v.II(1): 5–28.

Lucas, K. (Ed.) (2004). *Running on Empty: transport, social exclusion and environmental justice*. Bristol, Policy Press.

Lucas, K. (2012). Transport and social exclusion: Where are we now? *Transport Policy*, 20: 105–113.

Lucy, W.H. (1988). Equity planning for infrastructure: applications. In: J.M. Stein (ed.) *Public Infrastructure Planning and Management*. Newbury Park, Sage, pp. 227–240.

Muellner, B. (2002). The deviance of respectability: nineteenth-century transport from a woman's perspective. *The Journal of Transport History*, 23(1): 37–45.

Mumford, L. (1961). *The City in History: its origins, its transformations, and its prospects*. New York, Harcourt, Brace & World.

Murray, A.T. and R. Davis (2001). Equity in regional service provision. *Journal of Regional Science*, 41(4): 577–600.

Ong, P.M. and D. Miller (2005). Spatial and transportation mismatch in Los Angeles. *Journal of Planning Education and Research*, 25(1): 43–56.

Preston, J. and F. Rajé (2007). Accessibility, mobility and transport-related social exclusion. *Journal of Transport Geography* 15(3): 151–160.

Rawls, J. (1971). *A Theory of Justice*. Cambridge, MA, Harvard University Press.

Richardson, H.W. (1974). A note on the distributional effects of road pricing. *Journal of Transport Economics and Policy*, 8: 82–85.

Rimmer, P. (1985). Transport geography. *Progress in Human Geography*, 9: 271–277.

Rucker, G. (1984). Public transportation: another gap in rural America. *Transportation Quarterly*, 38(3): 419–432.

Sager, T. (2005). Footloose and Forecast-free: Hypermobility and the Planning of Society. *European Journal of Spatial Development*, September 2005(17): 1–23.

Sandel, M. (1982). *Liberalism and the limits of justice*. Cambridge, Cambridhe University Press.

Schaeffer, K.H. and E.D. Sclar (1975). *Access for all: transportation and urban growth*. Harmondsworth, Penguin.

Schiefelbusch, M. (2010). Rational planning for emotional mobility? The case of public transport development. *Planning Theory*, 9(3): 200–222.

Schweitzer, L. and A. Valenzuela (2004). Environmental injustice and transportation: the claims and the evidence. *Journal of Planning Literature*, 18(4): 383–398.

Smeed, R. *et al.* (1964). *Road Pricing: the economic and technical possibilities*. London, HMSO.

Talen, E. (2001). Access: geographical. *International Encyclopedia of the Social & Behavioral Sciences*, 1: 30–33.

te Brömmelstroet, M. and L. Bertolini (2010). Integrating land use and transport knowledge in strategy-making. *Transportation*, 37(1): 85–104.

Teuber, A. (1984). Bookreview of Spheres of Justice by Michael Walzer. *Political Theory*, 12(1): 118–123.

Trappenburg, M. (2000). In defence of pure pluralism: two readings of Walzer's spheres of justice. *Journal of Political Philosophy*, 8(3): 343–362.

Urry, J. (2000). *Sociology Beyond Societies: mobilities for the twenty-first century*. London/New York, Routledge.

Vigar, G. (1999). Transport for people: accessibility, mobility and equity in transport planning. In: C.H. Greed (ed.), *Social Town Planning*. London, Routledge, pp. 90–101.

Wachs, M. and T.G. Kumagai (1973). Physical accessibility as a social indicator. *Socio-Economic Planning Science*, 6: 357–379.

Walzer, M. (1983). *Spheres of Justice: a defense of pluralism and equality*, New York, Basic Books.

Walzer, M. (1995). Response. In: D. Miller and M. Walzer (eds), *Pluralism, Justice, and Equality*. Oxford/New York, Oxford University Press, pp. 281–296.

Wu, B.M. and J.P. Hine (2003). A PTAL approach to measuring changes in bus service accessibility. *Transport Policy*, 10(4): 307–320.

Young, I.M. (1990). *Justice and the Politics of Difference*. Princeton, NJ, Princeton University Press.

Zeitler, U. (1999). *Grundlagen der Verkehrsethik*. Berlin, Logos Verlag.

5 Accessibility as a Primary Good?

Introduction

John Rawls' theory of justice is widely considered a landmark in Western thought on the subject of social justice. Since the publication of *A Theory of Justice* in 1971, a huge body of literature has emerged, explaining the theory, exploring its consequences, or criticizing it. Robert Nozick, one of Rawls' fierce critics, underscores the importance of Rawls' work when he observes that "political philosophers now must either work with Rawls' theory or explain why not" (Nozick 1974, p. 183). This in itself is sufficient reason to explore in-depth the possible implications of Rawls' theory for the transportation domain. The fact that transportation researchers have referred more to Rawls' theory of justice than to any other theory of social justice is another reason to do so (see Rooijakkers 2012 for an excellent overview).

This chapter is organized as follows. I will first briefly describe the main components of Rawls' theory of justice. Then I will explore three possible ways of incorporating accessibility within his theory. Each of these approaches has been pioneered in the domain of health care. By discussing these extensions of Rawls' theory in some detail, I will clarify the (im)possibilities of incorporating accessibility into a Rawlsian framework. I end the chapter with an overview of key concepts from Rawls' theory that will aid the development of a theory of fairness in accessibility.

Justice as fairness

Rawls' theory of justice, termed 'justice as fairness', covers enormous ground. For my purposes, two core elements of Rawls' theory are most important (see also Green 1976). The first element consists of the procedure Rawls has developed for arriving at the principles of justice. The second part consists of the set of principles of justice that, Rawls argues, emerge if the procedure for arriving at principles is properly executed.

The theory's procedure for selecting principles of social justice follows the tradition of social contract theory. It involves a thought experiment of an imaginary contract situation which Rawls calls 'the original position'. The original position provides the setting in which free, equal, mutually disinterested and rational persons seek to come to an agreement regarding the principles of social justice that will define the basic structure of society. The persons, as parties to a contract, are mutually disinterested in the sense that their decisions are assumed not to be influenced by concerns of compassion or guilt vis-à-vis others. Rather, each person in the original position is assumed to be merely concerned about his own interests. The persons are considered to be rational in the simple sense that they can select the best means to any desired end. Rawls furthermore assumes that the persons in the original position are placed behind his famous 'veil of ignorance'. Because of this veil, the persons in the original position lack any knowledge of the particularities that distinguish them from one another, such as age, gender or race. It also prevents them from knowing their particular natural advantages or disadvantages (such as their level of intelligence or physical strength), their particular social position at birth, or even the particular ends and values they actually wish to pursue. The parties to the contract are permitted, however, to know the true general facts about the human condition and natural and social laws.

The purpose of the original position and related veil of ignorance is to insure strict impartiality in the choice of the moral principles that are to shape the basic structure of society. The notion of impartiality has been drawn on before in philosophical thought, notably in the form of the 'impartial spectator' (Hare 1973; Smith 2010 [1759]; Sen 2006; Denier 2005; see also Chapter 3). The original position differs from this and comparable notions in two important respects (Green 1976). First, it avoids the problem of one person, albeit an imaginary one, choosing the principles of justice. The distinction between persons is maintained in Rawls' original position, and while they are stripped of knowledge of their particularities, they can still defend their most vital interests. Second, the device of the original position assists our thinking by remarkably simplifying the moral choice process. This is achieved through stripping the parties to the contract of knowledge about their particularities. Since the parties do not know about their particular ends and values, or 'plans of life' in the words of Rawls, they do not fall into the trap of weighing one perspective of the good life against another. And because they do not know their place in society once the veil of ignorance is lifted, they will take into account the possible differences between persons that may emerge in society once the veil of ignorance is lifted and the selected principles of justice are actually implemented. The device of the original position thus converts the complicated task of moral choice into the much simpler procedure of rational prudence. Rather than having to engage in the complicated and often fruitless process of weighing one moral intuition against another, the original position makes it possible to only ask one simple question: What principles would I, as a rational agent in the original position, find advantageous to myself? Green concludes that "[b]ecause of the constraints that this position imposes on our choice, the results of this prudent deliberation will be acceptable moral principles" (Green 1976, p. 114).

Rawls then analyses what principles of justice the contract parties in the original position would choose. He starts his analysis by arguing that these principles should address the basic structure of society, or the unified system of the major political, social and economic institutions that distribute fundamental rights and duties and determine the appropriate distribution of the benefits and burdens of social cooperation. A theory of justice should address this basic structure, rather than allocations of particular bundles of goods, because the basic structure itself shapes all subsequent decisions and actions. This also implies that Rawls' principles of justice should be understood in relation to the basic structure and cannot simply be transposed to everyday allocative decisions. As Rawls makes clear, principles suitable for individual allocations may not be suitable for the long-term functioning of a society's major institutions, and vice versa (Rawls 2003, p. 11).

The parties to the contract are thus to decide about the principles that determine the basic structure of society. Rawls simplifies this abstract notion by introducing the concept of so-called 'primary social goods'. Rawls defines primary goods as "things ... a rational man wants whatever else he wants" because with more primary goods "men can generally be assured in carrying out their intentions and in advancing their ends, whatever these ends may be" (Rawls 1971, p. 92). Drawing on a shared conception of rationality, as well as some uncontroversial appeals to psychology and beliefs about human nature, he argues that "wanting [primary goods] is part of being rational" (Rawls 1971, p. 223), because primary goods enable free and equal citizens to advance their conceptions of the good (Rawls 2003, p. 61). The parties to the contract, although they do not know their particular ends and values, thus have a general interest in a distribution of these primary goods that is most beneficial to themselves.

Rawls distinguishes five primary social goods (Rawls 1971; 1982; 2003):

a. A set of basic rights and liberties, including freedom of thought and association, freedom defined by the integrity of the person, and so on.
b. Freedom of movement and free choice of occupation against the background of diverse opportunities.
c. Powers and prerogatives of offices and positions of responsibility, particularly those in the main political and economic institutions.
d. Income and wealth, understood broadly as all-purpose means for achieving directly or indirectly a wide range of ends, whatever they might be.
e. The social bases of self-respect. These are those aspects of the basic structure that are normally essential if citizens are to have a lively

sense of their own worth as moral persons and to be able to realize their highest-order interests and advance their ends with self-confidence.

These goods are *primary* because they are things that persons need in their status as free and equal citizens, and as normal and fully cooperating members of society. They are *social* primary goods as they are the product of human cooperation and not a natural fact. They differ from 'natural goods', such as health and vigor, intelligence and imagination. Rawls argues that the distribution of these natural goods is not so directly shaped by the basic structure of society. As such, they are morally arbitrary: "The natural distribution is neither just nor unjust ... These are simply natural facts. What is just and unjust is the way that institutions deal with these facts" (Rawls 1971, p. 102). A just society would be one in which every person receives a fair share of the primary social goods, thereby compensating for the arbitrariness embodied in the natural lottery.

The parties to the contract are to select the principles that guide the distribution of these primary goods. They do so from the standpoint of the original position. Thus each contractant selects those principles governing the basic structure that are most likely to maximize his own share of the primary goods (Green 1976, p. 114). Since each contractant finds himself in the same position, each contractant will reach the same conclusion based on rational prudence alone. Hence, the principles selected will be mutually agreed upon.

Given that the original position and the veil of ignorance create contractants that are fundamentally similar, the outcome of the unanimous choice process is principles that equally protect the vital interests of everyone. As a result, the principles are strongly egalitarian. The final principles, according to Rawls, will seek to maximize the worst possible outcome for each contractant once the veil of ignorance is lifted, since each contractant is zealously protective of his most vital interests in the situation of uncertainty created by the original position. The selection of principles that maximize the minimum outcome is especially rational, Rawls argues, if three conditions obtain: when knowledge of the probabilities of various outcomes is limited or non-existent; when the prospects of gain are not particularly attractive; and when the possibility of losing is intolerable (Rawls 1971, p. 153–155). In his later work, Rawls underlines that the contractants in the original position do not decide under risk, in which probabilities are known, but in a situation of uncertainty. Hence their decision-making cannot be guided by calculations about expected pay-offs, but is guided by the understanding that the contractants must protect the fundamental interests of the citizens they represent (Rawls 2003, pp. 106–107). Furthermore, Rawls underscores the strains of commitment into which the contractants enter once they agree on a particular set of principles of justice. The contractants "must ask themselves whether those they represent can reasonably be expected to honor the principles agreed to" over an entire life (Rawls 2003, p. 103). Hence they must select principles that all members of society, irrespective of their position in that society once the veil of ignorance is lifted, can willingly accept. The chosen principles have to achieve a stable society, i.e. a society from which no one wants to withdraw, because everyone's fundamental interests are already cared for.

Based on this line of reasoning, Rawls then draws up the following set of principles of justice (Rawls 2003, pp. 42–43; based on the earlier formulation in Rawls 1971, pp. 60–90):

1. Each person has the same indefeasible claim to a fully adequate scheme of equal basic liberties, which scheme is compatible with the same scheme of liberties for all (*principle of greatest equal liberty*).
2. Social and economic inequalities are to satisfy two conditions: first, they are to be attached to offices and positions open to all under conditions of fair equality of opportunity (*principle of fair equality of opportunity*); and second, they are to be to the greatest benefit of the least-advantaged members of society (*the difference principle*).

These principles of justice are lexically or serially ordered: "[t]his is an order which requires us to satisfy the first principle in the ordering before we can move to the second, the second before we consider the third, and so on" (Rawls 1971, p. 43).

The first principle relates to the primary social goods under (a) and (b). Rawls maintains that the liberties arranged by this first principle are so important to many different life plans that even a slight decrease or relative loss of them is a severe threat for the individual: "a basic liberty covered by the first principle can be limited only for the sake of liberty itself, that is, only to insure that the same liberty or a different basic liberty is properly protected" (Rawls 1971, p. 204). The absolute priority of the basic liberties means that they cannot be traded against, for example, a higher average level of income and wealth. Thus, within the original position, where contractants have no information about the chances of winning or losing a greater share of liberties, they will rationally agree on granting the most extensive equal share of these liberties to everyone (Green 1976, p. 115). The lexical order of the principles of justice, and the insistence that basic liberties be guaranteed to everyone, are of vital importance for the contractants to buttress their self-respect (Green 1976, p. 116).

The principle of fair equality of opportunity relates to the distribution of the primary social goods under (c). The principle requires that people have an equal chance of getting a particular position relative to their capacity for that position. The importance of this principle goes beyond mere fairness in the labor market, as it relates first and foremost to powers and prerogatives of offices and positions of authority. Thus the principle is of key importance in guaranteeing a fair system of self-governance, i.e. fair access to positions of power. Furthermore, since offices and positions are closely linked to self-respect, and self-respect is ultimately the most important social good because it determines whether a person can pursue a plan of life without sinking into "apathy or cynicism" (Rawls 1971, p. 440), fairness in the distribution of jobs and offices is of the utmost importance. It not only requires that an applicant with the relevant qualifications should not be excluded from the position for reasons of gender, sexual orientation, religion, class or other morally arbitrary characteristics (Denier 2007, p. 106). Rawls argues that the contractants would go further than mere formal equality of opportunity and understand that other morally arbitrary factors, most notably a person's position at birth and related social circumstances, should not play a key role in the distribution of these offices and positions. They would argue that formal equality of opportunity, i.e. the mere absence of formal discrimination in the competition for jobs, would not protect their most vital interests. The parties actually have an interest in guaranteeing that the competition is as fair as possible, so as to guarantee the best possible worst-outcome once the veil of ignorance is lifted. "The thought here is that positions are to be not only open in a formal sense, but that all should have a fair chance to attain them" (Rawls 1971, p. 73). This implies, for Rawls, the provision of education so that all, irrespective of social circumstances, have equal opportunity to obtain an education and develop their skills and talents. This is a prerequisite to move from mere formal equality of opportunity to what Rawls terms fair equality of opportunity.

The difference principle relates to the distribution of primary social goods under (d), i.e. income and wealth. These goods are of key importance in taking advantage of the basic liberties guaranteed by the first principle and as a means of pursuing a particular life plan. The difference principle states that inequalities in the distribution of these goods are acceptable as long as they are to the benefit of the least-advantaged members of society. The reasoning behind the contractants' choice differs somewhat from the arguments for the first two principles. The contractants in the original position are assumed to know true basic facts about economic systems: they know, for example, that human beings naturally differ in their productive abilities and that economic systems can sometimes be more efficient by employing various incentives (such as differences in payment) to elicit the exercise of economically valuable talents and skills (Green 1976, p. 115). Given these facts, the contract parties could insure a higher overall level of economic prosperity by permitting unequal shares for different members of society. But since the parties behind the veil of ignorance are assumed to be only concerned about their own interests, this is in itself not a reason to allow differences in income and wealth. The contract parties are only interested in their possible worst outcome, as they understand that once they agree on the principles of justice, they have to live an entire life under the strains of these commitments, even if they do not work out well for them. Thus, Rawls argues, the contract parties are only willing to allow differences in income and wealth if these differences work to the advantage of the worst-off group. This is the famous difference principle, which states that when choosing between several alternative basic structures for society, one is to choose the alternative that maximizes the expectations of the worst-off representative man over the course of an entire life. The principle thus goes beyond the mere requirement that the worst-off benefit from economic development, for instance through the 'trickle down' effect. Rather, the worst-off group, and then the next worst-off, and so on, must be made as well off as possible, not merely somewhat better off. Formulated differently, at a given point in time a one unit increase in inequality in income and wealth is only acceptable if this directly translates into a higher level of income and wealth for the worst-off, and if no better alternative is available in which the worst-off are even better off (e.g. a more egalitarian society). All other increases in inequality in income and wealth are unacceptable.

Note that Rawls defines the least-advantaged groups as those members of society with the lowest prospects of enjoying primary social goods over an entire life. Since in Rawls' society all citizens have equal liberties, and fair equality of opportunity is also guaranteed, and positions of power tend to go hand in hand with high levels of income and wealth, the basic metric for identifying the least-advantaged members of society (or the so-called 'representative worst-off man') is the index of income and wealth. The fact that Rawls can identify the worst-off with this simple index is of crucial importance for the strength of his theory, and actually inhibits its extension to include transportation, as I will show below.

Expanding justice as fairness to include transportation

What lessons could be derived from Rawls' theory of justice for the domain of transportation? Is it possible to develop principles for the fair distribution of accessibility based on his theory? What is clear from the outset is that Rawls' difference principle cannot be simply applied to transportation (contrary to, for instance, Khisty 1996; Langmyhr 1997; Viegas 2001; Tyler 2006). The principles of justice put forward by Rawls relate to the basic institutions of society and not to each and every allocative decision (Rawls 1971, p. 64; Arrow 1973, p. 249). In other words, Rawls does not claim that the set of principles he proposes, or a subset thereof, can be transposed to a particular domain of society without further argumentation. In referring to his theory of justice, he explicitly states that he is interested "in only one instance of its application", namely its application to the basic structure of society (Rawls 1971, p. 8). Rawls even claims that the application of the difference principle as a single principle by itself leads to "nonsense" (Rawls 2003, p. 72).

The development of principles of justice for the domain of transportation thus requires a fundamental expansion of Rawls' theory. In the literature, three different paths can be distinguished to include additional goods into the Rawlsian framework. Each of these paths has been developed for the domain of health care; none has addressed the domain of transportation. In the following sections, I will take up each of these answers, drawing on the arguments from the health care domain but using transportation as the area of concern.

Accessibility as an additional primary good

The first and most obvious way to incorporate additional goods into Rawls' theory of justice is by extending the index of primary goods. This path has been suggested by a number of authors in relation to health and it seems, at first sight, also promising for the transportation good. Like income and wealth, accessibility can be seen as an "all-purpose good", a good "every rational man is presumed to want" (Rawls 1971, p. 62). Like income and wealth, accessibility has "a use whatever a person's rational plan of life" (Rawls 1971, p. 62). It could even be argued that accessibility is more important than income and wealth, as it is a prerequisite for obtaining not only income and wealth but also offices and positions. Like income and wealth, accessibility is a *social* good: it is the product of human cooperation and its distribution is determined by the rules of the (major) institutions of society. Furthermore, accessibility requires travel and travel may be quite expensive, so that it is by no means certain that the least-advantaged individuals will always be able to secure accessibility from their level of income and wealth as guaranteed by the difference principle. In light of these observations, it seems a promising path to incorporate the transportation good defined as accessibility into the index of primary goods.

This line of reasoning has been followed by Ronald Green (Green 1976; see also Denier 2007, pp. 125–126) for the domain of health care. I briefly summarize his line of argument here, as it can shed light on the possibilities of following a similar path in the domain of transportation. Green argues that health care stands near to basic civil liberties, since mental and physical well-being is rationally just as important as these primary social goods, and arguably more important than income and wealth. Hence, he argues, we could expect the rational agents in the original position to opt for a principle of equal access to health care. This could then be understood as a third principle of justice, being lexically prior to both the fair opportunity principle and the difference principle. He argues that such a principle would imply that "each member of society, whatever his position or background, would be guaranteed an equal right to the most extensive health services the society allows" (Green 1976, p. 117).

The problem with this line of argumentation lies in the delineation of the set of 'most extensive health services'. Since the number of health services has rapidly expanded over the years, the requirement to guarantee an equal right to the most extensive set of health services seems to imply that we are required to give up a large part of a society's wealth in return for even small improvements in health. Green qualifies this requirement and only proposes an equal right to the most extensive health services that *society allows*. He notes that a right to health care "must eventually be defined in terms of its permissible claim on other resources" (Green 1976, p. 119). Green argues that, while it may be difficult to determine exactly how much of a society's resources are to be reserved for health care, it is likely that the contractants in the original position "would certainly want to set some upper and lower limits on the availability of health services" (Green 1976, p. 119). Green then proceeds to show how these upper and lower limits may change as a society develops over time and becomes more affluent. He argues that in all stages of economic development it is rational for members of the original position to sacrifice some health care services for economic considerations (Green 1976, p. 121). Yet, in all circumstances, *equality* in access to a basic set of health services will be required as the contractants would want to secure the highest minimal level of health care for themselves after the veil of ignorance is lifted. Thus the size of the health basket may be changed, but rational actors would always want to guarantee equal access to a basic set of health services irrespective of a person's social position. Green furthermore argues that contractants would only be willing to reduce the size of the health basket if the economic resources that are freed in this way benefit all members of society: "[n]o rational individual, after all, would agree to expose himself to grave health risks without at the same time requiring that the benefits produced by these risks be distributed in ways that he can accept" (Green 1976, p. 122).

The way in which Green has inserted health into the Rawlsian framework, while intuitively appealing, is at odds with the classic problem of interpersonal comparison. This problem has been intensively debated in economics (e.g. Kaldor 1939; Harsanyi 1955; Scanlon 1991). Interpersonal comparisons "have been thought to involve value judgments of a kind that are not only out of place in positive economic science but also inappropriate as a basis for decisions of social policy" (Scanlon 1991, p. 17) and, hence, for claims of justice. The problem lies in the fact that people may differ in the relative value they attach to different goods. Hence, if a *set* of goods is used as an indicator of fairness, it becomes impossible to compare the relative position of two different persons without making (paternalistic) value judgments regarding the relative importance of the different goods that make up the set. Green cannot avoid the problem of interpersonal comparison, as he actually requires the contractants in the original position to *weigh* the importance of one primary good against the other, i.e. health services against income and wealth.

Rawls has carefully designed his theory so as to avoid such value judgments as much as possible (Rawls 1971, pp. 91–92). He has done so, first, by developing a theory in which a clearly delineated set of principles are lexically ordered. In this way, Rawls avoids weighing, for instance, individual liberties against wealth and income. Second, he has chosen a relatively simple index of goods by which persons are to be compared: income and wealth. As Scanlon (Scanlon 1991, pp. 19–20) rightly points out, for such an index no further value judgments are necessary because interpersonal comparison "would simply be a process of empirical investigation ... – literally a matter of *comparison*" (Scanlon 1991, p. 19 —italics in original). Third, Rawls is only interested in identifying the worst-off representative man, which implies that only ordinal judgments of the relative position of individuals are required. In this way, he avoids the far more complex assessment, and cardinal measurement, of the relative position of all individuals or groups in society.

Now, if a right to health services were to be added to the Rawlsian set of primary goods, these advantages of Rawls' theory are erased. This is because the addition of this 'right' would require a balancing of health services against income and wealth, as Green explicitly acknowledges. Green's proposal implies that the simple index of income and wealth has to be supplanted by a composite index that includes both income and wealth and health services. This implies that the assessment of the relative position of representative men or social groups will involve value judgments and would require too much information on the preferences of individuals. As a result, "the identification of the least advantaged becomes impossible" (Denier 2007, p. 126) and therefore also the identification of the most fair basic structure of society. Thus what seems a simple addition of health care to the set of primary goods actually implies a fundamental challenge to Rawls' theory. It cannot be a 'simple' addition. Adding health care to the set of primary goods would require a major rethinking of Rawls' theory of justice—a path no author has yet followed. There is thus no simple way to add a good—whether it is health care or accessibility—to the index of primary goods.

There is another argument as to why Green's proposal is of little help in defining fairness in the domain of transportation. That argument runs as follows. Even if it were possible to 'simply' add accessibility to the set of primary goods, it would still leave ill-defined how accessibility should be distributed. In contrast to health care, equality cannot be achieved in the domain of accessibility. But if not equality, what principle should guide the distribution of accessibility? Rawls has defined a set of principles of justice. Which of these principles, if any, would be suitable to guide the distribution of accessibility? The answer to this question would require the development of a full-fledged understanding of fairness in the domain of transportation. Thus the addition of accessibility to Rawls' set of primary goods, even if it were possible, does not present an answer, but only reformulates the question.

xpanding the notion of fair equality of opportunity

Norman Daniels (Daniels 1985; 2008) has proposed another, more promising, way to incorporate an additional good into Rawls' theory of justice. Like Green, Daniels focuses on the domain of health, but, in contrast to Green, he has developed an elaborate theory of justice and health. Here, I briefly summarize his argument and draw lessons for the domain of transportation.

Daniels' argument starts with his exploration of the special moral importance of health. Building on the 'biostatistical' account of health, Daniels upholds that "health is the absence of pathology", with pathology understood as "any deviation from the natural functional organization of a typical member of a species" (Daniels 2008, p. 37). In other words, pathology is a departure from normal functioning; health, by implication, means normal functioning. A biological function "can be defined as a causal contribution to a species-typical goal, such as survival or reproduction" (Daniels 2008, p. 38). What is normal, in turn, is to a large extent a matter of statistics: "a statistical deviation from the causal contribution of the relevant part" to species-specific functioning (Daniels 2008, p. 38). While Daniels acknowledges that norms may play a role in the identification of departures from normal functioning, he underscores the importance of identifying normal functioning based on the "biological facts of nature without value judgments" (Daniels 2008, p. 38, quoting Boorse 1997). Daniels argues that this approach makes departures from normal functioning as objective and value-free as possible, enabling public agreement about what counts as a departure and what does not. The subsequent challenge is to reach "normative judgments about which dysfunctions are worthy of treatment" (Daniels 2008, p. 39).

The special importance of maintaining normal functioning derives, according to Daniels, from the relationship between normal functioning and the protection of the normal opportunity range. Persons, Daniels argues, have a special moral interest in protecting the normal opportunity range, which he defines as the array of life plans persons can reasonably develop for themselves in a given society (Daniels 2008, pp. 58–59). Deviations from normal functioning may directly affect people's opportunity range. They may actually affect people's ability to obtain offices and positions, thereby obstructing Rawls' fair equality of opportunity for jobs and positions. Daniels therefore argues that Rawls' principle of fair equality of opportunity does not only require a comprehensive program of education to correct for unfortunate social conditions, as Rawls has underscored. The principle also requires a comprehensive set of health services to avoid and correct unfortunate health circumstances.

Daniels then moves on to expand the notion of opportunity. Rawls has reserved the notion for positions and offices only, given their great strategic importance in relation to the primary goods of income, wealth and self-respect. Daniels needs to expand the notion of opportunity, as limiting it to jobs and positions would imply an "age-biased and morally objectionable account of health care" (Daniels 2008, p. 60), as job and career opportunities are more important in the early and middle stages of life, but health care needs arise throughout a person's life. By broadening the notion of opportunities, Daniels is able to link health policy to Rawls' fair equality of opportunity principle. He argues that "institutions meeting health needs quite generally have a central impact on individual shares of the opportunity range and should therefore be governed directly by the opportunity principle" (Daniels 2008, pp. 59–60). In other words, given the often pervasive impact of ill health on the size and scope of a person's opportunity range, the delivery of health policies should be governed by the goal to restore health *in order to guarantee* fair equality of opportunity. Health services in their broadest sense are as strategic in importance as education to mitigate the morally arbitrary influences of the social and natural lotteries on prospects in life (Daniels 2008, pp. 54–62). Based on this framework, Daniels argues that the goal of health policy is to guarantee fair equality of opportunity through, first, the avoidance of deviations from normal functioning through prevention, second, the correction of deviations from normal functioning through cure, and, third, through care and compensation for deviations from normal functioning when cure is not possible.

Daniels' solution is elegant, as it avoids the need to add another good to the set of primary goods and leaves Rawls' powerful overarching framework intact. Yet, on a closer reading, Daniels' approach does not succeed in its goal. It either creates a so-called 'bottomless pit' or it requires the introduction of highly problematic interpersonal comparisons. The bottomless pit emerges because Daniels' argument implies that any (statistical) deviation from normal functioning, no matter how small, should be treated whenever it has an impact on fair equality of opportunity. The application of the principle of fair equality of opportunity thus implies that a virtually unlimited share of a society's resources should be dedicated to health policies. Indeed, the argumentation suggests that fair equality of opportunity should be restored, even if this depletes the income and wealth resources of all members of society, including the worst-off groups, to a bare minimum. The only way to avoid this intuitively unappealing implication is by introducing interpersonal comparison, i.e. by comparing and weighing the benefits of health interventions' contribution to restoring fair equality of opportunity against the costs of such interventions for society as a whole and in particular for the income and wealth of the least-advantaged group. Daniels is well aware of the limitations of his line of argumentation. He acknowledges that his approach only gives "general guidance in the design of systems that meet health needs", but "does not tell us how to meet health needs fairly when we cannot meet them all" (Daniels 2008, pp. 102–103). As a way out, he proposes to supplement his general principles of justice with a fair process for setting limits on the resources that are dedicated to health policies.

This conclusion regarding health and health policies holds as much for the domain of transportation as it does for health care. Thus Daniels' theory, while elegant and rich, does not provide a basis for the incorporation of transportation in Rawls' theory of justice. The approach cannot avoid the problem of interpersonal comparison, but can at best provide only 'general guidance' regarding a fair distribution of goods that do not belong to Rawls' initial set of primary goods. Daniels' solution of introducing a fair process is at odds with my ambition to develop a substantive and prescriptive theory of justice for the domain of transportation (see Chapter 1). Following the procedural path would *de facto* imply abandoning the entire endeavor of this book.

There is yet another reason why Daniels' approach can be of little help in defining fairness in the domain of transportation. Daniels accepts and follows Rawls approach of developing a fundamentally a-spatial account of social justice, a path which is in line with virtually all leading theories of social justice (see Chapter 3). For that reason, neither Rawls nor Daniels has to be concerned with the challenge posed by the structuring impact of space. Yet any account of social justice that takes space seriously is likely to expose a range of problems in Rawls' theory of justice and Daniels' extension of it. The most obvious problem relates to the principle of fair equality of opportunity. It is only because Rawls ignores the fundamental spatiality of the human condition that he can disregard the morally arbitrary influences of space on equality of opportunity, to paraphrase Rawls' own words. Likewise, Daniels can only assume the universal role of health policies in restoring fair equality of opportunity by ignoring the structuring impact of space. Yet over the past decades an abundance of literature has emerged uncovering the often pervasive influence of space on opportunity, health and health care. Indeed, geographers and other scholars have collected a large body of evidence regarding the large differentials in employment and related powers and prerogatives across space (see e.g. Massey 1995) and the sometimes striking geographical disparities in the uptake of health care (e.g. Neutens 2015). By ignoring space, Rawls and Daniels can avoid the question of whether and to what extent the morally arbitrary influences of space have to be mitigated. Clearly, any approach to justice in the domain of transportation cannot ignore space; it can only start from the fundamental role space plays in the lives of persons.

Taken together, these arguments suggest that Daniels' elegant expansion of Rawls' theory of justice cannot deliver the necessary foundations for the demarcation of justice in the domain of transportation. Hence I will not explore Daniels' path any further, but will instead turn to Rawls' own proposition for extending his theory of justice beyond the set of initial primary goods.

Rawls' solution

Does Rawls himself provide a direction to incorporate transportation within his theory of justice? In most of his work, Rawls has hardly explored the implications of his framework for goods that fall outside his set of primary goods. However, in his *Restatement*, he briefly takes up this challenge. In line with Green and Daniels, he develops a line of reasoning for addressing health needs within his theory (Rawls 2003, pp. 171–174).

Rawls starts his argument by emphasizing that the index of primary goods is an index of the expectations regarding these goods over the course of a complete life. That is, the contractants in the original position are to reach an agreement about the principles of justice based on the assessment regarding the goods they expect to receive over an entire life. Since Rawls has powerfully argued that the contractants will agree on equality in liberties and opportunities, the assessment will primarily relate to the expectations regarding income and wealth. These life-long expectations are viewed as attached to the relevant social positions in the basic structure, including the position of the least-advantaged group.

Rawls acknowledges that people belonging to each social group may show differences in need arising from illness and accident over the course of a complete life. He explores how his framework can be applied to the medical and health needs of citizens "whose capacities for a time fall below the minimum" of normal cooperating members of society (Rawls 2003, p. 173). He suggests that, in order to finance health services for the worst-off groups in society, we need to take some of the wealth and income of the better-off groups through, for example, taxation. This redistributive policy —a reduction in income for better-off groups to the benefit of health services for the least-advantaged groups—can continue "up to the point where further provision would lower the expectation of the least advantaged" (ibid.). The thinking here is similar to that underlying the difference principle per se, but now the expectations of the least-advantaged include not only income and wealth, but also "the provision of health care at a certain level (calculated by estimated cost)" (ibid.). The idea is that taking income and wealth from better-off groups may not only lower the income of these richer groups directly, but may also reduce the total wealth in a society as incentives for hard work are lessened. Thus, by taking some income from the best-off groups and using it for health care, the least-advantaged gain in health care but may lose in income and wealth. The understanding of this dynamic and its detrimental impact on the least-advantaged groups creates an intuitive 'cap' on the use of society's resources for health services.

Rawls' line of reasoning provides an intuitively appealing answer to setting limits regarding expenditures on health care, but it comes at a cost. The cost lies in the need to assess the situation of the least-advantaged based on an index of goods, comprised of income and wealth and health (care) services. Since some members of the least-advantaged group may prefer a higher income over better health, while others may prefer the opposite, the introduction of an index of primary goods implies that value judgments cannot be avoided. Thus this extension of Rawls' framework to health also leads to the introduction of the problem of interpersonal comparisons of an index of goods. Rawls is well aware of this problem and explicitly points out that the decisions regarding expenditures on health care are not to be made in the original position. Rather, it is up to the real-world representatives of citizens, who must strike a balance between income and wealth, health care, and many other worthwhile expenditures, such as those for education, retirement and so on (ibid., p. 174).

In spite of this limitation of Rawls' solution, it is worthwhile transposing Rawls' approach to the domain of transportation. The line of reasoning is slightly different, for three reasons. First, where the need for health care is related to the unpredictable occurrence of illness and accidents, the need for accessibility is universal, although citizens may differ in the intensity of the need. Second, where health services tend to be provided on an individual basis, transportation services tend to serve collectives rather than individuals. Thus the benefits of transportation expenditures tend to be reaped by many. Third, health expenditures are generally perceived as a cost that reduces the level of income and wealth at the disposal of the members of society. Transportation expenditures, in contrast, can actually improve the functioning of the economy and thereby increase the overall income and wealth of society.

In light of these differences, let me now try to transpose the Rawlsian approach to health care to the domain of transportation through three simple examples. For reasons of simplicity, each example concerns a society consisting of only a few groups, including a least-advantaged one. Note that in this fictive society, income and wealth are arranged according to the difference principle and the position of the worst-off group is judged based on a composite index consisting of income and wealth and accessibility, in line with Rawls' extension to health care.

In the first example, society comprises of a rich and a poor population group. Figure 5.1 depicts the development of accessibility and income levels over time, for two groups. In the initial situation (T_0), the only means of transportation is walking and all members of society are able to walk. Rich and poor thus experience identical levels of accessibility. In order to improve accessibility levels, it is necessary to raise taxes to finance investments in transportation infrastructure. For this purpose, the rich group incurs a tax increase from point T_1 onwards. In this first example, it is assumed that any improvement in the transportation infrastructure can be used by all individuals, so an investment always results in an accessibility improvement for both groups. The improved accessibility triggers an increase in productivity that exceeds the investment costs in improved infrastructure. The investments thus lead to an increase in overall income and wealth. Since the basic structure of our society lives up to the difference principle, the extra income and wealth also comes to the benefit of the worst-off. In the figure, it is assumed that maintaining a stable after-tax level of income and wealth for the rich generates the highest overall-productivity and thus the highest level of income and wealth for the worst-off members of society. Note that the assumption of a stable income for the rich group is not relevant to the argument, as the difference principle directs the attention to the least-advantaged group and accepts lower incomes for the richer groups if this benefits the least-advantaged members of society. This pattern of accessibility improvements repeats itself over time: investments are made in transportation infrastructure, and accessibility levels for the rich and the poor, and income and wealth for the poor, go up. However, the increase in income and wealth drops over time, as the positive impacts of transport investments on productivity become smaller as the transport network develops (due to decreasing returns on investment). At a certain point (T_2 in Figure 5.1), a transport investment still increases accessibility for both the rich and the poor, but the impact on overall income and wealth is lower than the costs of the investment, leading to a reduction in overall income and wealth. As a result, income and wealth go down for both the rich (due to taxes for infrastructure investment) and the poor (due to lower transfers). Thus, beyond point T_2, the problem of interpersonal comparison emerges: accessibility improvements have to be weighed against decreases in incomeand wealth. This is obvious, but it

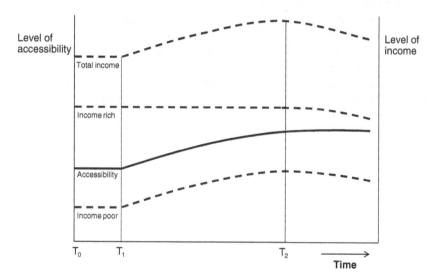

Figure 5.1 Rawls and accessibility: trade-off between improvements in accessibility and increases in income and wealth in the first fictive society. Beyond T_2, improvements in accessibility have to be weighed against decreases in income and wealth.

also highlights a more striking observation: to the left of point T_2 no such weighing is necessary. Thus, as long as transport investments improve the accessibility levels of the least-advantaged group and generate sufficient economic growth to at least maintain the income levels of that group, no weighing between the different components of the index (income and wealth versus accessibility) is necessary, and contractants in the original position could agree to these investments. In other words, all investments in transport infrastructure up to point T_2 live up to Rawls' perspective! Beyond point T_2, weighing is necessary and decisions can no longer be made in the original position.

Let me now turn to the second example (Figure 5.2). As in the first example, walking is the only means of transportation for all members of society in the initial situation (T_0) and rich and poor thus experience identical levels of accessibility. However, in contrast to the first example, new investments in transport infrastructure can only be used by the rich group (e.g. because use of the infrastructure is expensive). The rich group thus experiences an increase in accessibility from T_1 onwards, while initially the accessibility level of the poor remains unchanged. The improved accessibility for the rich triggers an increase in productivity and thus in overall wealth and income of society. Since the basic structure of society lives up to the difference principle, the extra income and wealth also comes to the benefit of the worst-off in the maximum possible way (it is, again, assumed that maintaining the income and wealth of the rich leads to the highest gains in overall wealth and income and thus to the highest income for the least-advantaged group). Thus, in the early stages of the investments in transportation infrastructure, the poor experience an improvement in their situation: while their accessibility levels do not improve, they do receive an increasing level of income. As time moves on, more and more funds are invested in transportation infrastructure. This leads to a further increase in accessibility for the rich, in improvements in productivity, in overall income and wealth, and ultimately in increases in income and wealth for the poor. However, as land uses start to reorganize around the fast transportation mode, to better cater for the rich group (which obviously has most purchasing power), the accessibility level of the poor population group gradually decreases. Beyond this point $(T_2$ in Figure 5.2), the poor are confronted with an increase in income and wealth, but a drop in accessibility. Thus the same situation occurs as in the first example, but much 'earlier in time'. Only in the very early stages of the development of the society, when transport improvements have not yet affected land use patterns, do transport improvements live up to Rawls' perspective. As soon as transport investments start shaping land use patterns, the problem of interpersonal comparison emerges: decreases in accessibility have to be weighed against improvements in income and wealth. As discussed, this weighing falls outside the scope of the Rawlsian framework of justice, and, thus, Rawls' theory has to remain silent about the fairness of transport investments that lie beyond point T_2.

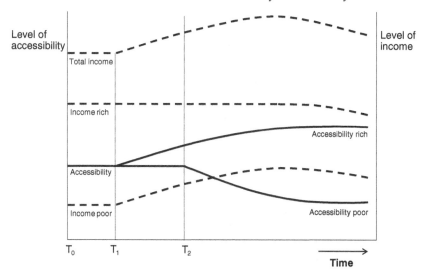

Figure 5.2 Rawls and accessibility: trade-off between improvements in accessibility and increases in income and wealth in the second fictive society, in which accessibility improvements only accrue to the rich population group.

So far, the role of space has been limited in the two examples, as it has been assumed that transport improvements can improve accessibility levels across the board. Typically, however, such investments will improve accessibility for some areas, and thus for some groups, but not for others. This differential effect of space is taken into account in the third example. In this case, society is comprised of three groups: the rich, the poor, and the peripherals. The peripherals have the same income and wealth as the poor group, but have a lower level of accessibility due to their peripheral location. In line with the other examples, in the initial situation (T_0) the only means of transportation is walking and it is assumed that all members of society are able to walk. The rich and poor groups, who both live in the center, experience identical levels of accessibility, which lie above those experienced by the peripherals. In line with the first example, investments in infrastructure can be used by all population groups. However, in contrast to the other examples, the impacts of infrastructure are spatially confined: they either benefit the groups living in the center or those residing in the periphery. In this situation, the peripherals are clearly the least-advantaged group as measured by the composite index. They have the same level of income and wealth as the poor group, but a lower accessibility level. This situation directly introduces the problem of interpersonal comparison.

To see why, consider the ways in which the index of the least-advantaged group could be improved. There are basically two ways. The first is by taxing the rich and improving the accessibility experienced by the peripherals. Such transport investments improve the situation of the peripherals if they lead to a higher level of productivity sufficient to at least maintain the overall level of income and wealth in society. If that is the case, the level of income and wealth of both the peripherals and the poor can be maintained, while the accessibility level of the peripherals is improved. Note that the income and wealth of both the poor and the peripherals have to be maintained in order to avoid the problem of interpersonal comparison between these two groups. This way of improving the accessibility level of the peripherals can continue as long as the improvements lead to a sufficiently large increase in productivity, and as long as peripherals' accessibility level does not surpass the accessibility level of the poor living in the center. Once the peripherals have achieved the same level of accessibility as the poor, the accessibility levels of both groups will have to be increased, again to avoid the problem of interpersonal comparison between the poor and the peripherals.

The second way to increase the index of the least-advantaged group is through increasing the group's income and wealth. Let us assume that this can be done most efficiently by taxing the rich and improving the transport infrastructure for the rich and the poor living in the center. The increased productivity and related overall income and wealth are then used to improve the income and wealth of the peripherals as the least-advantaged group. In order to avoid the problem of interpersonal comparison, it is also necessary to improve the income and wealth of the poor group living in the center. Otherwise, the peripherals would outperform the poor in terms of income and wealth, while the poor would have a higher accessibility level than the peripherals, and the taxing and investment strategy would implicitly contain a weighing of income and wealth versus accessibility levels.

While these two taxing and investment strategies may avoid the problem of interpersonal comparison, the mere existence of two strategies reveals that the problem of interpersonal comparison cannot be avoided. The first strategy implicitly assumes that increasing the accessibility level of the least-advantaged is the best strategy to improve their index, while the second strategy suggests that increasing their income and wealth is the preferred way to go. The choice between the two strategies requires interpersonal comparison and thus falls outside the scope of the Rawlsian framework of justice. The choice cannot be made by the contractants behind the veil of ignorance, but has to be made when the veil is lifted and "the full range of general economic and social facts is brought to bear" (Rawls 1999 [1971], p. 175); in other words: when sufficient information is available on the actual state of affairs and the preferences of members of society.

It may be clear that, while each of the examples represents a strongly stylized society, the third example most closely resembles real-world settings. Indeed, in any real-world context, population groups will differ in terms of both the height of their income and the level of accessibility. Hence, Rawls' own approach to include health care in his theory of justice as fairness runs into the same problem of interpersonal comparison as the approaches developed by Green and Daniels. This may be a disappointing conclusion, but Rawls' theory is sufficiently rich to provide other insights on which a theory of justice for the domain of transportation can build.

Conclusions

In this chapter, I have explored whether Rawls' theory of justice could provide the bedrock for delineating fairness in the domain of transportation. It has taken a long path to reach a disappointing conclusion: Rawls' theory cannot provide clear demarcation points regarding a fair distribution of accessibility. The paths suggested by Green, Daniels and Rawls himself to extend the original theory all run into the same problem of interpersonal comparison. Even if only the situation of the least-advantaged group is taken into consideration, improvements in accessibility will have to be weighed against improvements in income and wealth. It was precisely this process of weighing one moral intuition against another that Rawls sought to avoid in his theory of justice. By expanding his theory to other domains, including transportation, weighing returns in full force. The consequence is that an expanded version of the theory cannot provide guidance regarding the fair distribution of accessibility.

In spite of this disappointing outcome, the elaborate discussion of Rawls' theory of justice as fairness does not leave us empty-handed. Rawls' theory and its extension to health provide a number of building blocks that can be employed for the development of a theory of fairness in accessibility. Let me briefly highlight these building blocks.

First, Rawls' theory suggests that accessibility should be seen as one of the benefits of social cooperation and that its distribution should thus be guided by principles of justice. By underscoring that accessibility is a benefit of social cooperation I do not refer to the fact that most transportation infrastructures and services tend to be provided by governments and are typically perceived as a public good. What I refer to is the fact that accessibility is, in its very essence, an asset that is jointly produced by all. It is only because of the spatial concentration of members of society that accessibility emerges. The concentration of persons allows the emergence of businesses, shops, hospitals, schools, and so on. Each member of society thus has some share in the production and reproduction of accessibility. Accessibility is therefore *par excellence* a benefit of social cooperation. This would even hold if all transportation infrastructures and services were to be delivered through private, for-profit, entities. It is precisely because accessibility is a product of social cooperation that all members of society may lay claim to a fair share of the advantages that accessibility confers to persons. This, then, is an additional argument for setting accessibility apart as a good with a distinct social meaning, whose distribution should be subject to principles of justice.

Second, Rawls stresses that agreement about principles of justice is fundamentally different from agreement about matters of practical policy-making. In contrast to the latter, principles of justice should be designed so that persons can be expected to honor the principles *over an entire life time*. The weight of these 'strains of commitment' avoids persons from agreeing all too easily on principles of justice. Principles of justice are too important to be subject to the whims of the day and should be delineated taking these (theoretical) strains of commitment into account.

Third, Rawls' focus on primary goods is related to the fundamental interest of persons in shaping and, where necessary, adjusting their own life plans. Indeed, Rawls argues that his primary, all-purpose, goods should be distributed in such a way that persons can pursue a wide range of life plans. This enabling character of primary goods resonates strongly with the enabling character of accessibility (see Chapters 1 and 4). It suggests that the distribution of accessibility, as an all-purpose good, should also take into account the special moral interest of persons to determine their own path of life.

Fourth, Rawls' notion of the 'worst-off representative man' or the 'least-advantaged group' will prove to be valuable in the explorations that follow. The focus on the worst-off group eliminates the need to assess the share of each and every member of society and thus gives direction to the assessment of fairness in a particular domain. The notion of the least-advantaged group will also be of use in analyzing and assessing accessibility patterns, as I will show in the last part of this book.

Finally, in what follows I will also draw on Daniels' approach to define the notion of normal functioning. Daniels does not seek an objective definition of deviations from normal functioning. He rather proposes a statistical one, claiming that the statistical approach makes it possible to determine departures from normal functioning in a way that is as objective and value-free as possible. This, he argues, enables public agreement about what counts as a departure and what not. This 'biostatistical' account of health can also be useful in the domain of transportation, as I will show in the discussion on the relationship between accessibility and activity participation in Chapter 7.

The relevance of each of these 'building blocks' for a theory of justice for the domain of transportation will be discussed in more detail in the chapters to come.

References

Arrow, K.J. (1973). Some ordinalist-utilitarian notes on Rawls's theory of justice. *Journal of Philosophy*, 70(9): 245–263.

Boorse, C. (1997). A rebuttal on health. In: J.M. Humber and R.F. Almeder (eds), *What is Disease?* New York, Springer, pp. 1–134.

Daniels, N. (1985). *Just Health Care*. Cambridge, Cambridge University Press.

Daniels, N. (2008). *Just Health : meeting health needs fairly.* Cambridge, Cambridge University Press.

Denier, Y. (2005). On personal responsibility and the human right to healthcare. *Cambridge Quarterly of Healthcare Ethics*, 14(2): 224–234.

Denier, Y. (2007). *Efficiency, Justice and Care: philosophical reflections on scarcity in health care.* Dordrecht, Springer.

Green, R.M. (1976). Health care and justice in contract theory perspective. In: R.M. Veatch and R. Branson (eds), *Ethics and Health Policy.* Cambridge, MA, Ballinger Publishing Co.

Hare, R.M. (1973). Review of Rawls' Theory of Justice–I. *The Philosophical Quarterly*, 23(91): 144–155.

Harsanyi, J.C. (1955). Cardinal welfare, individualistic ethics, and interpersonal comparisons of utility. *The Journal of Political Economy*: 309–321.

Kaldor, N. (1939). Welfare propositions of economics and interpersonal comparisons of utility. *The Economic Journal*: 549–552.

Khisty, C.J. (1996). Operationalizing concepts of equity for public project investments. *Transportation Research Record: Journal of the Transportation Research Board*, 1559: 94–99.

Langmyhr, T. (1997). Managing equity: the case of road pricing. *Transport Policy*, 4(1): 25–39.

Massey, D.B. (1995). *Spatial Divisions of Labor: social structures and the geography of production.* Hove, Psychology Press.

Neutens, T. (2015). Accessibility, equity and health care: review and research directions for transport geographers. *Journal of Transport Geography*, 43: 14–27.

Nozick, R. (1974). *Anarchy, State, and Utopia.* New York, Basic Books.

Rawls, J. (1971). *A Theory of Justice.* Cambridge, MA, Harvard University Press.

Rawls, J. (1982). Social unity and primary goods. In: A. Sen and B. Williams (eds), *Utilitarianism and Beyond.* Cambridge, Cambridge University Press.

Rawls, J. (1999 [1971]). *A Theory of Justice, Revised Edition.* Cambridge, MA, The Belknap Press of Harvard University Press.

Rawls, J. (2003 [2001]). *Justice as Fairness: a restatement.* Cambridge/London, The Belknap Press of Harvard University Press. (Edited by Erin Kelly.)

Rooijakkers, A.F.M. (2012). Rawls in beweging; een theoretisch literatuuronderzoek naar een mogelijke overeenstemming tussen de subjectie van Rawls' rechtvaardigheidstheorie en transport in zijn maatschappelijke betekenis. Unpublished Master's thesis, Radboud Universiteit, Nijmegen; http://gpm. ruhosting.nl/mt/2012-MA-PL-17RooijakkersAndreas.pdf

Scanlon, T.M. (1991). The moral basis of interpersonal comparisons. *Interpersonal Comparisons of Well-being*: 17–44.

Sen, A. (2006). What do we want from a theory of justice? *The Journal of Philosophy*, 103(5): 215–238.

Smith, A. (2010 [1759]). *The Theory of Moral Sentiments.* Harmondsworth, Penguin.

Tyler, N. (2006). Capabilities and radicalism: engineering accessibility in the 21st century. *Transportation Planning and Technology*, 29(5): 331–358.

Viegas, J.M. (2001). Making road pricing acceptable and effective: searching for quality and equity in urban mobility. *Transport Policy*, 8(4): 289–294.

6 Insuring for Lack of Accessibility

Introduction

In this chapter, I will continue to build on the contractarian approach to social justice in order to develop a theory of justice for the domain of transportation. I will take up Ronald Dworkin's theory of equality of resources and explore its possible consequences for transportation.

Dworkin presented his theory in two early papers and further elaborated the approach in his book *Sovereign Virtue* (Dworkin 1981a; Dworkin 1981b; Dworkin 2000). In these works, he developed a complex line of argumentation, invoking auctions and insurance schemes, in order to determine what it means to devote an equal amount of resources to each person's life. Like Rawls and other philosophers of justice, Dworkin's approach is a-spatial in nature. Yet, as I will show in this chapter, the employment of auctions and insurance schemes enables the explicit treatment of space in reasoning about justice. This makes the Dworkian line of argumentation particularly suited for the development of a theory of justice for the domain of transportation.

In what follows, I will start with an outline of the main elements of Dworkin's theory of justice. I will present in some detail Dworkin's fictive example of shipwreck survivors on a deserted island who seek to distribute the resources on the island in a fair way. I will then expand this example to incorporate transportation as well as location. Through a series of fictive examples, I will develop a number of insurance schemes that aim to protect persons against various forms of accessibility-related bad luck. Taken together, these insurance schemes result in the outline of a set of principles of justice for the domain of transportation in the concluding section of this chapter.

Fairness as envy-free distributions

Dworkin proposes to use resources, rather than Rawls' primary goods, as the proper metric of fairness. He conceptualizes resources as the sum of material resources owned privately by individuals. A society is fair, according to Dworkin, if an equal amount of resources is devoted to each person's life (Dworkin 2000, p. 70; see also p. 89). He argues that under equality of resources "people decide what sorts of lives to pursue against a background of information about *the actual cost their choices impose on other people* and hence on the total stock of resources that may fairly be used by them" (ibid., p. 288; italics KM). The best device to take these costs into account, according to Dworkin, is the idea of an economic market.

Dworkin then takes a fictive example in order to develop his theory. In the example, a number of shipwreck survivors are washed up on a deserted island with abundant resources and no native population. These immigrants accept the principle "that no one is antecedently entitled to any of these resources, but that they shall instead be divided equally among them" (ibid., pp. 66–67). They also accept a particular test of an equal division of resources, which Dworkin calls the envy test: "No division of resources is an equal division if, once the division is complete, any immigrant would prefer someone else's bundle of resources to his own bundle" (Dworkin 1981b, p. 285; Dworkin 2000, p. 67; see Varian 1985 for a discussion of the application of the envy test in the field of economics).

Dworkin argues that an equal division of resources will not deliver a distribution that will live up to the envy test. This is because an identical combination of the resources on the island may well cater better for some tastes or preferences than others, and hence may give the immigrants reason to challenge the equal division. While, in this case, one immigrant may not literally envy another person's bundle, for the simple reason that the bundles are identical, the immigrant might point out that the other person's tastes are better served by the equal division of resources. After some trial and error, the immigrants to the island realize that an auction is the only proper way to achieve a truly equal division of the available resources. Dworkin proposes that each of the immigrants is handed over an equal amount of some form of currency—100 clamshells in his example —and uses this amount to bid for those resources that best suit his or her life plan. Since each person has equal 'wealth', each person plays an equal role in determining the ultimate distribution of the resources on the island. However, it is also clear that resources preferred by many members of society will be more 'expensive' in the auction. Hence, a person who wants to purchase such a resource will have to give up more of his clamshells in order to do so. Dworkin claims this is fair, because "the true measure of the social resources devoted to the life of one person is fixed by asking how important, in fact, that resource is for others" (Dworkin 2000, p. 70). In other words, if one person obtains a resource and thus excludes others from enjoying that resource, this has a cost in terms of reduced preference satisfaction. The size of this cost should be reflected in the 'price' of the resource, according to Dworkin. The auction enables immigrants to deal with the implications of scarcity for fairness: "Under equality of resources ... people decide what sort of lives to pursue against a background of information about the actual cost their choices impose on other people and hence on the total stock of resources that may be fairly used by them" (ibid., p. 69). Given the limited availability of resources, 'popular' choices are more expensive than 'unpopular' ones, and this should be reflected in the bundle of goods that is held by the respective members of society. In light of this scarcity, the auction enables each immigrant to obtain a bundle of goods that best matches his preferences, while taking into account the preferences of the other immigrants to the island. If the auction is properly executed, no one will envy another person's set of purchases after the auction, because he could have bid for that bundle of goods, rather than the goods he actually bid for. The auction not only outperforms an equal division of resources, in which each person has an identical bundle of resources, in terms of fairness, but also in terms of efficiency, as the auction enables all persons to purchase a bundle of goods that best matches their preferences.

After presenting the initial auction, Dworkin goes on to ask how his approach to equality of resources can be generalized to more complex cases involving labor, investment, trade, and so on. He first explores how his scheme of equality of resources can deal with luck. Dworkin distinguishes between two forms of luck: option luck and brute luck. Option luck is a matter of how deliberate and calculated gambles turn out —whether somebody gains or loses "through accepting an isolated risk he or she should have anticipated and might have declined" (ibid., p. 73). Brute luck refers to cases in which the person has no influence on the occurrence of a particular event. While Dworkin recognizes that the difference between both types of luck is not always easy to draw, he maintains that differences in a person's life-time bundle of goods due to option luck are in line with his notion of equality of resources. That is, persons who gamble and win, and thus expand their bundle of goods, are entitled to keep these goods, as other persons could have made the same gamble and could have won (or lost). The chance of losing is the price the gamblers pay for the opportunity to win, and a person who declines to gamble has preferred not to pay this 'price' in favor of the certainty of another bundle of goods. So differences in persons' life-time resource bundles due to option luck are in line with equality of resources and thus do not warrant any form of redistribution.

The situation is different for brute bad luck, Dworkin argues. Brute bad luck, such as blindness or other impairments, will limit a person's ability to engage in production and trade and thus will affect a person's life-time resource bundle. Dworkin develops the concept of the hypothetical insurance scheme as a way to solve this issue. Again, he presents an imaginary society in which each person is given an equal share of some currency. In order to develop his argument, he assumes that everyone has the same risk of developing a physical or mental impairment in the future.

Subsequently, each person can decide to set some clamshells apart for purchasing insurance to protect him from this risk. Persons can also choose different levels of coverage, each with a different price tag attached to it. By offering such insurance to all persons against the same conditions, irrespective of a person's actual chance of developing some type of impairment in the future, brute luck is turned into option luck: persons make the deliberate decision to insure or not to insure against brute luck.

Subsequently, each person entering the imaginary society is asked how much he is willing to spend, from his clamshells, on insurance to protect for the natural disadvantages one may suffer, in addition to the purchase of the other resources up for sale in the auction. How much coverage would the average person purchase? Dworkin argues that this question would provide a workable baseline from which to work out a premium. This will be so, even though particular persons differ in the risks they are willing to take and the insurance premiums they would be prepared to pay. People would, Dworkin argues, make roughly the same assessment of the value of insurance against impairments such as blindness or loss of limbs, as is currently the case in at least part of the actual insurance market. On average, for instance, people might be willing to spend ten percent of their income. Consequently, we should compensate those who develop impairments, or are born with them, accordingly, out of some fund collected by income taxation or other compulsory insurance scheme with a fixed premium.

Dworkin acknowledges that in real life people do differ in their chances for brute bad luck and that insurance schemes take these differences into account. He argues, however, that by making the simplifying assumption of equal chances for brute bad luck, the idea of a market in insurance can provide a counter-factual guide through which equality of resources might face the problem of impairments in the real world. He also recognizes that, even if persons are assumed to have equal chances for brute bad luck, they may differ in their willingness to set resources aside to turn that brute bad luck into an option luck. Yet, since there is no reliable way to obtain information on each person's willingness to insure in the hypothetical situation once brute bad luck has struck, he proposes to use the average willingness to insure as the benchmark for the insurance scheme and suggests that persons who perhaps would have purchased more insurance in the hypothetical situation settle for that average.

Dworkin then moves on to address the issue of labor and wages. He acknowledges that different types of labor are likely to deliver different pay-offs and may thus disturb the initial equality of resources. He points out that, if talents and skills are equal among the members of society, reasons to engage in a particular job are a matter of preferences. A person who prefers a job that delivers products highly appreciated by others may collect more resources over an entire life than a person who prefers a job producing a service that is hardly sought after. Dworkin argues, in line with his argument regarding option luck, that these differences are acceptable. For the latter person could have taken up the former person's position and could have obtained a larger set of goods. He has decided not to do so, because he prefers the other job, even given the consequences in terms of resources. In other words, the person has no complaint if we expand the envy test to include both occupation and resources. The test now requires that no one should envy the bundle of occupation and resources at the disposal of anyone else over an entire life-time. Dworkin concludes: "If everyone had equal talents..., the initial auction would produce continuing equality of resources even though bank-account wealth became more and more unequal as years passed" (ibid., p. 85).

Obviously, in any real-world setting, skills and talents are unequally distributed. Dworkin develops another type of insurance scheme to deal with this issue. He points out that in the initial auction, people would be offered the possibility of insuring against 'lack of skills'. He argues that this issue boils down to uncertainty among people about the "economic rent" of their talents, i.e. about the level of income their talents may produce (ibid., p. 94). Dworkin subsequently proposes a hypothetical insurance scheme in which people are radically uncertain about the economic rent of their talents. Rather, they can only assume that they have the same chance as everyone else of occupying any particular level of income in the economy. They can subsequently purchase an insurance from multiple insurance companies, who sell insurance against failing to have an opportunity to earn whatever level of income a person names. It may be clear that the premiums for insuring against not receiving the highest income in the society will be extremely high, as the chances that a person will earn less than the highest income is close to one. Hence, few people will purchase such an insurance. But the willingness to purchase an insurance will substantially increase with lower levels of coverage, for two reasons. First, the premiums will be substantially lower when coverage falls, as the chances that the insurer actually has to pay will become smaller. Second, and related, the penalty of losing the insurance bet, in terms of insurance premiums paid that in the end do not lead to any payment in income increment at all, becomes smaller and smaller in relation to the actual income of the person, since the premiums drop with the decrease in the coverage level. Thus Dworkin concludes that people are very likely to insure at some level of income. While people will differ in terms of the coverage that they will want to purchase, even under complete uncertainty about the economic rent of their talents, Dworkin argues that it would be possible to determine some average level of coverage which most people would be willing to purchase. This level can then serve as the benchmark for a tax scheme to enable unemployment and other welfare payments. Dworkin finally develops an argument that the tax rate does not have to be equal across income levels, showing that it is beneficial for both the insurer and the insured to link the insurance premium to a person's actual income level. The resulting Dworkian world thus exhibits substantial income inequality, but would guarantee a sufficient level of income for everybody, based on a progressive tax system.

Dworkin's approach to justice is attractive, as it makes scarcity an intrinsic element of reasoning about fairness. It shows that equality has a price, a price that a rational agent is only willing to pay to a limited extent. The result is that the notion of equality of resources is actually on a par with substantial differences in resources over a person's life time. This is not, as Dworkin emphasizes, because equality is only relevant at the outset, when the immigrants land on the deserted island, but because equality of resources accepts, within a certain range, a variety of distributions (ibid., p. 108). This is so because the insurance device "aims to make people equal in their ex ante risk of bad luck, but not in their ex post circumstances once bad luck strikes"—or does not strike (ibid., p. 346). The insurance approach defines the 'bottom' of a variety in distributions, at least in an abstract way, by defining what level of compensation is owed to people experiencing impairments, limited skills and talents, or other forms of brute bad luck. Above the minimum, large differences in resources are allowed.

Extending Dworkin's insurance scheme to transportation

What can we learn from Dworkin about fairness in the domain of transportation? In what follows, I will pursue Dworkin's line of reasoning to explore these consequences.

Before doing this, it is important to underline the relevance of Dworkin's approach. Dworkin seeks to develop an approach that sets limits on the intuition that society should fully compensate people who are confronted with brute bad luck. "The effect of the hypothetical insurance strategy is not to eliminate the consequences of brute bad luck ... but only to the degree and in the way that prudent insurance normally would. The strategy aims to put people in an equal position with respect to risk, rather than to negate risk altogether" (Dworkin 2000, p. 341). Dworkin's argument is that eliminating risk altogether would imply that a society would have to spend so much on persons who are struck by brute bad luck that it would have no resources left to make life worth living. The insurance approach sets rational limits on this intuition to rule out the effects of brute bad luck altogether.

The approach is in a crucial way comparable to Rawls' veil of ignorance (Roemer 2002). The device of the veil of ignorance makes it possible to avoid, as much as possible, the complicated and often fruitless process of weighing one moral intuition against another. Instead, the contractants in the original position merely need to ask themselves the question: What principles would I as a rational agent in the original position find

Table 6.1 Overview of the hypothetical scenarios designed to extract principles of justice for the transportation domain.

Number	Pages	Title of scenario	Description
1	91	The basic case	Immigrants bid for a residential location and residence, against the background of a singular transportation system that can be used by all
2	95	Bidding for transportation services	Immigrants bid for various transportation service packages, as the transportation system on the island is not pre-given
3	100	Bidding for impairment-proof transportation services	Immigrants bid for various transportation service packages in the understanding that they may be excluded from using particular packages in case of travel-related impairments
4	105	Insuring under fair income differentials	In contrast to all previous scenarios, immigrants know that they risk receiving only the floor income once life on the island commences; they can bid for an additional insurance against this risk
5	109	Insuring under unfair income differentials	In contrast to the previous scenario, immigrants run the risk of receiving an income well below the floor level once life on the island commences; they can bid for an additional insurance against this risk
6	116	Insuring for random location assignment	*Case of insufficient accessibility* In contrast to all previous scenarios, immigrants cannot choose their residential location but run the risk of being allocated a peripheral location with an insufficient level of accessibility; they can bid for insurance to protect themselves against this risk
7	117	Insuring for random location assignment	*Case of travel-related impairments* In contrast to all previous scenarios, immigrants cannot choose their residential location but run the risk of being allocated a peripheral location providing sufficient accessibility by the dominant transportation mode but insufficient accessibility by the alternative transportation mode accessible for persons with travel-related impairments; the immigrants can bid for insurance to protect themselves against this risk
8	118	Insuring for random location assignment	*Case of inhibitively expensive location rents* In contrast to all previous scenarios, immigrants cannot choose their residential location but run the risk of being allocated a residential location with a sufficient level of accessibility but an inhibitively expensive location rent; the immigrants can bid for insurance to protect themselves against this risk

advantageous to myself? The hypothetical insurance approach has the same effect: a person merely has to ask how much of his resources he would be willing to set aside to mitigate some form of brute bad luck. Rather than using a veil of ignorance, Dworkin uses the device of 'counterfactual reasoning', i.e. assumptions regarding equal initial resources (clamshells) and uniform distributions of brute bad luck that make it possible to draw conclusions regarding the type of insurance scheme prudent persons would willingly purchase.

In what follows, I will extend Dworkin's auction scheme to the domain of transportation. I will do so by defining a number of fictive scenarios in which immigrants are exposed to different forms of accessibility-related bad luck (Table 6.1). For each scenario, I will explore whether prudent immigrants would seek protection through the purchase of an insurance scheme and, if so, what form that insurance scheme might take. Based on the resulting insurance schemes, I will outline a set of justice principles for the domain of transportation in the final section of this chapter.

The basic case

Let me start with the ideal case of a hypothetical island state the size of a medium-sized metropolitan area, to be settled by a group of immigrants who can purchase whatever goods that are available on the island from an identical set of clamshells. Let us assume, first, that our immigrants need to settle for an extensive period of time on our island. Hence, they are particularly concerned about their future residential location. Second, that the locations of the destinations our immigrants would like to visit during their stay on the island are given. And third, that there is only one mode of transport available on the island and that all immigrants arriving at the island are able to use this transport mode. The immigrants can then use their clamshells to bid for four interrelated goods: a residential location, a residence, transport infrastructure, and trips (Table 6.2). The residential location only relates to the location of the residence, while the residence itself relates to the properties of the building including its size. Transport infrastructure refers to the facilities necessary to travel to desired destinations. Let us assume that the immigrants have to pay a fixed fee for the use of these facilities, which varies according to the accessibility level of the selected residential location, with fees increasing as accessibility levels decrease (because more infrastructure has to be provided to link the residential location to the destinations on the island). Transport expenditures are the expenses an immigrant incurs when actually traveling to a destination on the available transport infrastructure. In addition to these four goods, the immigrants to the island can purchase all other available goods with their equal shares of clamshells.

Table 6.2 Key goods for which the immigrants to the island can bid in the auction.

Goods	Type of cost	Total cost for the immigrant	
Residential location	Location rent	Depends on selected location and selected plot size	} Housing costs
Residence	Housing rent	Depends on specifics of selected residence	
Transport infrastructure	Infrastructure fee	Depends on selected location	} Transportation costs
Trips to destinations	Travel expenditures	Depends on selected location and actual number of trips	

Given the fact that people arriving to our island state will differ in terms of their desire to participate in out-of-home activities, their enjoyment of travel, their preferences regarding time use, as well as their preferences for all other goods that are up for sale, they will also differ in their location preferences. Some will be willing to spend a substantial share of their clamshells on a location with a high level of accessibility, in close proximity to the destinations, because they have a strong preference for participating in out-of-home activities and strongly dislike travel. Others may prefer other goods over participation in out-of-home activities and thus prefer to spend fewer of their clamshells on purchasing a high-access location. Depending on the distribution of preferences among the immigrants to the island, particular locations will be more expensive than others. Since it is unlikely that the immigrants will attach a negative value to accessibility, locations with a higher accessibility level to desired destinations will always be more expensive than identical locations with a lower level of accessibility. This is so because immigrants with a strong preference for out-of-home activities will want to purchase these locations in order to limit their travel expenditures. They would thus be willing to outbid other immigrants in the competition for the high-access residential locations. Immigrants who attach less importance to out-of-home activities will, in turn, prefer to put fewer clamshells aside for the purchase of a residential location, in order to preserve more of their resources for other goods. They will thus be willing to settle for a lower-access location, as long as the total costs of location rent and transportation are lower at that location than at a higher-access location. This way, they maintain as many clamshells as possible for the purchase of other, more preferred, goods. Thus the lower an immigrant's preference for participation in out-of-home activity, the less she will be willing to spend on a residential location in order to obtain accessibility. Then, after the initial auction is over, a situation emerges of differential, but fair, accessibility levels (Figure 6.1). After all, each of the immigrants could have bid for somebody else's bundle of goods, including the location.

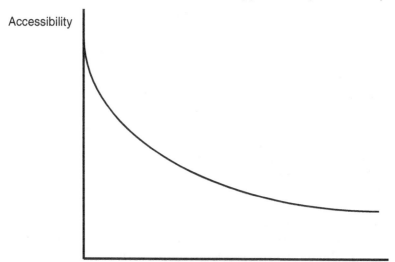

Accessibility

Range of locations

Figure 6.1 Hypothetical range of accessibility levels experienced by the immigrants to the island after the fair auction.

This result is, obviously, in line with Alonso's famous bid-rent model. Alonso, too, underscores the importance of competition over locations as the cause for the emergence of particular land use patterns. Location theory, in Alonso's perspective, is not a matter of optimal location, but one of competition for the right to occupy the land (Alonso 1967, p. 41). In light of competition, firms or other land users do not minimize transport costs or transport costs plus land rent. Rather, they maximize profits. This is, obviously, exactly what is happening in our island state. The immigrants do not maximize profits, but maximize the fulfillment of their preferences through the purchase of a particular bundle of goods, including a particular residential location. What makes the island case special is the fact that all parties enter the competition over the right to occupy the land with an identical set of resources. Because of this, the resulting location pattern is both fair and efficient at the same time. It is efficient, because all immigrants have been able to fulfill their preferences as much as possible, given the actual cost of their choices for other people. It is fair, because any of the immigrants could have purchased with his set of clamshells the bundle of goods which was bought by any of the other immigrants. Thus, the arrangement lives up to Dworkin's envy test.

Note that the actual cost of immigrants' choices depends on the distribution of preferences over the entire population of immigrants. If few immigrants are interested in engaging in out-of-home activities and few immigrants resent travel, the willingness to pay for locations with high levels of accessibility will be relatively low. If, on the other hand, many immigrants like to participate in out-of-home activities or strongly dislike travel, immigrants will have to pay a larger share of their clamshells to obtain a high-access location. In the former case, the rent-gradient will have a lower peak and slope downward more gently. In the latter case, it will have a higher peak and steeper slope. Both cases, however, are equally fair and efficient, given the initial distribution of preferences over the immigrants, as the slopes reflect the cost of an immigrant's choices for other people.

Note furthermore that immigrants who bid for low-access locations will have to spend a larger share of their clamshells on transport infrastructure fees and travel expenditures. This, obviously, will reduce their willingness and ability to bid for these low-access locations. Thus these locations will not only be cheaper because they provide a lower level of accessibility and the positive value the immigrants ascribe to accessibility, but also because of the additional costs related to transport infrastructure and travel expenditures. Clearly, the location rent will drop with the level of accessibility. Yet, for immigrants with a strong preference for participation in out-of-home activity, for a given plot size a move towards a lower accessibility location may well lead to higher total costs spent on location rent, infrastructure fees, and travel expenditures, because of a strong increase in the latter due to increased travel distances to destinations. Furthermore, as in Alonso's bid-rent model, the higher the transport costs, the steeper the rent gradient for residential locations. The bidding process also underlines the importance for the domain of transportation of Dworkin's claim that "the true measure of the social resources devoted to the life of one person is fixed by asking how important, in fact, that resource is for others" (Dworkin 2000, p. 70). If few immigrants prefer to live on the periphery, that choice is both more and less expensive than if a large number of immigrants preferred that option. It is more expensive, because fewer persons would have to carry the total costs of financing the necessary transport infrastructure to connect the periphery to the destinations in the center. However, the choice would also be less expensive, because fewer immigrants will actually bid for a plot of land on the periphery. How these opposite tendencies work out for each immigrant depends on the preferences of all other immigrants, as well as on the costs of providing infrastructure.

This first description of the island state obviously represents a strongly simplified case with a number of idealized assumptions. Nevertheless, it is possible to draw some first lessons which hold under the stated conditions of full equality of resources and a fair auction. Under such circumstances:

- Any differences in actual accessibility levels experienced by persons are fair.
- Any differences in the share of income (clamshells) spent on transportation costs (infrastructure fees and travel expenditures) and housing costs (location rent and housing rent) are fair.

- Fairness requires that each person carries his full share of the total costs related to the provision of transport infrastructure resulting from a particular choice for a residential location (i.e., fairness does not require any form of cross-subsidy between population groups in different geographical areas).

- Fairness requires that each person pays the full costs of his actual travel (i.e., fairness does not require any form of cross-subsidy of travel expenditures—as often seen in the pricing of public transport tickets—between population groups in different geographical areas).

These observations shed light on several of the contentious debates on transport finance, notably the differences in subsidies reaped by long-distance rail commuters versus low-income bus users (Grengs 2002), but I will only return to this after additional explorations of fairness in the island state.

Bidding for transportation services

In the base case, described above, the immigrants to the island had no choice but to accept the transport service available on the island. Let me now complicate the case and assume that the immigrants also have to bid for transportation services in a fair auction in which each immigrant has an equal number of clamshells.

Let us assume that in the initial auction the immigrants are free to purchase any type of transport service. The services are provided by companies, termed 'transportation providers', which compete for customers in a perfectly competitive market without entry barriers, as is the case for Dworkin's insurance companies. Since it is highly inefficient to provide a completely individual transportation service to single customers, the transportation providers will offer a particular type of collective service jointly with the rights to use that service. For instance, some transportation providers may offer a 'road service', consisting of the right to use a road network for immigrants who have access to an appropriate motorized vehicle. Other transportation providers may offer the right to use a network of, for example, buses, trams and trains, as well as suitable access and egress options, which can be used by the immigrants without the need to have a vehicle. Still other providers may offer the right to use a network of cycle paths to immigrants with access to a suitable bicycle. The services offered by the providers to the immigrants will not only differ in terms of the (main) transportation mode, but also in terms of the quality of the service as reflected in, for example, door-to-door travel times, convenience, or safety. Obviously, in a truly competitive market, the number of offerings might well proliferate, at least in the initial stage of the auction. For instance, the providers of the road service may offer a complete package encompassing the right to use the network as well as a vehicle. It can also be imagined that multi-modal services will be offered by 'niche providers', who develop a package based on the services of the mode-specific providers.

Clearly, the transportation providers will seek to offer transportation service packages that are as attractive as possible in terms of the balance between service and costs, in order to entice as many immigrants as possible to bid for their package. This may induce transportation providers to undertake strategic behavior, for instance by offering their services in the initial round of the auction at a price below the cost of providing the transportation service, in an effort to attract immigrants and push out possible competitors from subsequent rounds of the auction. I assume that the providers will refrain from such market distorting strategies, disciplined as they will be by the existence of a truly competitive market. Note that if we assume that the Rawlsian 'strains of commitment' also apply to the providers (and not only to the immigrants, as will be discussed below), this strategy may also be too risky for providers, because the auction process may well come to an end after a round in which the provider has offered its services at a loss-making price.

In order to develop the argument, we will assume that at the auction stage the transportation providers have not yet built the transportation infrastructure or deployed the transportation services. Rather, they are merely offering the service, which will then miraculously be provided instantly to the immigrants once the auction has ended. Furthermore, the providers can be expected to offer a range of 'service packages' to the immigrants, analogous to the market for mobile phone services, ranging from a flat-fee subscription enabling the use of a particular transportation service without limitations, to a lower fixed fee in combination with variable user charges, to an offering without a subscription fee in which the user only pays when actually using the transportation service. However, even in the latter case the immigrants will still have to set aside sufficient clamshells in the auction in order to be able to carry out the preferred number of trips once the auction is finalized and life on the island commences. Before analyzing the possible results of an auction under these circumstances, let me recall two more assumptions from the base scenario which are also relevant for this case. First, the location of destinations that the immigrants may want to visit is assumed to be given and fixed. Second, all immigrants are assumed to be able to use all transportation services offered by the transportation providers (i.e., immigrants do not experience any travel-related impairments). Hence the immigrants are free to choose between all the transportation services and service packages offered by the providers.

How will the auction work out for the provision of transportation services on the island? In order to explore the possible consequences, it is important to underscore that the immigrants not only enter the auction with equal clamshells, but also with different preferences. In the base scenario, it was stressed that the immigrants differed in their preferences for participating in out-of-home activities, their enjoyment of travel, and their preferences regarding the use of time. These differences will obviously have consequences for the type of transportation service package that immigrants will want to purchase in the auction. For instance, immigrants with a strong preference for out-of-home activities will be more likely than more 'sedentary' immigrants to purchase a service package that allows unlimited use of the selected transportation service. More important are the possible differences in immigrants' preferences regarding the type of transportation service. For instance, immigrants may differ in their enjoyment of driving or cycling; immigrants with a low preference for out-of-home activities may prefer a cheaper transportation service that does not require the purchase of a possibly expensive vehicle; or immigrants may value their time very highly and therefore prefer either the fastest transportation service or the service which allows the traveler to make productive use of travel time. The exact distribution of the preferences over the entire immigrant population will obviously strongly influence how the competition between the transportation providers, and hence the services, will work out.

In order to understand how the relationship between the preference distribution and the outcomes of the auction may play out, it is important to note that the transportation providers are likely to set a price for their service packages in the initial round of the auction, on the condition that sufficient immigrants will purchase the particular service they have on offer. This is likely because the transportation services will be used by multiple immigrants whose expenditures jointly have to cover the costs of providing the service. If, in the initial round of the auction, fewer immigrants prefer to bid for the transportation service than the provider initially expected, the provider has two basic ways to respond, assuming that he has already tweaked his service packages to make the service as attractive as possible. He can either raise the price for the service so that the smaller-than-expected group of immigrants bidding for the service will shoulder the entire costs of providing the service, or he can reduce the quality of the service in order to reduce the total costs of providing the transportation service. Either strategy is likely to lead to a decrease in the number of immigrants willing to bid for the particular transportation service. It will depend on a number of factors, including the distribution of the preferences among the immigrants (as translated into a price elasticity for the particular service) and the cost structure of the provider, whether further rounds of price increases or quality adjustments are necessary for the transportation provider to attract sufficient immigrants in order to offer its service without a loss. Note that this dynamic does not necessarily lead to an equilibrium; i.e., it may well turn out that the provider will not be able to offer its service without a loss under the prevailing distribution of immigrants' preferences and prevailing competing transportation services. Now the opposite dynamic may obviously occur for transportation services that prove to be highly popular among the immigrants in the initial round of the auction. The transportation provider that attracts a larger number of immigrants than initially expected will be able to decrease its prices in the second round of the auction, thereby attracting additional immigrants to its service. These providers may experience a further positive feedback loop in the following rounds of the auction until a stable situation is reached.

This dynamic process of action and reaction between immigrants and providers may quickly lead to a reduction in the total number of providers that can still offer competitive service packages in the auction process. Whether the process will eventually lead to a monopoly, i.e., to a situation in which only one transportation service remains, will depend on a number of circumstances, notably (1) the distribution of immigrants' preferences regarding the transportation services; (2) the differences in the cost structure between the transportation services; (3) the size of the economies of scale of each transportation service, in particular at substantial levels of use; and (4) population size. I shall discuss a number of possibilities to highlight the interrelationships between these circumstances. The distribution of preferences obviously strongly influences the emergence of a monopoly. If all transportation services are identically priced in the initial round of the auction and have comparable economies of scale, then a slight bias in the preference distribution among the immigrants towards one transportation service may lead to a positive feedback loop in favor of the preferred transportation service, resulting in the emergence of a monopoly. If immigrants show a clearer preference pattern, the dynamics are more difficult to predict, because it will depend on the willingness of the immigrants to pay for their preferred transportation service. If a group of immigrants is large enough and has a high level of willingness to pay, i.e., if the immigrants in this group are willing to spend a substantial share of their clamshells to purchase their preferred transportation service even if it is more expensive than the alternative(s), and thus give up a substantial amount of the other goods on the island in favor of their transportation preference, then a situation may emerge in which multiple transportation services will co-exist, catering for the same destinations. But if the immigrant group with a preference for a relatively expensive transportation service is small, these immigrants may nevertheless be tempted to give up their preference if the transportation provider continues to increase the price of the service package over several auction rounds in an effort to reach a break-even point. It follows that the emergence of multiple transportation services connecting the same set of destinations is highly dependent on a particular condition: the 'proportional' relationship between the size of immigrant groups with roughly homogenous preferences regarding transportation services or the strength of their preferences on the one hand, and the costs of providing particular transportation services on the other hand. This condition of proportionality states that when the transportation services on offer differ in cost structure and economies of scale, which is highly likely, the preference pattern would have to be in line with those differences, with more immigrants having a (strong) preference for the more expensive transportation service, in order to create an outcome at the end of the auction process that includes the expensive transportation service.

Since it is highly unlikely that the condition of proportionality will hold, it may be expected that few transportation services will survive the auction process. Transportation services that are either substantially more expensive or provide substantially poorer service are likely to enter a negative feedback loop and ultimately lose out in the auction process. Transportation services that are preferred by only a small minority of the immigrants are likely to experience the same fate. The transportation services that remain till the later stages of the auction are either preferred by a substantial share of the immigrants and are reasonably priced for a given quality, or are extremely cheap while still providing reasonable quality. How the competition between these remaining transportation services will work out is a more delicate matter to establish. Here, population size may play a role. Recall that immigrants will bid for residential locations in the entire spectrum from the center to the periphery of the island state, depending on their preferences for out-of-home activities and travel, amongst other considerations. The bidding process will tend to lead to a relatively high density of immigrants in the center and lower densities towards the periphery, in part because immigrants with a preference for a large residence will tend to bid for the cheaper locations in the periphery. In addition, recall that it is more expensive to provide transportation services to the periphery, because of the larger distances that need to be covered to reach destinations in the center. As a result of both factors, i.e. lower densities and larger distances, the transportation providers will charge a higher price for the service packages in the periphery than in the center. This situation is no different from the base case, in which the immigrants had to pay differential transportation infrastructure fees. However, with multiple transportation services competing for the clamshells of the immigrants, small differences in the cost structure of transportation services may be exacerbated in the price of the service packages charged in the periphery. After all, in the periphery a smaller number of people will have to carry the total costs of the transportation service. Thus even small differences in costs structures between transportation services may well lead to substantial differences in service package fees to be paid by the immigrants in the periphery, shifting their preference towards the cheaper transportation service. It is thus more likely in the periphery that negative and positive feedback loops will occur, in which immigrants 'abandon' the slightly more expensive transportation service in favor of the cheaper offer, resulting in a monopoly for the cheaper service at the end of the auction process. Such a process is less likely to occur in the center of the island state, not only because the initial difference in service package fees is smaller, limiting the incentive to switch to a cheaper option, but also because the higher concentration of immigrants implies that a shift of one immigrant from the more expensive to the cheaper transportation service carries less weight and will thus have less impact on the price setting behavior of the transportation providers, suggesting that a double feedback loop is less likely to occur in the center.

What lessons can be drawn from this second auction process? While this second case underlines the importance of immigrants' preferences in the emergence of the transportation system on the island, the case also underscores that it is highly unlikely that a plethora of transportation services will be provided to serve the same origin–destinations relationships. Rather, it is highly likely that prudent agents will be willing to give up their initial transportation service preferences in favor of a cheaper option of comparable quality, in order to save resources for more important preferences. This agent behavior will then lead to a dynamic process in which at best a few parallel transportation services will remain. Under less favorable conditions, notably when a relatively small population needs to shoulder the costs of the transportation services, a monopoly is likely to emerge, in light of the vast economies of scale in the provision of virtually any transportation service.

These observations are important, because they are at odds with the increasingly vocal call to provide citizens with a 'choice' among multiple transportation modes (see, for instance, Banister 2008). These calls seem to be devoid of the understanding that providing choice comes at a substantial cost, which has to be carried by those same citizens. A call for more choice may well be warranted under conditions of a high population concentration, where multiple transportation options can be offered relatively efficiently, costs can be shared by many, and economies of scale of one transportation service may have been exhausted while substantial economies of scale can still be captured for another transportation service. However, under less favorable conditions, such a call seems to be hardly warranted at all. Once the costs of providing for choice are taken seriously, choice can hardly be seen as a general, overriding, argument in favor of investments in alternatives to the (currently) dominant car-road system. For such an argument, we need to look somewhere else, notably towards people with travel-related impairments, for which an alternative to the car-road system is often hardly a matter of choice but of sheer necessity.

Bidding for impairment-proof transportation services

In the first two scenarios, I have assumed that all immigrants to the island are equally able to use all the transportation services offered on the island. Let me now complicate that condition. Let us again assume that a group of immigrants arrives to the island state with a fixed location of destinations and thus a known pattern of accessibility. Each immigrant is handed an identical number of clamshells to bid for the goods that are available on the island, including a diverse range of transportation services. In contrast to the first two scenarios, let us assume that the immigrants do not know, at the outset, whether they will develop a travel-related impairment over the course of their life, i.e., whether they will be able to make use of all the transportation services that may be offered by transportation providers. Let me now explore what type of transportation services the immigrants will bid for in the auction, if they are uncertain whether they will develop travel impairments.

In order to explore this scenario, it is important to stress the potential impact of a travel-related impairment on the life of the immigrants. If an immigrant decides to bid in the auction for a transportation service that can only be used by persons with a particular set of abilities, than she runs the risk of not being able *at all* to engage independently in out-of-home activities once life on the island commences. It may be assumed that prudent immigrants will want to avoid this situation and rather seek some protection against travel-related impairment. This will certainly hold, if we understand that the immigrants have to accept the Rawlsian 'strains of commitment': the auction process is not merely a bidding mechanism but is to determine the characteristics of the transportation services that will be available on the island. That is, after the end of the auction process the immigrants are only entitled to the level of accessibility provided by the transportation services for which they have bid in the auction. They cannot legitimately expect society to provide a higher level of service than that for which they have themselves set clamshells aside. Hence the immigrants will be careful to avoid choices that will leave them completely stranded in the future.

The transportation providers, well aware of this fact, will strive to offer services that address the risk of brute bad luck. Roughly, they can choose between two options. They can either offer transportation services that provide an identical level of service to all immigrants, irrespective of their spectrum of travel-related abilities. They can also offer a primary transportation service that can only be used by immigrants experiencing the 'normal' spectrum of travel-related abilities in conjunction with an alternative service for immigrants struck by brute bad luck. In the latter case, the difference between the accessibility levels provided to both groups may vary. In schematic terms, the accessibility provided to the immigrants experiencing a travel-related impairment could be defined as a percentage of the accessibility to be received by the other immigrants. Thus a range of possibilities could be defined, starting from a first-best inclusive transportation service providing all immigrants with the same level of accessibility irrespective of their spectrum of travel-related abilities, through a range of second-best services in which immigrants experiencing travel-related impairments receive a particular share of the accessibility level provided to the immigrants experiencing the 'normal' spectrum of travel-related abilities, down to the worst possible service that only provides accessibility to the immigrants experiencing the 'normal' spectrum of travel-related abilities while all immigrants struck by brute bad luck do not receive any accessibility at all.

Generally speaking, the choice of the immigrants for a particular transportation service package will depend on five interrelated factors: immigrants' preferences; the risk of experiencing travel-related impairments; the cost difference between the inclusive and a second-best service; the level of accessibility provided by the second-best service in case brute bad luck strikes; and the wealth of society. Let us assume, for now, that the inclusive and the second-best services provide identical levels of accessibility to immigrants experiencing the 'normal' spectrum of travel-related abilities. If this condition applies and risk is low and cost differentials are high, then some share of the immigrants may be expected to prefer the second-best service over an inclusive service. This is so because immigrants will be selective in using their clamshells, weighing the possible benefits of a high accessibility level in case of brute bad luck against the (certain) benefits of fulfilling other preferences. If indeed a substantial share of immigrants prefers the second-best service, a feedback loop may once again occur, with more and more immigrants 'abandoning', in subsequent rounds of the auction, the inclusive service in favor of the ever-cheaper second-best service. Thus even if immigrants can choose their transportation services and are all equally ignorant about their future spectrum of travel-related abilities, it is by no means certain that prudent immigrants will always select a transportation service that lives up to the standards of universal access. But the argument also holds the other way around: if an inclusive transportation service is not substantially more expensive and such a service can provide a roughly comparable service in terms of accessibility as the second-best transportation service, than prudent immigrants are likely to prefer the inclusive service (which may, in turn, trigger a positive feedback loop).

Note that the total level of wealth will also shape the choice behavior of the immigrants. It would require the design of an entire economic system for the island state to fully develop this point. But even without taking up that endeavor, it can be seen intuitively that a high level of wealth will lead to the purchase of a wider range of insurance schemes or a higher level of coverage. In the case of Dworkin's island, a high level of wealth equals an island with an abundance of goods and thus low prices for many goods (but not for goods that remain by definition scarce, such as central locations). The immigrants therefore need a smaller share of clamshells to purchase goods to fulfill their most basic preferences (and needs) and can reserve more of their clamshells for less pressing preferences. Given the fact that the immigrants to the island have to set the conditions under which they will live their entire life, these less pressing preferences are unlikely to only encompass various forms of truly conspicuous consumption. Rather, they are likely to include insurance schemes against various forms of brute bad luck. Thus, while not all immigrants would want to use their abundance of clamshells to rule out all forms of brute bad luck, most immigrants may be expected to use at least some of their spare clamshells to lower the consequences of brute bad luck in comparison to a situation of austerity. So the higher the level of wealth in a society, the more likely immigrants are to set a larger share of their clamshells aside for the purchase of an inclusive or almost-inclusive transportation service package.

Let me add one more dimension. So far, I have assumed that the price the immigrants have to pay for an (inclusive) transportation service package is independent of their other choices. This clearly is not the case. As in the first two scenarios, the transportation providers will relate the price of their transportation service packages to the cost of providing the service. Thus, in the initial auction, providers will charge higher prices for a transportation service package in the periphery of the island than in the center, irrespective of the exact particularities of the package, because the cost of providing the service in the periphery is higher. Furthermore, given some economies of scale, it may be expected that the price differential, as defined in absolute numbers of clamshells *per* immigrant, will go up with an increase in service level, because lower densities in the periphery imply that a smaller number of immigrants will have to carry the total cost of the transportation service. In addition, immigrants with a preference for a central location will tend to show a higher willingness to pay for any given transportation service and are likely to purchase a more generous service package in the auction than their peripheral counterparts. The central immigrants will tend to pay more because they typically have a preference for participation in out-of-home activity (hence their choice for a central location). Similarly, they will tend to purchase a more generous transportation service package, i.e. a package guaranteeing a relatively high level of accessibility to immigrants struck by brute bad luck, because they will attach a higher value than the peripheral immigrants to the protection of a particular level of out-of-home activities. The result of these differentials in costs and preferences may well be that central immigrants will purchase a more generous transportation service package against a lower price than the immigrants opting for a more peripheral location. Certainly, the difference between the preferred level of accessibility and the 'insured' level of accessibility will vary across space.

Given the additional costs of a residential location in the periphery, not only in terms of the number of clamshells that have to be reserved for the purchase of a reasonable service package but also in terms of the larger deviation from the preferred accessibility level and thus also in terms of the more severe restrictions on activity participation when brute bad luck strikes, the immigrants arriving at the island state will be likely to change their bidding behavior. They will be less likely to bid for peripheral locations and purchase more central locations instead. This pattern will strengthen itself to some extent, because a decrease in the number of peripheral immigrants due to the high cost also implies that a smaller number of immigrants will have to carry the total cost of the transportation service in the periphery. The shift in bidding behavior may lead to an increase in the costs of the transportation services in the periphery, inducing additional immigrants to prefer a location closer to the center. The exact outcome of this dynamic feedback loop obviously depends on the strength of the location preferences of the immigrants, the preferences of the immigrants regarding risk protection, and the costs of the various transportation service packages. But the general tendency is clear: if either transportation services have to be adapted to cater for all immigrants or multiple transportation services are required to guarantee accessibility for all, under conditions of fairness a denser spatial structure is likely to emerge. Here, considerations of justice and efficiency point in the same direction.

The crucial points that emerge from this third scenario of our island state may be clear. First, prudent persons will always want to guarantee some minimal level of accessibility in case brute bad luck strikes. Second, under most circumstances it is rational for prudent agents to accept a lower level of accessibility in case they are struck by brute bad luck. Thus some level of disparity in accessibility between persons experiencing the 'normal' spectrum of travel-related abilities and persons experiencing travel-related impairments is fair. Only if the additional costs of providing identical accessibility levels to persons with travel-related impairments are very low will prudent persons accept these additional costs. Third, the higher the risks, the smaller the accessibility disparities that prudent persons will accept, ceteris paribus. Fourth, the same holds with increasing wealth in a society: the higher the level of wealth, the smaller the accessibility disparities that prudent persons are willing to accept. Finally, prudent persons will accept a spatial variation in accessibility disparities between persons experiencing the 'normal' spectrum of travel-related abilities and persons experiencing travel-related impairments.

While these lessons do not provide exact demarcation points regarding the accessibility level to be provided to persons experiencing travel-related impairments, it does underscore a number of practical points. First, a sufficient level of independent accessibility is to be provided to persons with travel-related impairments, even though this level may be substantially lower than the accessibility level provided to persons experiencing the 'normal' spectrum of travel-related abilities. Second, in aging societies, with an increasing population experiencing various forms of travel-related impairments, more resources should be set aside *per person experiencing travel-related impairments* to enable independent accessibility. Third, societies experiencing economic growth should set aside some of that wealth for improved services for persons with travel-related impairments so that accessibility disparities are *reduced*. The argument also holds the other way around: under conditions of economic austerity, some reductions in transportation services provided to persons experiencing travel-related impairments are acceptable and some increase in accessibility disparities may be accepted, as long as a sufficient level of accessibility is maintained for persons with travel-related impairments.

Insuring under conditions of income differentials

The case of fair income differentials

Let me now turn to a fourth scenario. Let us again assume that the immigrants enter an auction with equal clamshells. As we have seen, these immigrants will purchase a substantial set of insurance schemes to protect themselves against forms of brute bad luck that may strike them once life on the island commences. These schemes include a minimum income insurance, a health care insurance, as well as some form of travel-related impairment insurance (as presented above). Would the immigrants want to purchase additional types of insurance? In general, the immigrants would want to do so for types of brute bad luck that cannot be dealt with from the fair income shares guaranteed by the minimum income insurance. This holds, for instance, for health care risks, because it is by no means certain that the guaranteed floor income is sufficient to cover the costs of health care. Indeed, even immigrants with income levels substantially above the floor income will not always be able to pay for health care costs in case brute bad luck strikes in the form of a serious illness. Hence, prudent persons would want to purchase health insurance to protect against this form of brute bad luck *in addition to* the minimum floor income insurance. The question is whether the same line of argument applies in relation to immigrants' accessibility to destinations. In other words: Is it reasonable for the immigrants to assume that the floor income will always be sufficient to cover all access-related costs (location rent and transportation costs), or can forms of brute bad luck be identified that would require substantial additional income to cover all access-related costs?

In order to answer this question, we need to understand the situation that may emerge if income differentials in society are organized along Dworkian lines. In such a (fair) society, some citizens will find themselves unlucky on the job market and as a result at the bottom of the income distribution. Recall that the Dworkian floor income insurance is assumed to guarantee a sufficient level of income for everybody. This is so because prudent agents would purchase an insurance that would provide them with a sufficient income to live a life of dignity (Dworkin 2000, p. 335). In line with classical formulations, this floor income will enable the immigrants not only to obtain goods "indispensably necessary for the support of life" but also to purchase "whatever the custom of the country renders it indecent for creditable people, even of the lowest order, to be without" (Smith 1887, p. 117). This will certainly hold if we add the

Rawlsian 'strains of commitment' to the argument: once the immigrants understand that the insurance scheme they purchase determines the minimum income they can rightfully claim during their entire life, no prudent immigrant would purchase an insurance package that would not guarantee a sufficient income level. The citizens who are struck by bad luck and receive a low income will obviously have to give up some of their consumption of goods in order to make ends meet. Yet it is assumed that the insurance purchased by prudent immigrants would limit the scope of these sacrifices in order to guarantee a reasonable quality of life.

To explore the validity of this assumption, let us take a closer look at the expenses that need to be covered from the minimum floor income. Five types of goods and related expenses have been distinguished above (see Table 6.1):

- location rent, which is determined by the location of residence and selected plot size;
- housing rent, which depends on the size and quality of the residence (but not on the location);
- infrastructure fee, which depends on the location of residence;
- travel expenditures, which depend on the location of residence and the actual number of trips;
- all other expenditures, which depend on the actual consumption level of these goods.

The floor income guaranteed by the Dworkian scheme is supposed to cover the costs of a sufficient level of consumption of all these goods. Clearly, the immigrants may differ in their opinion of a sufficient level. For instance, immigrants with a strong preference for a convenient residence, who would set aside a relatively large share of their equal clamshells in the fair auction to purchase such a residence, may have a higher standard of sufficiency regarding the quantity and quality of housing than immigrants who attach less importance to their residence. Likewise, immigrants with only a weak preference for participating in out-of-home activities would probably be willing to settle for a smaller number of trips and thus lower transportation expenses than persons with a strong interest in activity participation. Dworkin's implicit assumption is that, on average, these differences in the delineation of a reasonable minimum for different goods will equal out in the total, leading to a rough agreement between the immigrants about the level of the floor income.

This assumption is crucial to understanding the fairness of the patterns of accessibility that may emerge in a society with differential, but fair, income levels. Let us consider the situation of two immigrants to the island. Let us denote them as A and B. Immigrant A has a strong preference for participating in out-of-home activities and would therefore be willing to set aside a substantial share of the equal clamshells in the fair auction for the purchase of a high-access location and to cover transportation costs. This would obviously come at the expense of his ability to purchase other goods on the island, such as clothing, wine, or expensive cheeses. Contrast this with immigrant B, who has a strong preference for good food and fashionable clothing and would reserve a substantial share of her equal clamshells for the purchase of these goods in the fair auction. This preference will obviously limit the amount of clamshells B can use to purchase a residential location and B may therefore settle for the location with the lowest level of accessibility on the island.

It may be expected that these differences in preferences will resonate in the definitions of a sufficient level of consumption. Thus A may be expected to maintain a higher minimum standard regarding participation in out-of-home activities, while B will maintain a higher standard regarding food and clothing. Both will want to purchase a floor income insurance that enables them to purchase a sufficient level of all the goods on the island. Yet it is not clear at the outset that both sets of preferences will imply a comparable level of floor income. Clearly, since a higher guaranteed floor income also implies a higher premium, there will be a tendency among immigrants to limit the coverage to the lowest possible level that will enable a life of dignity. Yet, since immigrants may differ in terms of the level of consumption of various goods that they deem necessary for a life with some dignity, the immigrants may also differ in terms of the minimum income insurance they will want to purchase. Dworkin does acknowledge this possibility, but argues that in the absence of full information on persons' preferences, accepting the average insurance level for all immigrants is the second-best option.

Let us assume that A and B purchase the same floor income insurance and that both are struck by brute bad luck. Since B accepted, at the outset, the location with the lowest accessibility on the island, the only way for her to reduce expenses to the required floor income is by decreasing consumption of other goods. The situation for immigrant A is somewhat different. Given the high level of location rent and transportation costs as a share of total income, it is not unlikely that the floor income will not even be sufficient to cover the costs of his location choice in the fair auction. A will thus have to reduce his expenditures on location rent and transportation costs. He can only do so by accepting a lower access location and at the same time reducing the number of trips to a lower, but still sufficient, level. While such a location would increase the costs of transportation for carrying out the sufficient level of trips, the location would still be cheaper in terms of total costs than a higher access location.

The situation that thus emerges is one in which the unlucky immigrants will not be able to choose from the entire set of residential locations available on the island. Rather, they will be confined to a sub-set of locations with a relatively low accessibility level. This process of income-based residential segregation in a capitalist society has been heavily criticized by, amongst others, Harvey (1973). Yet, while Harvey argues that this constitutes a form of injustice, the argument developed here suggests that income-based segregation in terms of accessibility levels can be a fair outcome. This is so for two reasons. First, it is fair because it emerges in a situation of equality of resources and the resulting fair income differentials. The argument is that prudent agents would be reluctant to set aside substantial resources to purchase a floor income insurance that would guarantee full freedom of choice regarding residential location and thus also regarding level of accessibility. Second, from the perspective of immigrants' preferences, residential segregation is no different from disparities in any other form of consumption. Prudent persons would not purchase a higher level of floor income insurance to guarantee a high level of consumption of expensive wines, but would rather settle for a lower level of consumption in case brute bad luck strikes. And so it is for accessibility: prudent persons would not want to pay a high premium just to guarantee a wider range of residential locations and thus of accessibility levels in case brute bad luck strikes. Rather, they would prefer a lower premium and enjoy the benefits of a higher disposable income, while accepting the (manageable) consequences in case brute bad luck strikes. Note that these consequences would not imply a lack of accessibility: as we have seen, all locations on the island provide by definition sufficient levels of accessibility.

This is a radical conclusion. It would imply that in a society with fair income differentials, systematic differences in accessibility levels between income groups are acceptable. It also implies that some level of sorting out of income groups over space is fair, at least from the perspective of accessibility. The extent of this sorting process will depend on at least two factors: the height of the floor income vis-à-vis the pattern of location rent, and the preference for accessibility among the entire population. With a relatively low floor income, the sorting effect will be stronger, as people with low incomes can only afford a small range of the available residential locations. Thus poorer societies, with a lower floor income level, may well show a stronger sorting effect than richer societies (but note that poorer societies will also show a different pattern of location rent than richer societies). The sorting effect will also be stronger if a population has relatively strong preferences for accessibility, as more people with incomes above the floor level will bid for locations with relatively high levels of accessibility, thereby driving up location rent and pushing out lower income households, including households living on the floor income level. Yet, even under these circumstances the sorting effect does not have to be complete, because some persons with earnings (well) above the floor income may still decide to trade off residential location and consumption of other goods. The segregation of income groups would thus be expected to decrease with a decrease in the level of accessibility.

This finding should not be seen as a justification for current accessibility differentials between other types of population groups or in favor of residential segregation per se. First, the argument does not suggest that differentials in accessibility levels across other dimensions than income, such as ethnicity, which can be found in many societies, are acceptable. Second, it has to be kept in mind that income differentials in virtually all existing societies are much larger than they would be in a Dworkian (or Rawlsian) world. In a society with fair income differences, the spatial sorting of income groups may be expected to be much more limited in scope than currently observed. As the detrimental effects of income differentials in other domains of life, such as education or health, will also be more limited in scope in such a fair society, the negative implications of spatial segregation of income groups may also be more limited in intensity. Third, recall that *all* locations in the fair society provide sufficient levels of accessibility. Thus the sorting out by income level does not push low income groups into areas with insufficient accessibility levels, as may be the case in current societies. Fourth, even in a society with fair income levels, the residential sorting out of income groups may be unfair on other grounds than justice in the domain of accessibility alone.

The case of unfair income differentials

The case of fair income differentials depicts a situation in which the floor income is at least sufficient to purchase a minimal level of goods to lead a life of dignity. Few societies, if any, live up to such Dworkian or Rawlsian income differentials. If we accept Dworkin's or Rawls' line of reasoning, these societies are thus unfair in the sphere of income and wealth. Yet, as Walzer's approach underscores, the lack of fairness in one sphere does not rule out progress towards fairness in another sphere. Arguably, many societies with vast and unfair income differentials have made substantial progress towards fairness in the spheres of basic liberties, education and health care. It is therefore of theoretical and practical relevance to explore what fairness in the transportation sphere might mean in the case of unfair income differentials.

Let us return to the island to explore this question. Let us again assume that the immigrants enter an auction with equal clamshells. Let us also assume that, for whatever reason, the immigrants cannot purchase a minimum income insurance in the initial auction. That is, once the auction is over, they will be randomly assigned an income level (and perhaps an accompanying job) that may or may not be sufficient to purchase the minimum level of goods necessary for a life of dignity. The question now is whether the immigrants would want to purchase *another* type of insurance, that is not an income insurance, to avoid the tragic consequences of being assigned an insufficient income level (i.e., an income level below the floor income that would be guaranteed by a fair income insurance).

In order to answer this question, we need to understand in more detail how the immigrants could respond to an insufficient income level, termed a 'subsistence income' in what follows. Clearly, an immigrant has a range of possibilities, the attractiveness of which depends in part on the immigrant's preferences. For instance, an immigrant can decide to live in a cheaper residential location in order to reduce the location rent, to purchase a smaller house to reduce the housing rent, to forgo some trips to out-of-home activities to reduce transportation expenditures, or to purchase less of the other goods available on the island. For analytical reasons only, two possible extreme responses can be distinguished. First, the immigrants can give absolute priority to their preferences in terms of residential location and level of activity participation and decide to use their available subsistence income to purchase, as far as possible, the residential location and number of trips that they would have purchased from the floor income guaranteed by the minimum income insurance. Second, the immigrants can give absolute priority to all their other purchases, with the exception of residential location and participation in out-of-home activities, and decide to purchase a bundle of other goods as they would if they had received the floor income, while using the remaining income, if any, to purchase a location and pay for trips to out-of-home activities.

Each strategy will, by definition, create substantial hardship for the immigrants. In the first case, the immigrants will not have sufficient income left to purchase a range of necessary goods. Depending on an immigrant's choices, he may experience a lack of healthy food, a lack of fuel for heating his house, or perhaps a lack of decent clothes to appear in public without shame. The immigrants who set aside sufficient funds for residential location and transportation costs may thus experience all kinds of poverty, such as fuel poverty, food poverty, 'dress-code poverty', or all of them combined. For lack of a better denominator, I will call this form of hardship consumption poverty, so that it can be easily distinguished from the second type of hardship. In this second case, the immigrants will have sufficient income to purchase a wide range of (necessary) goods, but will have to compromise in terms of residential location and level of participation in out-of-home activities. These immigrants will have to accept a residential location in a low-access area and reduce their number of trips in order to balance their budget. By accepting a low-access location, the costs per trip will go up. As a result, immigrants following this strategy may no longer be able to participate in a sufficient level of out-of-home activities. This coping strategy may thus result in financially-induced accessibility poverty (Mattioli 2014). The question is what type of insurance, if any, the immigrants would want to purchase in the initial auction to avoid either form of poverty.

Let me first explore the case of accessibility poverty. The immigrant adopting this strategy will have sufficient income to purchase most goods on the island, but will lack the necessary means to maintain a sufficient level of participation in out-of-home activities. He will seek an insurance, but not an income insurance, to cover him against that risk. Two possible types of insurance could relieve the hardship for the immigrant: a location affordability insurance and a transport affordability insurance. Note that both insurance schemes have to be defined in such a way that they do not constitute an increase in the subsistence income itself, because such an insurance would belong to the Walzer-type sphere of income and wealth and is not allowed in this scenario. This condition in a way reflects the political situation in many countries that hinders an increase in welfare payments or minimum income standards to a floor income in line with either Dworkin's or Rawls' approach.

The location affordability insurance scheme could roughly take the following form: in the case of an immigrant receiving an income level x below the floor income y, subsidize his location rent by z. In the initial auction, the immigrants could select the income threshold y and the subsidy level z. The higher the values of y and z, the higher the premium for the insurance. Clearly, prudent immigrants would be careful about spending too much of their clamshells on an insurance. At the same time, they may be expected to purchase an insurance that would guarantee them a sufficient level of participation in out-of-home activity, especially in light of the Rawlsian strains of commitment. Since the floor income insurance does guarantee this level, as we have already seen in the previous section, it may be expected that a prudent immigrant would purchase an insurance with an income threshold y that is roughly in line with the floor income guaranteed by the minimum income insurance.

It is also relatively easy to establish the level of the location subsidy z that immigrants are likely to purchase. The maximum size of z would be precisely equal to the difference between the minimum floor income y and the expected subsistence income x. More precisely, the immigrants would want to purchase a location affordability insurance that would link the location rent subsidy to the income shortfall, defined as $y - x$. In this way, the location subsidy would in all cases exactly compensate the income shortfall caused by the lack of a minimum income insurance and the situation for the immigrants would thus be exactly identical to the case in which fair income differentials apply and the immigrant is struck by brute bad luck in the income domain. The immigrants could also decide to insure for a lower level of z, but this would severely reduce their location choice. Since the immigrants did not decide to do so in the case of the minimum income insurance, there is little reason to assume that prudent immigrants would do so if they could only avoid accessibility poverty by purchasing a location affordability insurance. In light of the Rawlsian strains of commitment, prudent immigrants may be expected to purchase a level of insurance that would leave them some, although limited, room for flexibility.

The argument regarding the transportation affordability insurance is roughly the same. This insurance scheme could take the following form: in case an immigrant receives an income level x below the floor income y, subsidize his transportation expenditures by z. The immigrants would again be given the opportunity to select the income threshold y and the subsidy level z in the initial auction. Assuming that they do not purchase a location affordability insurance, they would use the transportation affordability insurance to fully compensate for their income shortfall created by the absence of a minimum income insurance. That is, they would tend to set the income threshold y at the level of the minimum floor income and link the level of the transportation subsidy z to the actual level of income shortfall experienced if brute bad luck strikes (i.e., at the level $y - x$). The immigrants would thus use the transportation affordability insurance to restore the situation that would obtain if the immigrants could have purchased a minimum income insurance.

The difference between the minimum income insurance and both the location and transportation affordability insurances is obviously that the latter types of insurance do not compensate the immigrants struck by brute bad luck with a financial payment, but with an earmarked subsidy that would leave the immigrants no choice regarding how they spend the subsidy. The earmarked subsidy could take the form of housing subsidies, as are common in many countries in Europe, or transportation fuel vouchers or reduced travel fares. Note that the drawback of this arrangement is limited, because a subsidy on location rent or transportation expenditures will obviously free up budget for other household expenses.

Let me now turn to the case of consumption poverty. The immigrants who have adopted this strategy will have a sufficient income to purchase a suitable residential location and a level of trips to enable a sufficient level of participation in out-of-home activities, yet will lack the means to purchase a sufficient level of a range of other goods on the island. Clearly, the immigrants will not be able to live a life of dignity under these circumstances and would thus be interested in using some of their clamshells to purchase an insurance to avoid this risk in the initial auction.

What shape could an insurance against consumption poverty take? Recall that in the current scenario it is not possible for the immigrants to purchase an insurance that would lead to an increase in the subsistence income. The immigrants can only purchase a type of insurance that would provide some form of earmarked subsidy for the purchase of particular goods or some form of in-kind support. The insurance could take the same shape as those proposed for residential location and transportation costs. That is, immigrants would seek to purchase an insurance that would provide a subsidy on the purchase of all other goods available on the island except for location rent and transportation costs. Since such a subsidy might be difficult to administer, insurance companies might be reluctant to offer such a general scheme and would rather prefer an insurance scheme that would target specific expenditures that take up a large part of the household budget. Typically, housing rent and energy costs belong to this category. Thus some of the immigrants might want to purchase an insurance for either costs along the lines of the insurance schemes presented above. The insurance companies might be willing to offer these two additional types of insurance for a low enough premium.

Thus the situation emerges that immigrants could protect themselves through a variety of insurance packages against the bad luck of obtaining only a subsistence income. Each package enables the immigrants to reclaim a sufficient income level, albeit through an earmarked subsidy or in-kind contribution. Clearly, the immigrants would not purchase all these insurance packages in parallel, but would either purchase one type of insurance or multiple partial insurances that jointly cover the income shortfall. The latter option might be preferred if immigrants expect the subsistence income to be so low that multiple subsidies are necessary to cover the resulting income shortfall. The number of insurance packages an immigrant is likely to purchase is thus largely dependent on the circumstances.

Before drawing conclusions, let me explore the insurance schemes from the perspective of the insurance companies. Each insurance company is interested in offering an attractive insurance package against the lowest possible cost, so that it can offer a competing premium vis-à-vis other insurance companies. The way to do this is by comparing the various possibilities available to the insurance companies to provide an earmarked or in-kind income supplement to the immigrants who receive a subsistence income. Rather than providing each entitled immigrant with an individual subsidy, an insurance company could also provide in-kind services to the immigrants. This is an especially relevant alternative for the transportation affordability insurance scheme described above. To understand this, recall that in our fictive scenario only one transport mode is available on the island. The insurance companies can increase the subsistence income of the immigrants by providing them earmarked subsidies to use this transportation mode. They can, however, also offer an alternative transportation service which would provide travel against lower costs to (entitled) immigrants. The latter strategy may well be cheaper for the insurance companies than the former, due to economies of scale. The insurance company would thus compare the two options in terms of their costs and their attractiveness to the immigrants seeking to purchase insurance. If paying individual earmarked subsidies would deliver the largest profits to an insurance company, then the company would prefer that option. If, however, it would be more profitable to offer a subsidized transportation service, the insurance company would offer this type of coverage to the insured. It may also be assumed that the profitability of these two insurance schemes may differ across space: it may be more profitable for the insurance companies to offer a subsidized service in high density areas, whereas it may be cheaper to give earmarked transportation subsidies in low density areas. The insurance companies may thus be expected to offer an insurance package that encompasses a variety of possible pay-offs to the immigrants. Let me call this the mixed transportation affordability insurance scheme, which would perhaps be offered alongside a separate location affordability insurance scheme as described above. Assuming for the moment that the subsidized transport service would provide the same level of service as the transportation system available on the island, the immigrants would be likely to purchase the mixed transportation affordability insurance scheme if it were offered at a lower premium than the regular transportation affordability insurance scheme. The cut-off point between areas in which the insurance companies provide an alternative transportation service and areas in which they provide an individual subsidy will depend on a number of conditions, most notably the number of people that are entitled to insurance 'payments', the costs of using the transport system available on the island, and the costs of providing an alternative transport service. The more persons are entitled to insurance payments (i.e., the larger the share of the population living on some level of subsistence income), the higher the cost of using the dominant transport system available on the island (i.e., the higher the costs for the insurance company of providing individual subsidies), and the lower the costs of the alternative service, the more reasonable it is to provide an alternative service rather than individual subsidies to complement income. Clearly, for any given society, these circumstances are more likely to prevail in high density areas than in low density areas.

The analysis presented here thus leads to the conclusion that in a society with unfair income differentials, citizens are entitled to in-kind provision of transportation services or earmarked transportation subsidies that would limit their income shortfall as much as possible. The former strategy does this by providing a transportation service that is cheaper to use than the dominant transportation system in society. The latter strategy limits the income shortfall by handing out subsidies, for instance on transportation fuels, vehicle expenses or transportation fares, to citizens with an income below the sufficiency level. Both strategies reduce the transportation expenses for households living on a subsistence income and thus de facto increase their disposable income. In this way, the financial barrier to sufficient accessibility is reduced or even eliminated, thereby reducing or avoiding accessibility poverty due to lack of income.

Translated to real-world settings, the analysis provides the moral underpinnings for subsidizing (public) transport. In a world of fair income levels, the floor income would be adequate to cover a sufficient level of consumption of transportation and all other goods. Direct or indirect transportation subsidies would thus not be necessary (except perhaps for paternalistic reasons). However, as long as a share of the population receives income levels below the sufficiency standard, justice *requires* transportation subsidies for them. The analysis also underlines that achieving fairness in transportation is possible under the 'second-best' circumstances of unfair income differentials. Indeed, it is very well possible to make progress within the sphere of accessibility while pervasive injustices exist in the sphere of income and wealth, as is currently the case in most societies. I will return to the issue of fair pricing of transportation in Chapter 10.

Insuring for random location assignment

Let me explore one additional scenario for the island state before drawing conclusions. In all previous scenarios of the insurance scheme, I have assumed that the immigrants to the island can choose a residential location in the initial situation. This even holds for the case of differential incomes, although the range of choice is substantially reduced for immigrants receiving only the floor income. Let me now explore the scenario in which immigrants are assigned a random location on the island. This scenario is to reflect the real-life situation of people being born and raised in a location they have not chosen themselves. Since persons may be expected to develop constitutive interests in the particular location in which they have lived a large part of their life and in which most of their social life takes place, they may be expected to be reluctant to leave their initial, *de facto* randomly assigned, location.

Before exploring the risks for the immigrants of a randomly assigned location, let me define the situation of the immigrants more precisely. I assume that the immigrants enter the island with the set of insurance schemes purchased in the fair auction with equal clamshells. These include a floor income insurance and a travel-related impairment insurance scheme, amongst others. The island offers a wide range of residential locations, including locations providing a level of accessibility that is below the sufficiency threshold, irrespective of transportation mode. The latter reflects the situation found in many peripheral regions of developed and developing countries, which offer limited accessibility to key activities like employment, advanced health care services, and higher institutions of education. The island provides two transportation modes, a dominant mode and an alternative mode that can be used by immigrants experiencing travel-related impairments (as well as others). The dominant mode is assumed to provide faster service, and thus a higher level of accessibility, than the alternative mode. Furthermore, it is assumed that the dominant mode provides excellent quality of service and that no further improvements in this mode, and thus in the accessibility provided by this mode, are possible. This, too, reflects the situation in many peripheral regions in developed countries, which may have a well-developed, and largely congestion-free, road network. When life commences on the island, immigrants are assigned a random residential location, in which they are assumed to be born and live the young years of their life. Because of this, the immigrants are assumed to develop a strong constitutive interest in their initially assigned location and thus to have a strong preference to continue their life in the same location, as long as the costs of doing so remain tolerable.

Given these circumstances, it is likely that the immigrants will be assigned a location that does not match their preferences. Some immigrants will be assigned a location with a higher level of accessibility than preferred, and thus with a higher location rent than they would have selected in a fair auction. Others will receive a location with an accessibility level well below their preferences. Yet, as long as the immigrants are also assigned an income level that can bear the higher location rent, or as long as the randomly assigned location provides sufficient accessibility, the costs of these deviations from their preferences will remain within a tolerable range for the immigrants. But not all randomly assigned locations may be acceptable to the immigrants to the island. On a closer look, the random location assignment may give rise to three different forms of more serious risks for the immigrants entering the island. In what follows, I will describe each form of risk and explore whether prudent immigrants would want to purchase an insurance to reduce these risks.

The first form of risk facing the immigrants consists of the chance of being assigned a location with an accessibility level *below* the sufficiency threshold. Recall that these locations have sub-standard accessibility levels irrespective of the transportation mode and that it is not possible to improve the accessibility of the location by upgrading the available transportation system(s). Furthermore, because it is assumed that the immigrants have a strong constitutive interest in their initial location, it is also assumed that they prefer not to solve their lack of accessibility by moving to another residential location. How could the immigrants to the island protect themselves against this risk? Clearly, the only way to improve the level of accessibility of these locations is by adding activities in the (vicinity of) the location. The immigrants will thus have a strong interest in seeking insurance that will upgrade the sub-standard accessibility levels to a sufficiency level by adding such activities. The insurance companies, however, will be reluctant to offer such an insurance across the board, because they are limited in their abilities to deliver. If they can collect sufficient premiums from the immigrants, they will be willing to provide services such as hospitals and schools to such areas, but they have much less influence on the location decisions of businesses and thus on the number of jobs in the area. They would thus be extremely reluctant to offer any insurance scheme that would provide coverage against a 'shortfall' in accessibility to employment. The insurance companies will derive lessons here from the highly problematic efforts of regional development policies in the past decades. At best, the insurance companies will be willing to offer an insurance scheme with a commitment to action, delineated in terms of costs. They will not, however, agree to any scheme that would oblige them to deliver a particular level of accessibility to employment. The willingness of the immigrants, in turn, to pay a particular insurance premium will depend on the size of the risk of being assigned a location with a sub-standard level of accessibility and the coverage provided by the insurance companies. The two are also closely related: the more immigrants who may be assigned a location with a sub-standard level of accessibility, the cheaper it will be to offer services such as health care in these areas, because of economies of scale. Thus if the risk is sufficiently high, prudent immigrants may be both willing and able to insure themselves for a sufficient level of accessibility (except for accessibility to employment). But in a low-risk situation the immigrants will be reluctant to set aside a large part of their clamshells for an additional insurance scheme, while the insurance companies will expect a high premium per immigrant to cover the costs of providing a service to a small population. It is thus rather likely that the immigrants will not purchase an insurance at all, but rather accept the hardships imposed on them by a location with a sub-standard accessibility level or move to a residential location with a sufficient level of accessibility. Note that all immigrants are assumed to have sufficient income and can thus afford themselves a location with sufficient accessibility.

The second form of risk facing the immigrants consists of two components. First, immigrants may be assigned a location that provides sufficient accessibility by the fastest mode of transportation, but insufficient accessibility by the slower, alternative, transportation mode. Second, immigrants may not be able to use the fastest transportation mode, because of costs or travel-related impairments. This situation would not occur when immigrants are in control of their residential location in the initial auction, as prudent immigrants would avoid selecting a residential location that provides them with an insufficient level of accessibility in case brute bad luck strikes in the form of a low income or a travel-related impairment. Yet in the real-world situation these locations clearly exist, partly because patterns of accessibility and standards of living—and thus expectations regarding participation in out-of-home activities—change over time. Indeed, as the accessibility literature shows, many suburban and peri-urban locations in metropolitan areas provide high levels of accessibility to car-owning residents, but often very low accessibility levels to residents without access to a car (see also Chapter 9). Given the existence of these locations and the risk of being 'assigned' to such a location, the question is whether immigrants would want to purchase an insurance to avoid this form of risk. The risk of not being able to use the fastest mode of transportation for reasons of cost can obviously easily be mitigated through the purchase of one of the affordability insurance schemes discussed in the previous section. Indeed, this situation is analytically the same as the one in which immigrants cannot purchase a floor income insurance scheme and thus seek to protect themselves against the risk of receiving only a subsistence income through the purchase of an affordability insurance scheme. It thus seems reasonable to assume that the immigrants would purchase an additional affordability insurance to guarantee themselves access to the fastest transportation mode in case they are 'assigned' to a location with a sub-standard accessibility level by the alternative mode.

The risk posed by travel-related impairments is of a different character, as this risk cannot be avoided through an affordability scheme. It requires the provision of an alternative transportation service that guarantees a sufficient level of accessibility, either through adapting the existing dominant transport system or through upgrading the existing alternative service. Whether it is possible to provide an adequate transport service either way depends on the state of the transportation technology; whether it is financially appealing to the immigrants depends on the costs of either option and the willingness to pay for these improvements among the immigrants. The willingness to pay, in turn, depends at least in part on the chances that an immigrant is struck by this type of brute bad luck. Clearly, if the risk for the immigrant is small and the costs of providing the service, in whatever form, are high, it is unlikely that an attractive insurance package will be offered by the insurance companies. The immigrants will then refrain from purchasing an insurance package and will be left with two choices: to remain in their initial location and accept the (harsh) consequences or to move to a location with sufficient accessibility. The latter may only be possible if immigrants have also been able to purchase a minimum floor income in the initial auction. If this is not the case, the immigrants run the risk of ending up on the island with both a travel-related impairment and a subsistence income. To avoid this risk, it may be expected that the immigrants will purchase one of the affordability insurances along the lines discussed above, which basically increases the subsistence income to the floor income, so that the immigrants can again choose a residential location with a sufficient level of accessibility provided by the alternative transportation mode. This insurance, however, will not address the immigrants' constitutive interests to continue their lives in the location in which they have been born and raised.

Let me now turn to the third form of risk. This consists of the chance of being assigned a location with an accessibility level well above the sufficiency threshold, but with an inhibitively expensive location rent. Such a situation may occur for immigrants receiving the floor income (or even slightly higher) once life on the island starts, as these immigrants cannot afford the entire range of locations on the island, as discussed before. What kind of insurance would the immigrants entering the island want to purchase to protect themselves against this risk? Clearly, these immigrants are likely to purchase some form of location affordability insurance. The insurance scheme will be somewhat different from the one discussed above, however. In the current scenario, it is assumed that immigrants do receive a sufficient level of income (i.e., the floor income or even slightly higher), but are assigned an expensive residential location that would normally be out of the range of possibilities for them. The immigrants will thus seek an insurance that would *increase* their disposable income beyond the floor level to allow for the payment of the location rent and the purchase of a sufficient level of all other goods on the island (including a sufficient level of trips). The insurance companies could offer various packages that would provide sufficient protection to the immigrants. The most obvious is a location affordability insurance that would take the following form: in case an immigrant may be expected to have expenses x above the floor income y for the purchase of a sufficient level of all goods on the island, then subsidize his location rent by z. As in the case of the location affordability insurance discussed above, it seems reasonable here that the immigrants would settle for a relatively modest level of subsidy z that would bring their level of consumption up to the sufficiency level for all goods but not beyond that. A few further points are in place here. First note that the immigrants living in high-access, expensive, locations may be expected to have lower transportation expenses due to their higher-access location, so that their disposable income after deduction of location rent and addition of location rent subsidy may be somewhat lower than the disposable income (after deduction of location rent) received by immigrants living on the floor income in a location that is within their range of possibilities. Second, it is important to stress that the location affordability insurance scheme is not grounded on considerations of fairness in the domain of accessibility, but solely on considerations regarding the ability of persons to continue their life in a location in which they have constitutive interests. Third, the income shortfall that befalls immigrants who experience this particular kind of bad luck could obviously also be alleviated by providing some other form of subsidy or in-kind contribution, such as a transportation expenditure subsidy or the in-kind provision of subsidized transportation services. It may be expected, however, that immigrants to the island would prefer an insurance scheme that clearly links between the cause of a risk and its protection. It is thus likely that they would prefer a location affordability insurance over any other type of insurance. Finally, it may be clear to the reader that this insurance scheme shows a strong resemblance to housing subsidy schemes that can be found in most developed countries. The argument provided here thus provides the moral motivation for such a scheme, but it may also be clear that additional and explicit explorations of fairness in a Walzer-like sphere for housing are warranted. Clearly, too, this effort is beyond the scope of this book.

What lessons can be drawn from the above? The analyses seem to suggest that the insurance schemes protecting against the various risks related to random location assignment are relatively expensive. This holds for the insurance scheme to protect against the chance of being assigned a location with an accessibility level *below* the sufficiency threshold, certainly if the chances of ending up in this situation are small. Furthermore, the insurance scheme against this risk will never be complete, as insurance companies cannot and will not guarantee a minimum level of accessibility to employment. The costs of insuring against the inability to use the fastest transportation mode on the island because of travel-related impairments, while being assigned a location with sufficient accessibility by that fastest mode but not by the alternative mode, can also be inhibitively high, in particular because of the costs related to the improvement of the dominant or alternative transport system. By contrast, immigrants may be expected to purchase an affordability insurance to protect themselves against the risk of being excluded from using the fastest transportation mode because of costs. Immigrants are also likely to purchase an affordability insurance, albeit of a different kind, to protect themselves against the risk of being assigned a high-access location with an inhibitively expensive location rent. The coverage against this risk would consist of a location affordability insurance, which is roughly in line with housing subsidy schemes common in many (developed) countries.

Conclusions

I have analyzed a wide variety of scenarios in which fictive but prudent (and perhaps in part fictive *because* prudent) immigrants to an island may find themselves. In each scenario, the immigrants face a different type of accessibility-related brute bad luck, against which they can protect themselves through the purchase of various types of accessibility insurance schemes.

Let me first describe the ideal, fair, pattern of accessibility as it emerges if immigrants purchase all the types of insurance schemes outlined in this chapter. In that fair society, all immigrants receive a floor income level that enables the purchase of a sufficient level of all necessary goods. This floor income also covers the costs of using the dominant transportation mode on the island. More precisely, it covers the transportation expenditures necessary for a sufficient level of trips with this dominant transportation mode, i.e., it covers the costs of a level of trips that enables participation in a sufficient number of out-of-home activities. The immigrants living on the floor income will be limited in the choice of residential location and will be priced out of expensive, high-access, locations. They will, however, maintain a range of choice among locations that all offer a sufficient level of accessibility. In the ideal situation, the dominant transportation mode can be used by all (adult) immigrants, irrespective of their abilities. However, the fair society may also feature a dominant transportation system that is not fully inclusive and thus cannot be used by all immigrants. In this fair society, some proportion of the immigrants may be struck by forms of brute bad luck that will prevent them from using the dominant transportation system on the island. These immigrants are obviously guaranteed a floor income. In addition, they are provided with an alternative transportation service that guarantees a sufficient level of accessibility. This alternative transportation service may take the form of an individualized service or of an alternative transportation system, depending amongst other factors on the population density and the risk of experiencing various types of travel-related impairments. The costs of using the system will be comparable to the costs of the dominant transportation system, so that persons experiencing travel-related impairments can pay for a sufficient level of trips from their floor income. Whenever the resulting user-generated revenues do not cover the entire costs of the alternative transportation system, the remainder of the costs will have to be carried by the entire society based on some form of progressive taxation.

Let me now turn to the situation typical for most developed countries and a rapidly increasing number of developing countries. This situation is characterized by a dominant car-road system shaping land use patterns, by a substantial share of the population excluded from the use of that dominant system, by a significant share of the population living on a subsistence income that is below a fair floor income, and by a *de facto* random assignment of residential locations. These conditions strongly shape patterns of accessibility as experienced by real-life persons. The argumentation line developed in this chapter has led to the identification of three basic forms of accessibility insurance that are to protect persons against the underlying forms of accessibility-related brute bad luck. Let me briefly summarize these forms of insurance.

The first form of accessibility insurance is to protect persons from being unable to use the dominant transportation system because of travel-related impairments (Table 6.3, insurance schemes 3 and 7). This insurance scheme guarantees a sufficient level of accessibility to all persons struck by this form of brute bad luck. The level of accessibility provided through the insurance scheme may be lower than that offered by the dominant transportation system; the difference between the two types of transportation systems or services may also vary across space. Yet all persons experiencing travel-related impairments should be guaranteed a sufficient level of accessibility (see below for the exceptions to this rule). The form of the transportation services offered to persons with travel-related impairments is open-ended in nature: it may consist of subsidized individual taxi services, accessible schedule-based public transport services, on-demand para-transit services, and so forth. Whatever the type of service offered, its qualities should be such that persons actually can and will use it to participate in out-of-home activities. This implies that services should be free of barriers that *de facto* reduce the accessibility level they provide, such as uncomfortable or unsafe bus stops, complex or dangerous walking routes, burdensome reservation systems, or extremely long reservation or travel times. In other words, sufficient accessibility implies sufficient accessibility as *experienced* by the persons using the system, which should be taken into account in the measurement of accessibility (see also Chapters 7 and 8).

The second form of accessibility insurance is to protect persons against the risk of being unable to use the dominant transportation system for reasons of cost (Table 6.3, insurance schemes 5 and 8). This insurance scheme guarantees that all persons can actually consume the sufficient levels of accessibility provided by the available transportation system(s), i.e., that they can actually engage in travel to participate in a sufficient level of out-of-home activities. The insurance scheme guarantees sufficient

Table 6.3 Overview of accessibility insurance schemes.

Number	Pages	Title of scenario	Description	Insurance scheme
1	91	The basic case	Immigrants bid for a residential location and residence, against the background of a singular transportation system that can be used by all	None; a situation of differential, but fair, accessibility levels will emerge
2	95	Bidding for transportation services	Immigrants bid for various transportation service packages, as the transportation system on the island is not pre-given	None; the auction is likely to result in a limited number of transportation services existing alongside each other, providing differential, but fair, accessibility levels
3	100	Bidding for impairment-proof transportation services	Immigrants bid for various transportation service packages in the understanding that they may be excluded from using these packages in case of travel-related impairments	Depending on circumstances, immigrants may purchase a partially exclusionary, but cheaper, transportation service rather than a fully inclusive service; in the former case, immigrants will also purchase an additional transportation service that guarantees a lower, but sufficient, level of accessibility for members of society excluded from the partially exclusionary transportation service
4	105	Insuring under fair income differentials	In contrast to all previous scenarios, immigrants know that they risk receiving only the floor income once life on the island commences; they can bid for an additional insurance against this risk	Immigrants accept the consequences of a floor income in terms of a lower range of choice regarding residential location; they do not purchase any additional insurance
5	109	Insuring under unfair income differentials	In contrast to the previous scenario, immigrants run the risk of receiving an income well below the floor level once life on the island commences; they can bid for an additional insurance against this risk	Immigrants will purchase an insurance scheme that is either used for in-kind provision of (low-cost) transportation services or for earmarked transportation subsidies to reduce income shortfalls

6	116	Insuring for random location assignment	*Case of insufficient accessibility* In contrast to all previous scenarios, immigrants cannot choose their residential location but run the risk of being allocated a peripheral location with an insufficient level of accessibility; they can bid for insurance to protect themselves against this risk	Immigrants are likely to accept this form of brute bad luck, as insurance schemes guaranteeing sufficient accessibility are expected to be inhibitively expensive; only if the chances of this form of brute bad luck are high, immigrants may purchase an insurance that guarantees some improvements in, but not a sufficient level of, accessibility
7	117	Insuring for random location assignment	*Case of travel-related impairments* In contrast to all previous scenarios, immigrants cannot choose their residential location but run the risk of being allocated a peripheral location providing sufficient accessibility by the dominant transportation mode but insufficient accessibility by the alternative transportation mode accessible for persons with travel-related impairments; the immigrants can bid for insurance to protect themselves against this risk	Depending on the circumstances, notably the wealth in society and the height of the risk, immigrants may either purchase an insurance scheme in order to secure an improvement of the alternative transportation mode, or refrain from purchasing an insurance and accept the consequences of insufficient accessibility, or change their residential location
8	118	Insuring for random location assignment	*Case of inhibitively expensive location rents* In contrast to all previous scenarios, immigrants cannot choose their residential location but run the risk of being allocated a residential location with a sufficient level of accessibility but an inhibitively expensive location rent; the immigrants can bid for insurance to protect themselves against this risk	Immigrants are likely to purchase a location affordability insurance in order to protect their constitutive interests to continue living in their initial residential location

accessibility either through in-kind subsidies that lower the costs of using the dominant transportation system or through the provision of an alternative, low-priced, transportation service. The latter strategy may be more cost-effective if a substantial share of the population cannot afford the costs of using the car-road system, if technological and economic circumstances enable the provision of an alternative service against relatively low costs, or when high population densities enable the efficient provision of such a service. The former strategy may be more cost-effective in the opposite circumstances. In practical terms, the insurance could take the form of a subsidized public transport system or of (earmarked) subsidies for the use of the car-road system. Clearly, both strategies can be observed in practice. Some governments subsidize car purchase or car use for low income households (see, for instance, 'wheels-to-work' type of programs in the USA; see Ong 2002; Cervero 2003), while virtually all developed countries subsidize public transport services to enable travel for persons on low incomes. While the latter form of subsidy is often provided to the entire population, the argument developed in this chapter suggests that only persons living on a subsistence income, i.e. persons with an income below the fair floor level, are entitled to this kind of support. Note that the very existence of unfair income levels in a society (in itself an injustice) thus implies a societal obligation to subsidize transportation. This, in turn, will imply a redistribution of income and will thus affect the sphere of income and wealth, directly through a progressive taxation scheme and indirectly through the (in-kind) subsidization of travel for persons with subsistence incomes, but without the radical and far-reaching implication of institutionalizing a Dworkian floor income or a Rawlsian fair income distribution. An injustice in one of Walzer's spheres can thus be partly corrected by strong principles of justice in another sphere, while maintaining much of the fences around each sphere.

Two more points are in place regarding this second form of insurance. First, the size of the support may well vary across space, as housing costs tend to be lower at low-accessibility locations (in line with Alonso's bid-rent model; see also Vidyattama, Tanton *et al.* 2013 for an interesting empirical exploration). This does not mean that housing and transportation costs should be equalized across space. Since persons tend to trade off housing costs and transportation costs, it only seems reasonable that persons living in low-access locations reap some of the benefits of the lower location cost as a compensation for lower levels of accessibility. Second, the argumentation line developed in this chapter suggests that persons with an income above the fair floor level should pay the full costs of using the transportation system(s). That is, any form of subsidy to lower the costs of using the transportation system for these persons is at odds with the demands of justice. I will return to this latter point in the final chapter of this book.

The third, and last, form of accessibility insurance is to protect persons against the risk of insufficient accessibility due to residential location

(Table 6.3, insurance schemes 6, 7 and 8). This is a complex type of insurance, as several situations can occur and each is related to the first two forms of insurance. First, persons may find themselves in a location providing an insufficient level of accessibility, but with a well-functioning transportation system. In this case, accessibility can only be improved through land use and service delivery interventions. These persons are only in principle entitled to an improvement in accessibility, as interventions in land use patterns are relatively expensive and sufficient accessibility to employment is virtually impossible to guarantee in market-based economic systems. The resulting accessibility insurance can thus only provide partial coverage. Second, persons may reside in inhibitively expensive locations due to high location rents or transportation costs. These persons are entitled to a location affordability or transportation affordability subsidy, in order to protect their constitutive interest in their residential location and safeguard the consumption of a sufficient level of accessibility. Third, persons may find themselves in a location with sufficient accessibility provided by the fastest transportation system, but an inability to use that system due to travel-related impairments. Here, too, only partial coverage may be guaranteed, as it may be inhibitively expensive to provide an alternative transportation service guaranteeing a sufficient level of accessibility across all locations.

From this summary it may be clear that the preference of persons, an important component of Dworkin's fair auction scheme, hardly plays a role in each of the three accessibility insurance schemes. This is so because in any real-world context it will be impossible to determine persons' preferences regarding activity participation without provoking strategic, free-rider type, behavior. Thus the insurance schemes cannot explicitly take into account the preferences of persons, but persons struck by various forms of accessibility-related brute bad luck will have to settle for the average level of coverage as agreed upon in society (cf. Dworkin 2000). I will return to the way in which this average level of coverage can be determined in the next chapter.

Taking a somewhat different perspective, the set of insurance schemes presented here can be seen as an embodiment of government's classical, and broadly supported, responsibility to protect citizens from violence. Willke (1992, pp. 242–246) powerfully argues that violence, in a modern society, should no longer be defined as merely direct physical violence of persons against persons, but has to include abstract forms of violence such as (preventable) illness, undernourishment, homelessness or environmental pollution. Willke argues that the damage these phenomena can inflict on persons does not differ fundamentally from the physical violence exerted by one person against another. Indeed, he argues, these abstract forms of violence may infringe a person's freedom in a more fundamental way than some forms of physical violence. If this broad conceptualization of violence is accepted, it becomes clear that transportation systems can be seen as powerful sources of violence. Indeed, it can be argued that a dominant transportation system exerts a nearly direct form of violence over persons excluded from using that transportation system. The social exclusion literature shows that this violence is not merely an abstract phenomenon; its impacts are real and fundamentally diminish the freedoms of affected persons. If this argument is accepted, the fundamental duty of a government to protect persons against violence thus also encompasses the violence exerted by transportation systems. Justice in the domain of transportation thus requires governments to protect citizens from the exclusionary violence that is embedded in non-inclusive transportation systems. The accessibility insurance schemes developed in this chapter should be seen as the practical manifestation of this classical government duty.

Let me end the chapter by summarizing the fundamental claims regarding justice in the domain of transportation that follow from the argumentation developed here:

1. An injustice is done whenever a person experiences an insufficient level of accessibility. This holds in virtually all cases.
2. All persons are entitled to a set of insurance schemes that guarantee a sufficient level of accessibility in virtually all cases. These insurance schemes are a key component of a fair scheme of mutual cooperation.
3. In order to achieve a sufficient level of accessibility for all, the proceeds from the insurance schemes are to be used to reduce and ultimately eliminate existing insufficiencies in accessibility in virtually all cases.
4. Interventions in the transportation system, in land use patterns or in service delivery policies are only just, and thus only justified, if they do not result in an increase in the number of persons experiencing insufficient accessibility levels or in a further reduction in the accessibility levels experienced by these persons.

The caveat 'in virtually all cases' refers to situations in which only a limited number of persons experience insufficiencies in accessibility and a reduction and elimination of these insufficiencies would be inhibitively expensive to society.

Taken together, these claims form the core principles of transportation planning based on principles of justice. The claims clearly pose a new question in need of an answer: What is a sufficient level of accessibility? Only based on an answer to this query, is it possible to systematically assess the fairness of transport-land use systems. This question will therefore be taken up in the chapter that follows.

References

Alonso, W. (1967). *A Reformulation of Classical Location Theory and its Relation to Rent Theory*. Papers of the Regional Science Association, Springer.

Banister, D. (2008). The sustainable mobility paradigm. *Transport Policy*, 15(2): 73–80.

Cervero, R.B. (2003). *Job access and reverse commute initiatives in California: a review and assessment*. Los Angeles, Institute for Transport Studies Berkeley/ University of California Transportation Center.

Dworkin, R. (1981a). What is Equality? Part 1: Equality of Welfare. *Philosophy and Public Affairs*, 10(3): 185–246.

Dworkin, R. (1981b). What is Equality? Part 2: Equality of Resources. *Philosophy and Public Affairs*, 10(4): 283–345.

Dworkin, R. (2000). *Sovereign Virtue: the theory and practice of equality*. Cambridge, MA/London, Harvard University Press.

Grengs, J. (2002). Community-based planning as a source of political change: the transit equity movement of Los Angeles' Bus Riders Union. *Journal of the American Planning Association*, 68(2): 165–178.

Harvey, D. (1973). *Social Justice and the City*. Bungay, Edward Arnold Publishers.

Mattioli, G. (2014). Where sustainable transport and social exclusion meet: households without cars and car dependence in Great Britain. *Journal of Environmental Policy & Planning*, 16(3): 379–400.

Ong, P.M. (2002). Car ownership and welfare-to-work. *Journal of Policy Analysis and Management*, 21(2): 239–252.

Roemer, J.E. (2002). Egalitarianism against the veil of ignorance. *The Journal of Philosophy*: 167–184.

Smith, A. (1887). *An Inquiry Into the Nature and Causes of the Wealth of Nations*. London, T. Nelson and Sons.

Varian, H. (1985). Dworkin on equality of resources. *Economics and Philosophy*, 1(1): 110–125.

Vidyattama, Y., R. Tanton and B. Nepal (2013). The effect of transport costs on housing-related financial stress in Australia. *Urban Studies*, 50(9): 1779–1795.

Willke, H. (1992). *Ironie des Staates: Grundlinien einer Staatstheorie polyzentrischer Gesellschaft*. Frankfurt am Main, Suhrkamp.

7 Defining Sufficient Accessibility

Introduction

The philosophical explorations thus far have delivered a fairly simple set of principles regarding fairness in the domain of accessibility. The bottom line of the argument is that all members of society should be guaranteed a sufficient level of accessibility under most, but not all, circumstances. A fair transport-land use system, in other words, provides sufficient accessibility to all members of society. The skeptical reader will argue that this is a mere reformulation of the question posed at the outset of the book. The question is no longer: On which principles of justice should transportation planning be based? Instead, the question now reads: What is a sufficient level of accessibility? Yet, as I aim to show in this chapter, this latter question can actually be answered by real-life agents through a deliberative democratic process.

For this purpose, it is important to delineate more precisely what is meant by the notion of a sufficient level of accessibility. I do not mean to say that it is possible, in general, to give an operational definition of sufficient accessibility, for instance in terms of the number of jobs a person should be able to reach within a given time and money budget. It would be absurd to expect such an operational definition from a theory of justice. Such a definition would radically, and unacceptably, constrain the scope of democratic decision-making (Walzer 1983, p. 67). But in line with Gutmann, I will argue that the argument developed in the previous chapter establishes a conditional right to sufficient accessibility. Like the welfare rights defended by Gutmann, the right to sufficient accessibility exists, in a way, "on the same level of principle as do free-speech rights" (Gutmann 1980, p. 201). Following Rawls, it could indeed be argued that the right to sufficient accessibility "falls under the general means necessary to underwrite fair equality of opportunity and our capacity to take advantage of our basic rights and liberties", just like the primary good of income and wealth (Rawls 2003, p. 174; see also Daniels 2008, p. 63, and Chapter 5). But while philosophical argumentation can sustain the argument that sufficient accessibility should be seen as a right or entitlement of members in a fair society, it is beyond the scope of a theory of justice to stipulate in any detail a particular sufficiency standard. That effort is the prerequisite of real-life agents who, in a democratic process, come to an agreement about the appropriate, context-sensitive, sufficiency threshold.

The exploration that follows therefore does not seek to define a particular sufficiency standard. The aim is rather to develop an approach that could be followed by real-life agents to reach an, inevitably time- and place-specific, agreement about what counts as sufficient and what as insufficient accessibility. Furthermore, I aim to define more precisely the duties that fall upon all members of society jointly in cases of insufficient and sufficient accessibility. Taken together, this provides a baseline for developing in the final part of the book a practical approach to transportation planning based on principles of justice.

The procedure for establishing a sufficiency standard

The argument developed so far has relied heavily on philosophical devices to answer the core question of the book: On which principles of justice should transportation planning be based? Following Dworkin, I have invoked a thin veil of ignorance to determine how prudent immigrants would deal with various forms of bad luck that might befall them in the domain of accessibility. The device of the veil of ignorance has its problems, however. The veil-of-ignorance approach asks "how we would allocate resources *if we did not know [the] actual distribution*" of abilities, skills or preferences over real-life persons (Roemer 2002, p. 183, emphasis in original). Roemer argues powerfully that it would be preferable to decide about (interventions in) resource allocations with as much information at hand as possible. Based on such information it is no longer necessary to rely on assumptions regarding the abilities, skills or preferences of persons under uncertainty, but it is possible to directly address the interests of the involved persons in the resource allocation at hand. As Kolm formulates it: "justice is not blind-folded egoism, but open-eyed and informed objectivity" (Kolm 1996, p. 20). This approach is also of relevance for the domain of accessibility: in order to set a sufficiency standard, it is necessary to have knowledge of the actual distribution of accessibility and its consequences for real-life persons. Without that knowledge, a sufficiency standard will necessarily remain an abstract construct, rather than a threshold with practical relevance. The 'blindfolded' thin veil of ignorance has served well as a device to establish the sufficiency principle, but is not suitable as a device for determining the sufficiency standard.

Lifting the veil of ignorance is not a simple matter from a philosophical perspective. It creates the risk of opening a Pandora's box of personal vested interests and group-based preconceptions, which may lead to biases in judgments. The literature proposes two possible solutions to prevent the

Pandora's box from determining the establishment of a sufficiency standard: the impartial observer, and democratic deliberation. I will not explore these approaches in depth here, but only provide a brief summary of the main ideas. The notion of the impartial spectator was first proposed, at least in writing, by Adam Smith in his book *The Theory of Moral Sentiments* (Smith 2010 [1759]). Like the veil of ignorance, the notion of the impartial spectator is a device that real-life agents can draw upon to assess the fairness of a decision. But there are three important differences with the veil of ignorance (see also Sen 2006). First, the impartial spectators are fully informed about the particularities of the situation. The veil of ignorance is fully lifted, so to say. Second, the spectators are to be disinterested observers who are not themselves parties to the societal decisions that are to be taken. They are, in this sense, truly impartial. Third, the spectators may represent voices from within the community, as well as voices from a distance, speaking from different (cultural) contexts altogether. The idea is that real-life agents take up the position of the impartial spectator, thereby examining how their own practices and conventions would look to others. While the notion of the impartial spectator has not been fully developed into a philosophical device to answer questions of fairness, it may be clear that invoking the perspective of an impartial spectator in real-life decision-making may assist in reaching fair(er) agreements (see Barry 1995 for an elaborate account).

Democratic deliberation is based on the understanding that "thinking about right and wrong is, at the most basic level, thinking about what could be justified to others on grounds that they, if appropriately motivated, could not reasonably reject" (Scanlon 2000, p. 5 cited in Sen 2002, p. 456). The body of literature addressing the notion of democratic deliberation and discussing its advantages and (im)possibilities is vast and it is beyond the scope of the book to critically engage with this literature (see Dryzek 1990 for an excellent early account; and for an early discussion of its relevance for the field of (urban) planning, Fischer and Forester 1993). For our purposes, it is sufficient to give a brief account of the body of knowledge captured by the notion of democratic deliberation. The approach requires that real-life processes of decision-making, in which relations of power and strategic use of information typically play an often pivotal role, are transformed into arenas in which well-informed and equally empowered citizens can make prudent decisions. The thought here is that deliberation based on arguments, referred to by Healey as "inclusionary argumentation" (Healey 1995), is the appropriate way to come to an agreement, rather than some form of majority voting or other democratic procedure. Yet, while the theory of democratic deliberation thus emphasizes the dominant role of arguments, the approach is ultimately a procedural one, prescribing the ideal setting within which deliberation should take place in order to reach the best, and fair, solution.

The real-life agents can draw on both these solutions in setting up a decision-making procedure to determine a sufficiency standard for accessibility. That procedure should adhere as much as possible to the, arguably rather idealistic, conditions required for inclusionary argumentation, while the perspective(s) of (multiple) impartial spectator(s) should be invoked in the democratic deliberations themselves. Such an approach may not result in complete agreement between the real-life agents involved in the deliberation and may thus fail to deliver a clear-cut stipulation of an accessibility standard. But, as Sen (2002, p. 456) underscores, "the demands of reasoned practice can, in one way or another, live with a good deal of incompleteness or unresolved conflicts". The idea here is that the real-life agents involved in deliberation can substantially reduce the scope of disagreement by focusing first and foremost on the domains where consensus can be reached based on argumentative reasoning. Sen argues that the remaining domain of disagreement may not hinder the parties from coming to "firm and useful statements" (ibid.). Indeed, democratic deliberation can assist in demarcating the domain within which some form of (pure) procedural justice, such as majority voting, may be applied.

The proposed procedure for demarcating a sufficiency standard thus consists of two stages. In the first stage of democratic deliberation, real-life agents engage in argumentation and seek to reach an agreement on a sufficiency threshold. They do so based on knowledge of the actual situation in their society, i.e. they are not placed behind a veil of ignorance. This deliberation may result in a general consensus about a singular sufficiency standard, thereby ending the decision-making procedure. It is, however, more likely that the deliberation will not result in such a clearly defined sufficiency threshold, but rather in the demarcation of a range of low accessibility levels deemed insufficient by all parties involved in the deliberation. The demarcation of this range may be adequate for policy making, thereby ending the process. But if it is not, the real-life agents enter the second stage of the decision-making process, the stage of democratic selection, in which they determine a singular, context-sensitive, sufficiency standard through some form of democratic procedure. The outcome of that democratic procedure is subject to the condition that it has to lie above the range of insufficiency delineated by the deliberative stage of the decision-making process.

This is clearly an extremely stylized description of the decision-making procedure that real-life agents could use to stipulate a sufficiency threshold. I will refrain from further developing this, essentially procedural, approach to fairness. Rather, in what follows I will return to substantive issues, thereby providing some guidance to the real-life agents involved in the decision-making procedure. I will first discuss how the real-life agents should engage with the relationship between accessibility and activity participation. I will then briefly discuss the knowledge base on which the real-life agents could draw in their democratic deliberations about the sufficiency threshold. Finally, I will describe the duties that follow from the demarcation of a (in)sufficiency threshold or range.

The relationship between accessibility and activity participation

Accessibility has been defined in Chapters 1 and 4 as a personal resource that bestows a person with the possibility of participation in out-of-home activities. The prudent immigrants to the island state have also perceived accessibility in this way. They have sought to insure themselves against forms of brute bad luck that would seriously affect their accessibility levels, because poor accessibility levels would limit their ability to participate in activities. This relationship between accessibility and activity participation raises the question whether real-life agents, involved in democratic deliberation as briefly outlined above, should focus on accessibility or directly on activity participation. In order to answer this question, I will discuss three possible perspectives on the relationship between accessibility and activity participation. I will subsequently argue that real-life agents concerned about persons' activity participation should focus their deliberations first and foremost on accessibility.

The first perspective on the relationship between accessibility and activity participation draws the attention towards the intensity or quantity of activity participation. The quantity of activity participation can be defined in terms of frequency (the number of out-of-home activities in which a person engages) and duration (the share of time a person spends on out-of-home activity participation). It may be hypothesized that the level of accessibility and the quantity of out-of-home activity participation are correlated. Clearly, at extremely low levels of accessibility a person's activity participation will be severely restricted. Indeed, although it is hard to imagine beyond the walls of a prison, a person with 'zero' accessibility is completely confined to her place of origin and is therefore unable to participate in any out-of-home activities (here, the basic liberty of freedom of movement and fairness in accessibility touch upon each other). But at any level beyond that absolute minimum, a person will be able to participate in at least some activities. It may also be assumed that there is no strict relationship between accessibility levels and the quantity of activity participation, as people differ highly in their need or desire to participate in out-of-home activities. For any given level of accessibility beyond the absolute minimum, we may thus observe persons with higher and lower intensities of activity participation. Yet it may be expected that the *average* level of participation in out-of-home activities, as an arithmetic average of all persons with a particular level of accessibility, will go up with an increase in the accessibility level. The relation will be a concave one, as the impact of one 'unit' of additional accessibility in a situation of high accessibility will have less influence on activity participation than a comparable 'unit' of improvement at a low initial level of accessibility.

Thus the variation in the quantity of activity participation may be expected to increase at a diminishing rate with every increment in accessibility.

The relationship between accessibility and activity participation is depicted graphically in Figure 7.1. Each point in the figure represents a person experiencing a particular level of accessibility and engaging in a particular number of out-of-home activities. The curve represents the average level of activity participation for persons experiencing different levels of accessibility. Clearly, accessibility can be measured in multiple ways and a person's accessibility level will typically depend on the particularities of the person (available transportation modes, income level, residential location, amongst others) and the characteristics of the transport-land use system (including the quality of the transportation systems and densities of destinations), making it difficult to identify persons experiencing identical levels of accessibility. Conceptually, however, it is possible to establish an average level of activity participation for each level of accessibility. As the shaded area in the figure indicates, a substantial variation in the quantity of out-of-home activity participation may be expected at high levels of accessibility, as a result of people's preferences and other factors. However, with decreasing accessibility, the relationship between accessibility level and activity participation will grow in strength and the variation in the level of activity participation will gradually decrease. At a certain point, it can be hypothesized, accessibility levels are so low that they directly limit the possibility of a person to participate in a normal range of activities. When this occurs, it could be argued, people experience an insufficient level of accessibility.

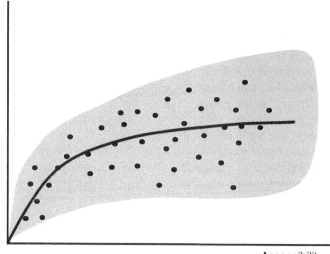

Figure 7.1 The relationship between accessibility and the quantity of activity participation.
Source: Based on Martens 2006.

This perspective leads to a reformulation of the question posed at the outset of this chapter. The question now reads: What is a sufficient level of activity participation? A fair transport-land use system would enable each citizen to engage in a sufficient level of out-of-home activities. The challenge is then to determine a sufficient level of activity participation. This is, in an important way, what the social exclusion literature has done in a qualitative way: to identify population groups that are unable to engage in a sufficient level of activities due to a poorly performing transport-land use system.

The second perspective underscores that persons are not merely interested in the quantity of activity participation, but also, and perhaps even more, in the benefits that participation in out-of-home activity brings to them. For instance, the value of participation in the job market is not merely a product of frequency and duration, but also depends on the type and quality of the employment. We can hypothesize that accessibility's relationship with the *benefits* of activity participation will be stronger than its relationship with the *quantity* of activity participation (Figure 7.2). Indeed, while the relationship between accessibility and the benefits of activity participation will also be a concave one, it may be expected that significant increases in benefits will be reaped over a larger range of initial accessibility levels. For example, a higher level of accessibility may enable persons to obtain a job that better matches their skills, to engage in leisure activities that more closely match their preferences, or to visit a more diverse set of family members and friends over a given period of time. Clearly, these benefits would not be captured by merely measuring the quantity of out-of-home activity participation in terms of frequency and duration.

This perspective leads to yet another reformulation of the question posed at the outset of this chapter. The question now reads: What is a sufficient level of benefit from activity participation? It may be clear that the level of benefit will be more difficult to determine than the actual level of activity participation. Out-of-home activity participation clearly generates a variety of benefits, which cannot simply be added up to produce the total benefit derived from such participation. At the same time, the social exclusion literature has also addressed this question, to some extent, in a qualitative way. By discussing the consequences of a poor transport-land use system in terms of unemployment, social isolation or poor health, the benefits rather than the frequency or duration of activity participation are addressed. This body of literature can thus help in demarcating the lower end of the accessibility spectrum, where accessibility becomes a barrier for achieving a sufficient level of benefits from participation in out-of-home activity.

Let me explore yet a third perspective. The focus so far has been limited to the relationship between accessibility and (the benefits from) activity participation. It can, however, be argued that this focus on what persons

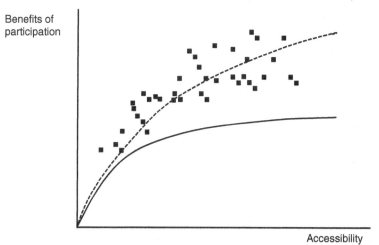

Figure 7.2 The relationship between level of accessibility and the benefits derived from that level of accessibility in terms of (a) the quantity of activity participation (straight line) and (b) the quality of activity participation (dashed line). The small squares represent the level of qualitative benefits derived by a particular person.
Source: Based on Martens 2006.

actually 'extract' from a particular level of accessibility—whether in terms of quantity or qualitative benefits—ignores the fundamental constitutive interest that persons have in not only the actual state they achieve, but also, and perhaps even more, in the range of states they could achieve. I draw here on the capability approach, a leading theory of social justice which I have not invoked so far. A key argument of the capability approach is that *"[d]oing x* and *choosing to do x* are, in general, not equivalent" (Sen 1988, p. 292—emphasis in original). Sen gives the example of fasting. The decision to stop eating can only be described as 'fasting' if the person really does have the alternative of eating more. Indeed, if the opportunity of normal eating disappears, the person may no longer be able to fast. The loss of the opportunity to eat freely is thus a substantive loss even for the person who chooses not to eat but instead to fast. The general point here is that persons have a constitutive interest in the range of states they could achieve. The value of the chosen option depends not merely on the characteristics of that option, but as much on the range of options from which it was chosen. For example, it makes a fundamental difference whether a person visits his grandmother everyday because she is the only family member he is able to visit given his time and money budget, or whether the same person consistently chooses to visit his grandmother from a range of other family members. The latter person is clearly better off, because he has the freedom to choose from multiple options and can execute his agency to give direction to his life. It would be fundamentally wrong to evaluate the situation of both persons merely based on their actual level of activity participation or even the benefits derived from activity participation, as it would fail to take into account the fundamental difference in their freedoms and in their ability to execute their agency. Likewise, it would be fundamentally wrong to assess a sedentary lifestyle under conditions of low accessibility in the same way as the *choice* for a sedentary lifestyle under conditions of high accessibility. This argument obviously also holds for other types of out-of-home activity participation, such as work or leisure.

It may perhaps be illuminating to rephrase this argument in the terminology of the capability approach (see Sen 1990; Sen 2011; Nussbaum 2000; Nussbaum 2003 for the most important formulations). The capability approach makes a distinction between so-called 'capabilities' and 'functionings'. Functionings represent what an individual has succeeded in being or doing, while the notion of capabilities captures the range of beings and doings a person could achieve. Translated to the domain of transportation, functionings can be equated with actual activity participation ('what a person has succeeded in doing'), while accessibility captures a person's capabilities ('the range of doings a person could achieve'). Sen and Nussbaum make the case that the assessment of the fairness of a situation should principally focus on capabilities rather than functionings, because the capability set reflects a person's freedom to choose between different ways of living. Defending the importance of capabilities, Sen refers to Marx's call to replace "the domination of circumstances and chance over individuals by the domination of individuals over chance and circumstances" (Marx 1846 in Sen 1990, p. 44). By focusing on capabilities, the person and her agency are given center stage. Likewise, by focusing on accessibility rather than the quantity or quality of activity participation, the person is given center stage in the assessment of transportation (and land use) interventions.

This analysis leads to yet another formulation of the question: What is a sufficient level of accessibility? The question now reads: What is a sufficient level of choice? The level of choice is then defined in terms of the range of out-of-home activities in which a person can participate. Clearly, in contrast with the two earlier formulations, this third question is literally a mere reformulation of the original question. This is so because the concept of accessibility incorporates the notion of choice: it has been defined as the potential of opportunities for interaction with locations dispersed over space (Chapter 1). Based on this definition, a higher level of accessibility by definition implies more choice; a decrease in accessibility inevitably implies a decrease in choice.

The analysis of the relationship between accessibility and activity participation suggests three reasons why it would be a mistake for real-life agents to focus their democratic deliberations on the actual levels of activity participation experienced by persons. First, low levels of activity participation may be as much the result of choice as of circumstance. Levels of activity participation, when analyzed in isolation, thus provide little insight into the service provided by the transport-land use system. Second, and related, even if low levels of activity participation are the result of circumstance rather than choice, these circumstances do not have to be related to the transport-land use system. For instance, persons may only infrequently visit a doctor due to the high cost of medical care or may not participate in leisure activities at all due to discriminatory selection practices. These are clear instances of injustices, but they do not point at any injustice in the transport-land use system (although the injustices might be related). Here, measuring only activity participation may lead to identifying a problem that is not relevant from the perspective of transportation (or urban) planning. Third, persons may actually show a fairly high level of activity participation while receiving an (extremely) low level of accessibility in comparison to the 'average' accessibility level across a particular society or population. This may be so, for instance, because a person happens to live in close proximity to key destinations, such as his job, a few shops and a number of friends and family members. Yet it would be wrong to ignore the situation of this person in the assessment of the fairness of a transport-land use system. That is so because a fairly high level of activity participation at a particular moment in time under conditions of low accessibility does not guarantee that a person will be able to maintain a sufficient level of activity participation as his plans, or the circumstances, change over time. In this case, limiting the assessment to the level of activity participation would fail to take seriously the constitutive interests of persons in the range of possibilities from which they can choose.

Taken together, these arguments suggest that from the perspective of justice it is crucial to measure persons' *possibility* of engaging in a variety of out-of-home activities rather than their actual participation in out-of-home activities. In other words, the assessment of the fairness of a transport-land use system should be based, first and foremost, on the measurement of accessibility. This implies that the real-life agents should also focus their deliberations on the level of accessibility and not on the quantity or quality of activity participation (see also Martens and Golub 2012; Martens 2016).

The knowledge base for setting a sufficiency standard

How can real-life agents determine what is a sufficient level of accessibility? I distinguish two approaches that could assist real-life agents in defining a sufficiency threshold. These approaches provide what I call the knowledge base for setting a sufficiency standard. Let me describe them briefly in turn.

In the first approach, the real-life agents base their deliberations on as much empirical knowledge as is available regarding the relationship between accessibility and activity participation. This will require data on accessibility levels as experienced by (groups of) persons and the related quantity of, and variety in, activity participation. It will furthermore require data on the benefits derived from activity participation, for instance in terms of (the quality of) employment, the intensity of social isolation, or the level of health care uptake. Based on these three sets of data, the real-life agents can seek to identify how accessibility shapes the quantity and quality of activity participation. This can subsequently feed their democratic deliberation regarding the sufficiency standard.

This first approach thus requires a deep understanding of the relationship between accessibility and activity participation, particularly at lower levels of accessibility. Perhaps surprisingly, but actually in line with the focus on revealed mobility in traditional transportation planning, few studies have systematically explored this relationship. The largely qualitative body of literature on transport-related social exclusion primarily addresses the (lack of) activity participation among vulnerable population groups, but without systematically exploring the relationship with accessibility. At best, these studies use rough proxies for accessibility, like proximity to a public transport stop (e.g. Cebollada 2008). The studies exploring the notion of stable travel time budgets do touch on the relationship between time and money expenditure on travel on the one hand and activity participation on the other, but typically refrain from analyzing the relationship with accessibility (see e.g. van Wee, Rietveld *et al.* 2006; Mokhtarian and Chen 2004; for an interesting recent study see Lucas, Bates *et al.* 2016). Only recently, studies have been conducted that explicitly investigate the link between accessibility and activity participation (Weis 2012; Weis and Axhausen 2012; Seo, Ohmori *et al.* 2013; Hu and Giuliano 2014). These studies provide a first, still limited, analysis of the relationship. Much more research will be necessary to gain a deep understanding of the relationship under a range of circumstances. The setting of a sufficiency standard will require a major research effort, certainly if it is taken into account that accessibility and (the benefits of) activity participation can be measured in multiple ways and that the relationship between accessibility and activity participation is likely to vary across time and space.

Given the lack of an empirical understanding of the relationship between accessibility and activity participation, the real-life agents may also rely on a second, and perhaps second-best, approach to determine the sufficiency level, building on Daniels' biostatistical approach to normal functioning (see Chapter 5). This approach avoids assessing the, in empirical terms perhaps elusive, relationship between accessibility and activity participation. Instead, it limits the empirical analysis to the measurement of accessibility as observed across an entire population. This approach is based on the understanding that the relative position or 'ranking' of a person vis-à-vis this range of actually observed accessibility levels will provide some indication whether the particular person receives a sufficient level of accessibility. The reasoning here is that persons with accessibility levels far below the average level for the entire population are likely to experience serious detrimental impacts in terms of quantity and quality of activity participation. In contrast, persons with an accessibility level at or well above the average for the entire population are likely to experience no serious limitations in their choice of activities and, ultimately, in their actual levels of activity participation. This second approach can build on a large body of literature analyzing accessibility levels across cities and (urban) regions (see e.g. Shen 1998; Kwok and Yeh 2004; Hess 2005; Kawabata and Shen 2006; Kawabata 2009; Benenson, Martens *et al.* 2011). This vast body of evidence regarding the range of accessibility levels observed in real-life contexts may help the real-life agents set a sufficiency standard in a pragmatic way. In this pragmatic approach, the real-life agents would define the sufficiency standard as a particular percentage of the average or median level of accessibility observed across a population. Depending on circumstances, which include the wealth of a society, real-life agents may reach consensus about a lower or higher percentage as the sufficiency threshold. Clearly, this second, pragmatic, approach has its own challenges. For one, it will require agreement regarding the measurement of accessibility, as different accessibility indicators may generate quite distinct accessibility patterns (although it is highly likely that largely identical population groups will be found at the bottom of the accessibility distribution irrespective of the way in which accessibility is measured). Furthermore, the approach is clearly only suitable in case of a generally well-functioning transport-land use system that provides accessibility to a substantial range of activities for a large part of the population. If the transport-land use system provides a poor level of accessibility across the board, the average level of accessibility may itself not be sufficient.

Establishing a sufficiency standard

The two approaches described above only suggest the knowledge base on which real-life agents can draw to stipulate a possible sufficiency standard. It is unlikely that the information derived from the proposed knowledge base will lead to an unequivocal answer to the question posed at the outset of the chapter: What is a sufficient level of accessibility? Yet I argue that either of these approaches can provide an adequate basis for real-life agents, if they seriously engage in inclusionary argumentation and invoke the perspectives of multiple impartial observers, to reach consensus about the 'extremes' of the accessibility spectrum: a lower range providing persons with a clearly *in*sufficient level of accessibility and an upper range conferring a clearly sufficient level of accessibility. At the same time, it may be expected that real-life agents will not be able to reach consensus in the deliberative stage of the decision-making process about the sufficiency of the accessibility levels in the range between these two extremes. Let me explore each of these ranges or domains in turn to clarify this argument.

The lower range of the accessibility spectrum captures accessibility levels that clearly, in the eyes of all real-life agents, provide insufficient choices for activity participation. It seems inevitable that real-life agents will agree that the absolute lowest level of accessibility, in which a person cannot engage in out-of-home activities at all, does not provide a sufficient level of choice. But for a substantial range beyond that absolute minimum, it seems reasonable to expect that real-life agents would also be able to reach such an agreement. The agents could draw here on the empirical relationship between accessibility and activity participation, as suggested above. Although data on this interrelationship will never be conclusive, as real-life provides a rich variation of circumstances and situations, the data may help to delineate the range of accessibility levels that unambiguously hinder activity participation. In line with the social exclusion literature, it may be expected that real-life agents would find an accessibility level insufficient if it would severely reduce a person's health care uptake, social contacts, job opportunities, and so on. The real-life agents could also draw on the second-best, comparative approach to demarcate a lower range of insufficient accessibility. This would relieve them from drawing on the often indeterminate knowledge about the complex interrelationships between accessibility and activity participation. It would merely require them to reach an agreement about unacceptable negative deviations from the average or median level of accessibility across a population. While it will certainly not be easy to determine which deviations are acceptable, it may be expected that real-life agents will be able to reach consensus on particularly large deviations from the average. Clearly, both approaches will leave room for multiple interpretations by the real-life agents, but it seems reasonable to assume that the agents, if following the procedures in the deliberative stage, will at least show some overlapping consensus and will thus be able to reach agreement about some range at the lower extreme of the accessibility spectrum, however minimal it might be.

The agents can use a comparable line of reasoning to determine an upper range of the accessibility spectrum. The upper range covers the set of accessibility levels that clearly, in the eyes of all agents involved in the democratic deliberations, provide a sufficient level of choice among out-of-home activities. Here, too, the real-life agents can build on the knowledge base described above, such as empirical studies that provide insight into the relationship between high levels of accessibility and levels of activity participation. Clearly the agents may be expected to agree that sufficient accessibility is provided if the vast majority of persons experiencing a particular level of accessibility are able to participate in a wide range of activities, certainly if these activities are dispersed over space and are carried out during various parts of the day and night. The cases of low activity participation under the condition of high accessibility will then be rightfully considered anomalies, as the result of choice rather than circumstance. Here too, real-life agents could use a comparative approach in which accessibility levels are compared across persons, and conclude that population groups with accessibility levels (well) above the average receive sufficient accessibility. Whatever approach the real-life agents adopt to identify a sufficient level of accessibility, it may be assumed that they can agree that some upper range provides sufficient accessibility.

This approach to boundary setting obviously leaves open an intermediate range of accessibility levels about which real-life agents will fail to reach an agreement, even if they properly engage in inclusionary argumentation and invoke the perspectives of impartial spectators from a range of (cultural) backgrounds (see Figure 7.3). Since it is unclear which obligations and responsibilities fall on the government (or any other collective actor) in the range of disagreement, it is likely that the real-life agents will agree that a further demarcation of the two ranges is necessary. Since democratic deliberation has already been exhausted, this can only be done in the second stage of the decision-making process, the stage of democratic selection. In this stage, real-life agents agree on some form of democratic procedure, such as majority voting, to determine the threshold between sufficient and insufficient accessibility. The possible outcomes of this stage of democratic selection are determined by the results of the stage of democratic deliberation: the sufficiency threshold *has* to lie within the range of disagreement. Easing such a constraint would turn the democratic deliberation stage into a superfluous and empty exercise. It might also lead to a disconnect between the decision-making process and the available knowledge base on the relationship between accessibility and activity participation. Clearly, real-life agents would be interested to protect the outcomes of the agreement they have been able to reach through an appropriate procedure of inclusive argumentation. Indeed, the identification of the ranges of sufficiency and insufficiency can be seen as Sen's "firm and useful statements" resulting from the democratic deliberation on sufficient accessibility (Sen 2002, p. 456).

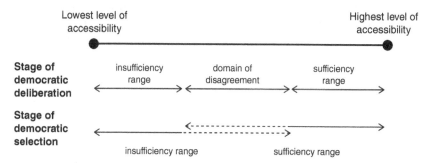

Figure 7.3 Graphic representation of the process of setting the boundaries of the range of sufficiency and the range of insufficiency, through the stages of democratic deliberation and democratic selection.

The domain of justice and the domain of free exchange

The delineation of the range of sufficiency and the range of insufficiency through the processes of democratic deliberation and democratic selection has profound consequences for the duties of members of society vis-à-vis each other. Let me explore each of these ranges or domains in turn to clarify these duties.

The lower range of accessibility captures the domain of risk against which the immigrants to the fictive island state would have insured themselves. The lower range thus represents the domain of justice: it is the domain in which persons are entitled to corrective measures to improve their accessibility level to the sufficiency level. The types of corrective measures are those defined by the types of insurances purchased by the prudent immigrants to the island. As shown in the previous chapter, these measures can encompass interventions in the transportation or land use systems. The financing of these corrective measures falls on the entire community and does not need to be shouldered (entirely) by the population segment suffering from insufficient accessibility. The need for corrective measures thus justifies a general taxation scheme that can finance them. In other words, the taxation scheme is the real-life materialization of the insurance schemes purchased by the immigrants to the island. The proceeds of the taxation scheme may *only* be used for financing measures that reduce the level of insufficiency or reduce the number of persons experiencing insufficient levels of accessibility. Since transportation infrastructures and services always imply continuous costs related to operation and maintenance, such a taxation scheme will be a permanent feature of any society with forms of brute bad luck as described in the previous chapter. I will return to the taxation scheme in the final chapter of this book.

The consequences of identifying an upper range are perhaps just as profound. This is so because that upper range falls outside the domain of the insurance schemes that have been identified in the island scenarios in the previous chapter. The segment of the population experiencing these sufficiently high accessibility levels is thus not entitled to accessibility improvements financed through some form of taxation. This is so because prudent agents will only accept a scheme of taxation if it resembles an insurance scheme which the prudent immigrants to the island would willingly purchase to protect themselves against a particular risk. Clearly, no prudent immigrant would purchase an insurance scheme to avoid a situation that does not pose a serious risk; prudent immigrants will prefer to reserve their clamshells for purchases with direct benefits rather than the purchase of an unnecessary insurance scheme with an uncertain, and perhaps zero, pay-off. Any taxation scheme that goes beyond the insurance schemes of the island is thus a form of coercion that is unacceptable to the prudent agents.

Does this imply that no accessibility improvements are possible for the population segment with an accessibility level above the upper accessibility boundary? No. Such improvements are still possible under two conditions. First, they are acceptable as long as they have no detrimental effects for population segments with (near) insufficient accessibility levels, i.e. as long as these accessibility improvements do not lead to transport or land use dynamics that reduce the accessibility levels experienced by the worst-off population groups. Second, these accessibility improvements are acceptable if they are self-financing, i.e. if they can be realized without an—inevitably coercive—scheme of taxation. This line of argumentation also holds for efforts to maintain accessibility levels well above the sufficiency threshold. Such 'maintenance' efforts—that is, traffic management measures to maintain travel speeds on major roads under conditions of increasing demand—should live up to the same standards: they are only acceptable if they have no detrimental accessibility effects for the groups with the lowest accessibility levels and if the efforts are self-financing. The self-financing requirement should be perceived in the broadest sense. The cost of investments or maintenance can be carried by both the users of the transportation system and by third parties benefitting from such improvements, for example through an increase in land values (e.g. Samsura and van der Krabben 2011). Clearly, because of the risk of free-rider behavior in the case of self-financing arrangements, any real-world financing scheme could well have some coercive features, but such features would only be acceptable if such a financing scheme did not force non-beneficiaries to co-finance and if such a scheme were the result of democratic decision-making among well-informed citizens.

The sizes of the two ranges may differ over time and between societies, depending on the level of wealth of a society and the available knowledge about the consequences of poor accessibility. The former condition emerges as relevant from the explorations of the island state: immigrants entering an island with an abundance of resources would be expected to reserve more of their clamshells for various insurance schemes than immigrants entering a situation of austerity. The more systematic the evidence base regarding the latter condition, the easier it will be for the prudent agents to agree on the ranges of sufficiency and insufficiency, thereby decreasing the range of disagreement and the role of democratic selection.

Conclusions

In this chapter I have sought to develop an approach that would answer the core question emerging from the preceding philosophical explorations: What is a sufficient level of accessibility? I have argued that the answer to this question is beyond the realm of philosophical exploration—the question can only be answered through a process of democratic deliberation and selection. I have briefly outlined the contours of the decision-making procedure that real-life agents could employ to stipulate a sufficiency threshold.

I continued my exploration by discussing the knowledge base on which real-life agents should draw in their deliberations about the sufficiency threshold. I argued that, while accessibility is only a means to an end, persons have a constitutive interest in the accessibility level they experience. Hence, transportation planning based on principles of justice should rely first and foremost on the measurement of accessibility levels. The delineation of a sufficiency threshold for accessibility can be based on either a detailed understanding of the empirical relationship between accessibility levels and the quantity and quality of activity participation or on a pragmatic approach of accessibility measurement and ranking of population groups in terms of their experienced accessibility levels. Based on either approach, it is possible to determine a range of sufficiency and a range of insufficiency. The stage of democratic selection is intended to bring these ranges together into a sufficiency threshold, resulting in the identification of a domain of sufficiency and insufficiency. Finally, I explored the moral obligations of persons vis-à-vis each other in both these domains.

The critical reader may argue that a sufficiency principle is in an important way elusive as well as expansive. Sufficiency standards can be easily adjusted upwards and so they may eat up resources. However, the conclusion should not be that sufficiency cannot be a distributive principle. Paraphrasing Walzer (1983, p. 67), it could be argued that the sufficiency principle is, rather, a "principle subject to political limitation; and the limits (within limits) can be arbitrary, fixed by some ... majority of voters". The proposal put forward here is fully in line with Walzer: the stage of democratic deliberation draws the boundaries within which a sufficiency threshold can be determined in the stage of democratic selection. The sufficiency threshold is in this sense arbitrary, but once it is set through the merging of the upper and lower ranges of accessibility into one threshold, the consequences are determined as well. The range below the threshold belongs to the domain of justice; here, improvements in accessibility are *required* in virtually all cases and should be financed by *a fair scheme of taxation*. The range above the threshold belongs to the domain of free exchange. Here, improvements in accessibility are optional and are *only allowed* if they are self-financing and do not increase the share of the population falling below the threshold.

This ends the philosophical explorations. Drawing on the conclusions of these explorations, in the final part of the book I will develop a practical approach to transportation planning based on principles of justice.

References

Barry, B.M. (1995). *Justice as Impartiality*. Oxford, Clarendon Press.

Benenson, I., K. Martens, Y. Rofé, *et al.* (2011). Public transport versus private car: GIS-based estimation of accessibility applied to the Tel Aviv metropolitan area. *The Annals of Regional Science*, 47(3): 499–515.

Cebollada, À. (2008). Mobility and labour market exclusion in the Barcelona Metropolitan Region. *Journal of Transport Geography*, 17(3): 226–233.

Daniels, N. (2008). *Just Health : meeting health needs fairly*. Cambridge, Cambridge University Press.

Dryzek, J.S. (1990). *Discursive Democracy: politics, policy, and political science*. Cambridge, Cambridge University Press.

Fischer, F. and J. Forester (eds) (1993). *The Argumentative Turn in Policy and Planning*. Durham, Duke University Press.

Gutmann, A. (1980). *Liberal Equality*. CUP Archive.

Healey, P. (1995). Discourses of integration: making frameworks for democratic urban planning. In: P. Healey (ed.), *Managing Cities: the new urban context*. Chichester/New York, John Wiley and Sons, pp. 251–272.

Hess, D.B. (2005). Access to employment for adults in poverty in the Buffalo–Niagara region. *Urban Studies*, 42(7): 1177–1200.

Hu, L. and G. Giuliano (2014). Poverty concentration, job access, and employment outcomes. *Journal of Urban Affairs*, first published online.

Kawabata, M. (2009). Spatiotemporal dimensions of modal accessibility disparity in Boston and San Francisco. *Environment and Planning A*, 41(1): 183–198.

Kawabata, M. and Q. Shen (2006). Job accessibility as an indicator of auto-oriented urban structure: a comparison of Boston and Los Angeles with Tokyo. *Environment and Planning B: Planning and Design*, 33(1): 115–130.

Kolm, S.-C. (1996). *Modern Theories of Justice*. Cambridge, MA, MIT Press.

Kwok, R.C.W. and A.G.O. Yeh (2004). The use of modal accessibility gap as an indicator for sustainable transport development. *Environment and Planning A*, 36(5): 921–936.

Lucas, K., J. Bates *et al.* (2016). Modelling the relationship between travel behaviours and social disadvantage. *Transportation Research Part A: Policy and Practice* 85: 157–173.

Martens, K. (2006). Basing transport planning on principles of social justice. *Berkeley Planning Journal*, 19: 1–17.

Martens, K. (2016). Why accessibility measurement is not merely an option, but an absolute necessity. In: C. Silva, L. Bertolini and N. Pinto. (eds) *Designing accessibility instruments: lessons on their usability for integrated land use and transport planning practices*. New York/Oxford, Routledge.

Martens, K. and A. Golub (2012). A justice-theoretic exploration of accessibility measures. In: K.T. Geurs, K.J. Krizek and A. Reggiani (eds), *Accessibility Analysis and Transport Planning: challenges for Europe and North America*. Cheltenham, Edward Elgar.

Mokhtarian, P.L. and C. Chen (2004). TTB or not TTB, that is the question: a review and analysis of the empirical literature on travel time (and money) budgets. *Transportation Research Part A: Policy and Practice*, 38(9-10): 643–675.

Nussbaum, M.C. (2000). *Women and Human Development: the capabilities approach*. Cambridge, Cambridge University Press.

Nussbaum, M.C. (2003). Capabilities as fundamental entitlements: Sen and social justice. *Feminist Economics*, 9(2-3): 33–59.

Rawls, J. (2003 [2001]). *Justice as Fairness: a restatement*. Cambridge, MA/London, The Belknap Press of Harvard University Press.

Roemer, J.E. (2002). Egalitarianism against the veil of ignorance. *The Journal of Philosophy*: 167–184.

Samsura, A. and E. van der Krabben (2011). Funding transport infrastructure development through value capturing: a game theoretical analysis. In: J.A.E.E. Van Nunen, P. Huijbregts and P. Rietveld (eds), *Transitions Towards Sustainable Mobility: new solutions and approaches for sustainable transport systems.* Springer, pp. 59–80.

Scanlon, T.M. (2000). *What We Owe to Each Other*. Cambridge, MA, Harvard University Press.

Sen, A. (1988). Freedom of choice: concept and content. *European Economic Review*, 32(2): 269–294.

Sen, A. (1990). Development as capability expansion. In: K. Griffin and J. Knight (eds), *Human Development and the International Development Strategy for the 1990s*. London, Macmillan, pp. 41–58.

Sen, A. (2002). Open and closed impartiality. *The Journal of Philosophy*: 445-469.

Sen, A. (2006). What do we want from a theory of justice? *The Journal of Philosophy*, 103(5): 215–238.

Sen, A. (2011). *Development as freedom*. New York, Anchor Books.

Seo, S.-E., N. Ohmori and N. Harata (2013). Effects of household structure and accessibility on travel. *Transportation*, 40(4): 847–865.

Shen, Q. (1998). Location characteristics of inner-city neighborhoods and employment accessibility of low-wage workers. *Environment and Planning B: Planning and Design*, 25(3): 345–365.

Smith, A. (2010 [1759]). *The Theory of Moral Sentiments*. Harmondsworth, Penguin.

van Wee, B., P. Rietveld and H. Meurs (2006). Is average daily travel time expenditure constant? In search of explanations for an increase in average travel time. *Journal of Transport Geography*, 14(2): 109–122.

Walzer, M. (1983). *Spheres of justice: a defense of pluralism and equality*, Basic Books.

Weis, C. (2012). Activity oriented modelling of short- and long-term dynamics of travel behaviour. Unpublished dissertation, Eidgenössische Technische Hochschule ETH Zürich, Nr. 20346.

Weis, C. and K.W. Axhausen (2012). Assessing changes in travel behavior induced by modified travel times: a stated adaptation survey and modeling approach. *disP-The Planning Review*, 48(3): 40–53.

Part III

A New Approach to Transportation Planning

8 Transportation Planning Based on Principles of Justice

Introduction

The aim of this chapter is to present the rules of transportation planning based on principles of justice. These rules are to give guidance to transportation planners and others on how to conduct proper transportation planning (see Chapter 2). They are to provide directions to the technical, yet inevitably political, process of preparing decisions regarding interventions in the transportation system.

Obviously the rules will be firmly rooted in the philosophical explorations presented in the previous chapters. In order to move from these explorations to practical rules for transportation planning, I will devote most of this chapter to an exposition of the underlying rationale of the rules. I will start with a discussion of the measurement of accessibility, as this is at the heart of transportation planning based on principles of justice. Since accessibility is not only shaped by the transportation system, but also by land use patterns and service delivery policies (see Chapters 1 and 4), I will continue by presenting an approach that will delineate the role of transportation planning in providing and guaranteeing a sufficient level of accessibility. I will then outline an approach to identifying population groups that experience an insufficient level of accessibility caused, at least in part, by a poorly functioning transportation system. The goal of transportation planning is to address the plight of these population groups.

Since not all problems can be solved at once, I will then turn to another key challenge of any approach to transportation planning: the setting of priorities. For this purpose, I develop an approach to assessing the fairness of transport-land use systems and identifying the population groups that suffer most from the unfairness embedded in those systems. This approach makes it possible to single out the population groups that are particularly affected by a sub-standard level of accessibility. I then turn to the last three steps of transportation planning based on principles of justice: the identification of the causes of sub-standard levels of accessibility, the generation of solutions to address these accessibility problems, and the assessment of the costs and benefits of these solutions.

I will end the chapter with an overview of the rules of transportation planning based on principles of justice. These rules or guidelines are not only useful for practitioners who prepare the day-to-day decisions regarding interventions in the transportation system. They are also intended as a source of inspiration for non-governmental organizations and citizen groups that seek to influence the process and outcomes of current practices of transportation planning. For them, the rules can provide a benchmark for their criticism and suggestions to improve the practice of transportation planning.

A final note is in order before commencing with the explorations. The rules of transportation planning based on principles of justice presented in this chapter only relate to the *physical* design of the transportation system—the set of infrastructures, facilities and services that enable movement and thus provide persons with accessibility and the possibility of participating in out-of-home activities. They do not address the *financial* design of the transportation system, i.e. the design of the *pricing* of transportation infrastructures, facilities and services. The latter topic can be administered separately from the physical design of the transportation system and thus deserves a separate treatment. I will reserve that effort for the last chapter of this book.

Measuring accessibility

The measurement of accessibility is clearly not a simple matter. In Chapter 1 accessibility was defined as the potential of opportunities for interaction. In line with this definition, the level of accessibility experienced by a person is determined by the spatial distribution of activities, by the available transportation systems, and by a person's ability to overcome spatial separation. That ability is, in turn, shaped by the resources available to a person, in terms of time, money, vehicle ownership, knowledge of the transportation systems, knowledge of the spatial pattern of activities, physical and cognitive capabilities, ability to handle discomfort, concerns about personal safety, and so on. Since persons will differ widely in terms of these resources and abilities, they will also differ widely in the accessibility level they experience. Furthermore, not all activities will be relevant to every person. Different persons will have different skills and preferences and thus experience different levels of potential for interaction, as different activities are relevant to them (Grengs 2015). Finally, the accessibility levels experienced by a person will vary over time. This is so because the level of service provided by transportation systems typically varies by time of the day and day of the week: roads are congested during rush hours, while public transport services often do not run at night. Accessibility will also vary over time because of temporal availability of activities, as reflected in opening hours of shops and other services (Neutens *et al.* 2014). Furthermore, differences over time may also occur because persons have different resources available at different moments in time, for instance because they do not have continuous access to a vehicle. Clearly, then, from the perspective of the person, accessibility has multiple dimensions and is likely to show substantial variation over time.

The question is whether the measurement of accessibility, as a prerequisite for the assessment of the fairness of a transportation system, should account for this enormous variation. Before answering that question, let me give a number of observations.

First, it may be clear from the description above that there is not one single and best way to measure accessibility. Since accessibility varies by purpose and changes over time and in accordance with circumstances, it would be a mistake to search for a measure that 'most accurately' captures accessibility as experienced by persons. There can be no such measure. The only way forward here is to explicitly acknowledge the multi-dimensional nature of accessibility by measuring it in multiple ways, for instance by measuring accessibility to jobs, services and social contacts, or assessing accessibility during peak, off-peak and evening hours. These measurements should not be perceived as the ingredients for an overarching indicator of accessibility, but rather as a rich source of information that can be drawn upon in the process of decision-making (see below).

Second, it should be understood that the suitability of an accessibility measure cannot be based on its ability to predict actual travel behavior, whether in terms of the quantity or quality of activity participation, the location of selected activities, mode choice, or any other characteristic. It would be fundamentally flawed to search for such a measure, as the relationship between accessibility and activity participation is loose at best, as was argued in the previous chapter. Searching for a measure with strong predictive power will therefore always violate the inevitable variety in patterns of activity participation. Such an approach might be useful, at best, at the lower end of the accessibility spectrum, where a stronger relationship between accessibility and activity participation may be expected. Yet even in this part of the accessibility spectrum, it may be a mistake to search for an accessibility measure that strongly correlates with the observed level of activity participation, given the fact that rich patterns of activity participation may still occur under low levels of accessibility. If anything, the suitability of an accessibility measure should instead be assessed based on its ability to capture the *range* of observed levels of activity participation, as this range reflects the states that persons may achieve. This range is of crucial importance because, as mentioned before, persons have a constitutive interest in protecting their opportunity range. Accessibility measures that reflect the opportunities a person could achieve, and can capture the richest patterns of activity participation, are thus to be preferred. Indeed, precisely because such an accessibility measure captures the range of possibilities, it will be particularly suited to assist in determining accessibility sufficiency thresholds.

Third, the measurement of accessibility should take into account the differences between persons, as these differences are directly shaping disparities in accessibility levels. Yet it is not necessary to take into account the entire variety in abilities and circumstances between persons. This is so because accounting for all the particularities of persons would ignore their fundamental interest in the range of states they can achieve. For instance, accounting for a person's possibilities of engaging in leisure activities, given her current job location, misunderstands the person's interest in the possibilities (or necessity) of changing her plans over time. Likewise, it would be a mistake to assess a person's accessibility to personal networks based on the particular locations of friends and family members, because these locations as well as the composition of the network may change over time. The measurement of accessibility should address the differences between persons, but primarily those differences which are of a structural character and reflect the situation of a substantial part of the population. Thus accessibility measurement should account for the set of transportation systems a person can use, as differences in access to transportation modes are a pervasive characteristic of any society and these differences have a profound impact on experienced accessibility levels. Likewise, accessibility measurement should account for the presence of children or other dependents in a household, as this presence shapes the accessibility of a substantial share of the population on a structural basis. Depending on the circumstances, concerns for personal safety when using transportation systems may also be a structural feature in a society, and may, for instance, shape the accessibility experienced by women or elderly residents in evening hours and during the night. Clearly, accessibility patterns may be shaped by other systematic features of a society. The assessment of the fairness of accessibility patterns should at least take into account the most prominent of these features, in terms of the size of the population affected and the impacts on accessibility levels (compare Daniels' approach to the socio-economic determinants of health; Daniels 1985; Daniels 2008).

Fourth, and supporting the conclusion of the previous point, the measurement of accessibility should stay within moral limits. As Rawls has powerfully argued, public policy should be based on information that is publicly available to all. The measurement of accessibility that takes into account the entire variety in persons' abilities and circumstances would violate this condition by requiring information that is not publicly available to all, thereby potentially infringing on the integrity of the person and jeopardizing persons' liberties and freedoms (Rawls 1971). This may apply, for instance, to 'rich' accessibility measures, such as measures based on Hägerstrand's powerful theory of time-geography (Hägerstrand 1970). Following Rawls' argument, it is not desirable, for instance, to account for persons' preferences for particular sorts of sports in assessing their accessibility to leisure activities, or to account for the residential location of family members and friends in assessing persons' accessibility to social contacts. The assessment of accessibility will have to be based on general proxies. However, this does not have to hinder the identification of the groups in society most likely to experience accessibility levels below the democratically stipulated accessibility threshold.

Fifth, it should be taken into account that transportation planning based on principles of justice requires, first and foremost, the identification of population groups experiencing an accessibility shortage (compare Rawls' worst-off representative man). For this purpose, it will not be necessary to measure in any 'exact' way the accessibility levels of each person. Rather, it will be satisfactory to gain an understanding of the general patterns of accessibility. If these general patterns, even if based on relatively simple ways to measure accessibility, enable the identification of the population groups at the bottom of the accessibility spectrum, this may well be sufficient for purposes of policy making. This will certainly hold if the results of this way of measuring accessibility can gain the support of the real-life agents engaged in democratic deliberation about accessibility.

The above arguments lead to the following conclusions. First, the assessment of accessibility patterns should be based on multiple accessibility measures. Second, it should take into account the differences between persons, although the assessment can suffice with addressing the systemic elements of these differences. Third, the arguments suggest that relatively simple measures of accessibility may well be adequate to identify population groups that are entitled to accessibility improvements. The use of such simple accessibility measures also has obvious advantages in terms of the interpretability and communicability of the results of the analyses (see e.g. Geurs and van Wee 2004), which is of special importance given the role of democratic deliberation in the establishment of a sufficiency threshold of accessibility.

Taken together, these arguments suggest that accessibility measurement must always capture a 'general' notion of accessibility and abstract from the variety in abilities and circumstances of persons. Such a 'general' measurement of accessibility can only be an indication of the actual level of accessibility experienced by any particular person. The measurement can therefore only provide an indication of the extent to which a person may experience accessibility-related problems in engaging in a sufficient level of out-of-home activities. Clearly, the lower the general level of accessibility experienced by a person, the higher the chances that the person will experience a low personal level of accessibility, the higher the chances that the person will not be able to participate in a reasonable set of activities, and the higher the chances of participation poverty, now or in the future. The measurement of accessibility is thus a measurement of the risk of participation poverty, i.e. of the chance that a person will experience a lack of activity participation due to problems in accessibility.

This formulation still leaves open exactly how accessibility should be measured. It may be clear from the above that there is no best way to measure accessibility. This remains true, even though the purposes of the accessibility measurement are well specified within the context of transportation planning based on principles of justice. In the next chapter, I will apply a relatively simple set of accessibility measures to assess the fairness of the transportation system in the Amsterdam region in the Netherlands. Clearly, a range of measures may be used and it will require a process of trial and error before a standard approach can emerge—if it ever does. Indeed, different circumstances may well require a different set of accessibility measures.

Measuring potential mobility

The argument developed throughout this book underscores that transportation planning should be concerned with the contribution of the transportation system, broadly conceived, to accessibility. The measurement of accessibility should thus be at the heart of transportation planning based on principles of justice. Yet accessibility is not only shaped by transportation systems, but as much by land use patterns. The measurement of accessibility thus provides no direct information on the contribution of the transportation system to accessibility. More precisely, the measurement of accessibility leaves underdetermined the extent to which respectively the transportation system and land use patterns contribute to a particular level of accessibility. Low accessibility levels may well be the result of poorly functioning transportation systems, a low density of desirable destinations, or both.

The way forward is not to replace the measurement of accessibility. The arguments provided throughout the book, notably in Chapters 4 and 7, underscore that accessibility should be the focal variable of transportation planning based on principles of justice. In order to delineate the contribution of the transportation system to accessibility it is necessary to complement accessibility measurement with an indicator that only addresses the contribution of the transport component to accessibility.

For this purpose, I turn to the assessment of the quality of transportation systems, i.e. to the assessment of the system's contribution to the potential mobility of persons. As argued in Chapter 2, such an indicator should be able to capture both the speed on the transport network and the network structure, as they jointly determine a person's potential mobility. I have developed such an indicator in previous work (Martens 2007; for an interesting parallel see Gutierrez, Monzon *et al.* 1998). This indicator can be best described as the Potential Mobility Index (PMI). For one origin–destination pair, the PMI is defined as the quotient of the aerial or Euclidean distance ('as the crow flies') and the travel time on the transport network between that origin and that destination. A PMI score can be calculated for each origin *i* by taking the average of the PMI values for all relevant destinations for that origin. In equation:

$$PMI(i) = \frac{1}{n} \cdot \sum_{i=1}^{n} \frac{d(i, j...n)}{T(i, j...n)}$$

where

PMI(i)	=	average aerial speed for zone *i*
d(i, j...n)	=	aerial distance between zone *i* and zone *j*
T(i, j...n)	=	travel time on the transport network between zone *i* and zone *j*.

Provided data is available, the measure can be applied to zones of any spatial scale, ranging from neighborhoods to transport activity zones and from census tracts to individual buildings.

The main advantage of the PMI measure is that it captures the impact of both the structure of the transport network and the speed on the links of the network. The measure has significant advantages over the widely used level-of-service criterion. A simple example can explain this. In the case where an area does not have its own entrance point to a highway, but is linked to the highway through a lengthy secondary road with low traffic volumes, the average speed on the transport network may well be relatively high. If the level-of-service index is used as an assessment criterion, travelers may not experience any 'transport problem' on origin–destinations pairs that include this secondary link. However, since drivers will have to make a detour to reach the highway, the actual potential mobility level of this area may well be relatively low. The PMI measure offers a more appropriate assessment of the quality of the transport network provided to such an area, as it links travel time to the lowest possible distance between two points in space (i.e. the straight line, aerial or Euclidean distance). Network inefficiencies are thus revealed by the PMI measure. This makes the measure particularly suited to determining the contribution of the transportation system to accessibility, as I will show below.

Delineating the role of transportation planning

As discussed, the measure of potential mobility is not intended to replace the measurement of accessibility, but rather to complement it. The goal here is not to develop some sort of multi-criteria analysis, but to define a framework that can help identify the role of transportation planning in addressing accessibility shortages and promoting a fair transportation system. This framework is meant to serve as a key step in transportation planning based on principles of justice.

In the framework, accessibility and potential mobility are juxtaposed on a set of axes (Figure 8.1). The horizontal axis represents potential mobility (measured in terms of PMI-scores), the vertical axis represents accessibility (which may be measured in various ways). Both axes represent a continuum from a low to a high level and create a coordinate system in which population groups can be positioned. The axes intersect in the middle, i.e. at the average level of potential mobility and at the average level of accessibility. This simple coordinate system enables the placement of population groups vis-à-vis both axes, based on the measurement of a group's potential mobility and accessibility. It also enables the introduction of a sufficiency threshold of accessibility, which would most likely be positioned anywhere below the origin of the coordinate system by the real-life agents involved in the process of setting the sufficiency standard.

The framework helps first of all to establish the role of transportation planning. That role is confined to the left-hand side of the quadrant system. This part of the quadrant system is 'populated' by population groups with a below-average level of potential mobility, i.e. by groups that are relatively poorly served by the transportation system. Yet not all

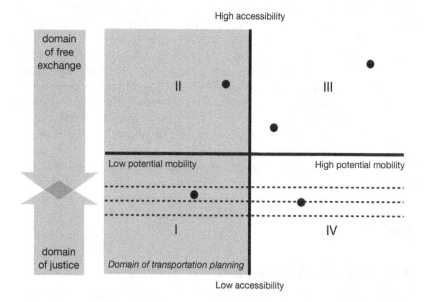

Figure 8.1 The coordinate system of potential mobility (horizontal axis) and accessibility (vertical axis). The coordinate systems allow the positioning of population groups (depicted as dots in the diagram) based on their observed levels of potential mobility and accessibility. The dashed lines represent possible accessibility sufficiency thresholds.

these groups are entitled to improvements in the transportation system. The domain of justice is only reserved for the population groups with an insufficient level of accessibility. As already mentioned, the sufficiency threshold is likely to be positioned somewhere below the horizontal axis (although under particularly unfavorable conditions real-life agents may well agree that accessibility levels above the average are also insufficient). This implies that the domain of justice also lies in the lower part of the coordinate system, whereas the domain of free exchange is positioned in the upper part of the diagram. This further delineates the role of transportation planning based on principles of justice: that role is not merely confined to the area to the left of the vertical axis, but to the population groups that are positioned in the bottom-left part of the coordinate system. These population groups experience a sub-standard level of accessibility that is caused, at least to a large extent, by a poorly functioning transportation system. Transportation planning based on principles of justice should, first and foremost, address the plight of these population groups.

Assessing the fairness of transportation systems

The approach to transportation planning described so far results in the identification of population groups experiencing insufficient levels of accessibility. These population groups fall under the regime of the domain of justice and thus are entitled, at least in principle, to improvements in accessibility. Clearly, in any real-world situation, it will not be possible to correct the injustices thus revealed in one big move, if only because of resource restrictions. It will thus be necessary to set priorities. I will now turn to an approach for setting these priorities and singling out population groups that should be served first. This approach requires the development of an index that can represent the level of fairness of a transportation system.

The proposed approach draws its inspiration from the measurement of fairness in the domain of income. In this domain, various approaches have been developed, including well-known indicators such as the Lorenz-curve and the Gini-coefficient. The economic approach that comes closest to the argumentation developed in this book is concerned with the identification and measurement of income poverty (see e.g. Ravallion 1992; Ravallion 1994). Like the approach developed here for the domain of transportation, the measurement of income poverty relies heavily on the identification of a sufficiency threshold, i.e. a level of income below which persons are considered to be poor. Based on such a sufficiency threshold, or income poverty line, the poor can be identified from among the total population and it becomes possible to assess the extent of income poverty in a community. In analytical terms, the income poverty line is identical to the accessibility sufficiency threshold presented in the previous chapter. The development of an index for setting priorities in the domain of transportation can thus benefit from the extensive body of literature on measuring income poverty. In fact, drawing on this body of literature, it is possible to define the notion of accessibility poverty and to develop an accessibility poverty index, as I have shown in earlier work with colleagues (Martens and Bastiaanssen 2015; Rofe, Benenson *et al.* 2015).

But an important observation is in place here. The measurement of income poverty is often seen as only one component of the assessment of fairness in the domain of income. This is so because considerations of fairness also tend to underscore the importance of the distribution of income. Indeed, a society without any poor persons but with a highly skewed income distribution, with most income and wealth concentrated in the hands of a relatively small share of the population, is often considered to be at odds with principles of fairness. This would most likely be the case if the Rawlsian perspective is adopted and also if the Dworkian line of reasoning regarding a progressive income taxation scheme is accepted. The mere existence of powerful theories of justice arguing that fairness in the domain of income and wealth requires more than the avoidance of income poverty, underscores that the measurement of income poverty is just that: an assessment of income poverty across a population. Without further justification it cannot be a comprehensive assessment of fairness in the domain of income.

The situation is quite different for the domain of transportation. Here, the measurement of accessibility poverty is *synonymous* with the measurement of fairness. This is so for at least three reasons. First and foremost, the extensive analysis presented in previous chapters suggests that prudent persons are principally interested in guaranteeing a sufficient level of accessibility and not in the actual distribution of accessibility over members of society. Second, disparities in accessibility are inevitable due to the structuring effect of space, underscoring that equality cannot serve as the idealized benchmark of an actual distribution, as is often the case in the domain of income. Third, differences in accessibility levels are unlikely to be as large as disparities in the domain of income, because time, as a key component of any conceptualization of accessibility, is a limited resource for everybody. In other words, the range of accessibility levels observed across a population will be relatively limited in scope. This observation, in turn, supports the claim that prudent persons will hardly be concerned about the distributive pattern of accessibility. Taken together, these arguments imply that the measurement of what could be called accessibility poverty is in fact the measurement of the fairness of a transportation system. In what follows, I will therefore develop an index of fairness in the domain of transportation.

Before presenting this index, let me return to the measurement of income poverty, as it has provided the basis for developing a practical index of justice in transportation. As mentioned above, the measurement of income poverty starts from the delineation of an income poverty line or sufficiency threshold. Several measures or indices have been developed to capture the extent of income poverty among a population and to compare poverty levels across societies (Foster, Greer *et al.* 1984; Ravallion 1992; Sen 1992). Probably the most powerful of these indices has been proposed by Foster, Greer and Thorbecke (1984). They have developed a poverty measure that not only captures the number of people below the poverty line, but also takes into account the distribution of income among the poor. The measure gives a weight to each poor person or group based on the size of the income shortfall, i.e. based on the difference between a person's income and the income poverty line. The lower a poor person's income, the larger his income shortfall and the larger his weight in the overall measurement of poverty. The measure thus generates an index of the *severity* of income poverty, taking into account both the number of persons with an income below the poverty line and the size of the income shortfall experienced by these persons. While different weights can be applied, I will confine myself to the so-called P_2 measure, since it has the clearest structure of all. The P_2 measure takes the weight of a person's or group's income shortfall to be the income shortfall itself. More precisely, with q number of groups with incomes no greater than the poverty line z in a total population of N persons, n_i representing the number of persons in the i-th group, and y_i representing the income of the i-th group, the P_2 measure is expressed as:

$$P_2 = \frac{1}{N} \sum_{i=1}^{q} n_i \cdot \left(\frac{z - y_i}{z} \right)^2$$

The value of P_2 ranges from 0 to 1, with a score of 0 indicating the case of an entire population with a sufficient income level, and a score of 1 the case of an entire population suffering from an insufficient income level. In other words, the larger the P_2 score, the greater the severity of income poverty.

The class of poverty measures developed by Foster and colleagues has a number of attractive properties. Most important, the measures are totally decomposable and subgroup consistent. This means that the contribution of each population group to overall poverty can be expressed as a percentage, with the contributions of all subgroups adding up to exactly hundred percent. By eliminating poverty in one subgroup, the overall poverty level will decrease by exactly that subgroup's rate (Foster, Greer *et al.* 1984; Ravallion 1992; Foster and Sen 2008). The P_2 measure thus makes it possible to rank subgroups by their contribution to overall income poverty. This, in turn, enables the setting of priorities. Clearly, groups with a large contribution to overall poverty are particularly deserving of mitigating policies, ceteris paribus.

In what follows, I will translate the P_2 measure to accessibility. As mentioned before, the measurement of accessibility poverty is identical with the measurement of the extent of fairness of a transport-land use system. In other words, the severity of accessibility poverty is identical with the extent of the unfairness of a transportation system. I have therefore termed the accessibility equivalent of the P_2 measure the Accessibility Fairness Index (AFI). Like the P_2 measure, this index requires the delineation of a sufficiency threshold and the distinguishing of population groups. Both components have been discussed elaborately before. In line with Foster, Greer *et al.* (1984) it is then possible to define the Accessibility Fairness Index for region r (AFI$_r$) as:

$$AFI_r = \frac{1}{N}\sum_{i=1}^{q} n_i \cdot \left(\frac{z-y_i}{z}\right)^2$$

where N represents the total population in region r; q the number of groups in region r experiencing accessibility levels below the sufficiency threshold z; n_i the size of the i-th group in number of persons; and y_i the accessibility level experienced by the i-th group below the sufficiency threshold z. The score on the AFI$_r$ denotes the *severity of the accessibility deficiency* in a region.

The score of a region on the AFI$_r$ measure is dependent on three components: the position of the accessibility sufficiency threshold; the share of the population that falls below the sufficiency threshold; and the exact level of accessibility experienced by persons below the threshold. Figure 8.2 depicts the three components of the assessment. The vertical axes in the figure depict a continuum of accessibility levels experienced by different persons and groups of a population in a region (or any other study area) and each includes an accessibility sufficiency threshold.

Figure 8.2a represents the so-called *prevalence* of accessibility shortfalls, i.e. the number of persons below the sufficiency threshold. In the figure, groups G_1 and G_2 experience an identical level of accessibility. Both are positioned below the accessibility sufficiency threshold, but the number of persons belonging to group G_2 is larger than the number belonging to group G_1, as depicted by the size of the circles. All else being equal, a study area with a larger group of persons below the sufficiency threshold provides a less fair transportation system to the area's residents. The size of group G_3 does not directly influence the prevalence of accessibility shortfalls, but it does influence the severity of accessibility deficiency: the larger the share of the total population that is located above the sufficiency threshold, the lower the accessibility deficiency and the fairer a transport-land use system.

Figure 8.2b represents the *intensity* or depth of accessibility shortfalls: person P_2 is farther removed from the accessibility sufficiency threshold than person P_1 and thus faces a more intense accessibility shortfall than person P_1. Person P_3 has an accessibility level above the threshold and thus faces no accessibility shortfall at all. Her situation should therefore not be taken into account in the assessment of the fairness of a transport-land use system, except indirectly as noted above.

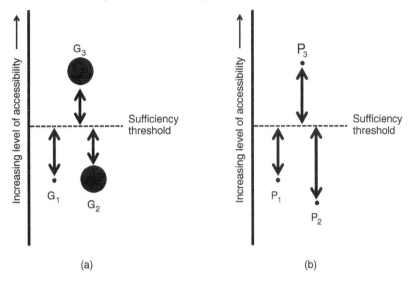

(a)   (b)

Figure 8.2 Visual representation of (a) the prevalence of accessibility shortfalls; and (b) the intensity of accessibility shortfalls. Taken together, they determine the severity of the accessibility deficiency in a study area.

The AFI_r measure captures both the prevalence and the intensity of accessibility shortfalls across a population. Taken together, the index thus captures the *severity* of the accessibility deficiency in a community (cf. Ravallion 1992). In other words, the measure generates an overall score of the fairness of the transport-land use system in a city or region, enabling the comparison of cities or regions vis-à-vis each other (although it will not be a simple matter, as different regions may (have to) set different sufficiency thresholds and accessibility will have to be measured in multiple ways).

For my purposes, it is more important that the AFI_r measure makes it possible to determine the contribution of each population group to the overall level of accessibility deficiency. By doing so, the measure generates information that can directly feed the process of priority setting, as it makes it possible to single out groups that are particularly affected by the accessibility deficiency in a region or city. The results of the measurement can only *feed* the process of decision-making, if only because the assessment of the fairness of a transport-land use system requires the use of multiple accessibility measures, as I have argued above. It is therefore not a simple and straightforward matter to generate a 'priority list'. Indeed, since any measurement of accessibility is always, in an important sense, a measurement of a *general* level of accessibility, it can only deliver an understanding of a person's risk of failing to achieve a sufficient level of activity participation. The results of the assessment of the fairness of transport-land use systems should therefore always be interpreted by decision-makers in consultation, broadly conceived, with the affected populations.

This does not imply that the information generated by the assessment of the fairness of a transport-land use system can be interpreted in a loose way by the parties involved in the decision-making process. Clearly, the larger the contribution of a population group to the accessibility deficiency in a region, the more a group is entitled to improvements in accessibility, all else being equal. The 'all else equal' caveat is important here, not only because of the reasons given above. It is also important, because a group's entitlement to accessibility improvements financed by an accessibility insurance scheme is in part dependent on the number of persons served by these improvements, as well as the costs of these improvements, as was concluded in Chapter 6. Since a population group may show a high contribution due to an extremely low level of accessibility rather than due to the size of the group, improvements in the accessibility level of such a group may well be inhibitively expensive. In such a case, another 'insurance scheme' (that is, another type of policy intervention) may be warranted instead of an accessibility improvement. This brings me to the last three steps of transportation planning based on principles of justice: the identification of the causes of accessibility shortfalls, the generation of solutions to address these shortfalls, and the assessment of the costs and benefits of these solutions. I will take up these steps in the next sections.

Identifying the causes of accessibility shortfalls

The rules of transportation planning presented so far result in a particular identification of 'the' transport problem, namely the lack of accessibility among particular population groups. Indeed, by following the rules described so far, it is possible to identify and prioritize population groups in terms of their contribution to the accessibility deficiency in a region, even though it is by no means a matter of simply applying the rules. The approach explicitly requires real-life agents to engage in democratic deliberation and use situational judgment in virtually every step of the approach. Yet even if the rules leave substantial discretion on the side of the agents, they also provide a clear direction on how to conduct proper transportation planning.

Ideally, the next step of the transportation planning process consists of the identification of the causes of the accessibility shortfalls experienced by the population groups most entitled to accessibility improvements. This is clearly not a simple matter. In contrast to traditional transportation planning, there is no direct and clear connection between the identification of 'the' transport problem and its causes. In traditional transportation planning, the identification of congested links is largely identical to the identification of the first-order cause of the problem: congestion is caused by an imbalance between supply and demand on a particular link. This excess demand may be the result of small increases in travel between a wide set of origin–destinations pairs or because of a major rise in travel between only a few areas; it may be the result of a growth in commuter flows or in travel for leisure purposes. Yet from the perspective of traditional transportation planning, these underlying causes are typically of little concern, as the first-order cause provides a sufficient basis for generating solutions.

The situation is entirely different for transportation planning based on principles of justice. Here, the identification of 'the' transport problem provides hardly any insight into the causes of the problem. This is so for multiple reasons. First, the process of transportation planning leads to the identification of population groups rather than particular parts of the transportation system. Second, the identification of population groups with insufficient accessibility is based on a composite index, which integrates the size of the accessibility shortfall with the size of the affected population. Population groups may thus show an identical contribution to overall accessibility deficiency for quite different reasons and be singled out for accessibility improvements for different reasons. Third, accessibility shortfalls may be the result of a wide diversity of causes. For instance, an area may experience a sub-standard level of accessibility because it lacks a connection with a major employment center in the region or because the transportation system is generally of sub-standard quality. Both causes may severely reduce the accessibility to employment opportunities. Yet in the former case the introduction of one dedicated transportation service to the major employment center may well eliminate accessibility shortfalls, while in the latter case a wider range of interventions may be needed. Fourth, since transportation planning based on principles of justice requires multiple ways of measuring accessibility, the causes of accessibility shortfalls may well vary between various ways of measuring accessibility. For instance, if accessibility is measured for a set of travel time thresholds (e.g. 15, 30 and 45 minutes), it is likely that the causes for observed accessibility shortfall patterns may well differ between these travel time thresholds. If the costs of using transportation services is taken into account in measuring accessibility, a further dimension will be added, because accessibility shortfalls may not only be the result of a poorly functioning transportation system, but also of an inhibitively expensive, but otherwise perhaps excellent, transportation system. Finally, and related, the identification of accessibility shortfalls inevitably has to be based on an assessment of a 'general' level of accessibility, as was argued at the beginning of this chapter. That implies that the identification of population groups entitled to accessibility improvements provides only partial insight into the particular accessibility problems experienced by persons belonging to these groups. Indeed, different persons belonging to the same group may well experience a lack of accessibility to quite distinct activities. For instance, some persons may experience poor accessibility to employment, while others are particularly affected by poor accessibility to health care services. Such fine-grained knowledge can inform subsequent policy making, as sufficient accessibility can never be restored in one sweeping move, but can only be achieved through a series of consistent interventions implemented over a range of years.

The above analysis suggests that the identification of the causes for accessibility shortfalls is not only a complex matter, it is also a crucial prerequisite for the development of solutions to address these shortfalls. Furthermore, the discussion underscores that the exploration of the causes for sub-standard accessibility levels has to be a combination of top-down and bottom-up analyses. A top-down, technical, approach may be necessary to detect the 'weak' components of the transportation system, such as missing transportation links, low travel speeds, long transfer times, low frequencies, and so on. This assessment will clearly require systematic analyses based on extensive data on the transport and land use system. This top-down, technical, approach to accessibility assessment should be complemented and enriched by a bottom-up approach to gain a deeper understanding of the causes for the accessibility shortfalls experienced by different population groups. If done through a proper process of local consultation, such a bottom-up approach may ensure that the generation of solutions will be based on a well-informed understanding of the most pressing accessibility concerns of the affected population groups.

Generating solutions to reduce accessibility shortfalls

Ideally, the next step of the transportation planning process consists of generating possible interventions to address the accessibility shortfalls experienced by the population groups most entitled to accessibility improvements. Like the identification of the causes of accessibility shortfalls, this is clearly not a simple matter. In contrast to traditional transportation planning, there is no straightforward connection between the identification of causes for the transport problem and possible interventions. In traditional transportation planning, the identification of congested links already points at possible solutions: enhancement of capacity on the transport link concerned. Clearly, there are more possibilities to eliminate or reduce congestion on particular links, such as the addition of a new link in the network, the improvement of an alternative transportation service, or through travel demand management measures. But even in these cases the (spatial) relationship between the transport problem, its causes and the solutions remains relatively strong. The identification of possible solutions can thus directly build on the identification of the (causes of the) transport problem.

The situation is quite different in the case of transportation planning based on principles of justice. For one, the analysis of the causes for accessibility shortfalls may well have led to the identification of a range of problems in the transportation system. Furthermore, population groups experiencing accessibility shortfalls may be located in quite different parts of a city or a region. These population groups may also lack accessibility to a variety of key destinations, which in turn may be dispersed over space. And even if accessibility shortfalls are spatially concentrated, they may be addressed through a variety of interventions, ranging from frequency increases of existing public transport services to subsidies on car purchases and maintenance, from the introduction of new public transport services to taxi vouchers at reduced prices, and from demand-responsive transport services to the provision of bicycle facilities in combination with bicycle training programs (for the latter, see van der Kloof, Bastiaanssen *et al.* 2014). Accessibility shortfalls could also be addressed through interventions in land use patterns and urban service delivery. While, strictly speaking, the latter type of measures fall outside the scope of transportation planning, it underscores that transportation planning cannot take place in a vacuum and that the process of generating solutions has to take a broad approach. It is therefore by no means clear at the outset of the search for solutions which measures would most effectively and efficiently address the concerns of the population groups experiencing accessibility shortfalls.

Generating solutions for accessibility shortfalls is thus not a simple matter. Like the identification of the causes of accessibility shortfalls, the generation of solutions cannot be a merely technical, top-down, exercise, but should be complemented with participatory, bottom-up, knowledge and expertise. The population groups that have been identified as experiencing sub-standard levels of accessibility may be expected to bring crucial knowledge to the table about the ways in which their particular accessibility problems can be addressed. This may well lead to the identification of a broad range of possible solutions, in part because the accessibility concerns of a population group may not be homogenous in nature.

This bottom-up approach may seem to suggest that addressing accessibility deficiencies is a matter of small-scale, tailor-made, measures to address specific accessibility needs, perhaps along the lines of solutions generated within the context of accessibility planning in the UK. Yet it should be remembered that prudent persons are interested in protecting the range of options they can achieve, that is, in their freedom. Small-scale, tailor-made, solutions often only address very specific accessibility needs at a particular time, in a particular place, among a particular group. In order to protect persons' interest in the range of possibilities for activity participation, the improvements in the transportation system should offer as much flexibility to persons as possible, because that flexibility determines in large part persons' potential for interaction with locations dispersed over space.

In his inspiring book on public transport for suburbia, Mees underscores that such flexibility can only be created by making use of the network effect of transportation systems (Mees 2010). That effect describes the phenomenon that the range of possibilities to access destinations increases exponentially with an increase in the number of connecting links of a network (see Levinson and Krizek 2008; Figure 8.3). The more links in a network (like roads or public transport lines), the more nodes of activities are connected (like neighborhoods, employment centers and so on), and the more destinations can be reached by persons with access to the system. This network effect is relevant across space and time. That is, given persons' constitutive interest in protecting the range of options they can achieve, they will not only be concerned about the range of locations that can be accessed, but also about the times of the day and days of the week that they can access these locations. Tailor-made solutions often ignore the importance of both types of network effect, as they tend to serve a particular transport need among a particular population group at a particular time. While such solutions may be called for under particular conditions, for instance in order to provide mobility services to persons experiencing severe travel-related impairments, they are generally undesirable, because they fail to add links to an existing transportation network serving multiple population groups. Such tailor-made interventions are thus 'lost' to the wider population.

Based on the above, it is then possible to outline two main rules that should guide the search for solutions to accessibility shortfalls. First, the search should take into account the inherent diversity of persons and therefore the differences in abilities to make use of various transportation facilities and services. The search should therefore focus on inclusive transportation interventions, which can be used by a wide range of

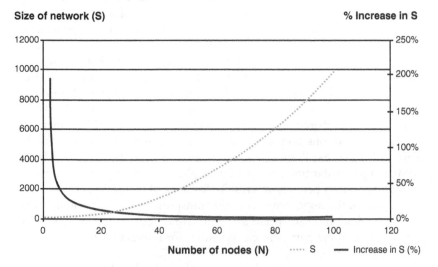

Figure 8.3 A graphic representation of the network effect.
Source: Levinson and Krizek 2008, p. 49.

persons independent of their particular spectrum of travel-related abilities. These interventions are to be preferred over more exclusionary types of solutions, provided the costs of the former are reasonable in comparison to the latter (see Chapter 6). Second, the search should take into account the importance of the network effect. Thus accessibility shortfalls occurring across a region or city should always be considered in conjunction, even if they affect different population groups, occur in different parts of the area, or relate to different types of destinations. It would be a fundamental mistake to take an approach in which accessibility shortfalls are addressed one population group at a time. Such an approach is likely to lead to small-scale solutions that will do little to reduce the accessibility deficiency in a region or city over time. Indeed, in the long run, such solutions may well be more expensive and less cost-effective than systemic interventions in the transportation system addressing the plight of multiple groups simultaneously (see also Helm 2013).

Evaluating interventions to move the transportation system towards fairness

Any solution to reduce accessibility shortfalls and move the transportation system towards fairness will have benefits and costs. In line with traditional transportation planning, the selection of the 'best' alternative solution will have to be based on a systematic comparison of these benefits and costs.

The dominant procedure for evaluating and comparing solutions in the traditional approach is social cost–benefit analysis, or simply cost–benefit analysis. However, this approach is not suitable for transportation planning based on principles of justice for a number of, partially overlapping, reasons.

First of all, in standard cost–benefit analysis all costs and benefits are aggregated to generate an overall assessment of a proposed intervention. This implies that cost–benefit analysis cannot provide any insight into the contribution of an intervention to the alleviation of accessibility shortfalls of particular population groups. Second, and related, the aggregate or 'lump-sum' approach implies that all costs and benefits have to be translated into monetary terms in order to be added up to generate an estimate of the net benefits of a project (Needham 2006). This, in turn, implies that even if cost–benefit analysis reports on the net benefits per population group, it leaves undetermined how these net benefits (or net costs) came about. For instance, a particular group may well reap net benefits because of a reduction in road fatalities or a decrease in air pollution. The translation of benefits and costs to monetary terms thus hides information which is crucial in order to assess whether a particular intervention addresses accessibility shortfalls.

Third, cost–benefit analysis is based on welfare theory and the related notion of consumer surplus and willingness-to-pay. Clearly, a person's willingness-to-pay is strongly dependent on a person's ability-to-pay, which in turn is largely determined by a person's income level. All else being equal, the higher the income, the more a person is willing to pay for a (non-inferior) good. Projects mainly benefiting population groups with a low ability-to-pay will thus tend to generate relatively modest surpluses, if at all. Since low income households will typically be over-represented among population groups with accessibility shortfalls, this implies that interventions seeking to address these shortfalls will tend to generate relatively moderate benefits. The consequence is that such interventions are likely to perform poorly in terms of their net benefits in comparison to other investments or policies (Martens 2006; Martens 2011).

Fourth, the most important benefit typically included in cost–benefit analysis consists of travel time savings. The argument developed so far underscores, however, that the evaluation of alternatives should not seek to capture the contribution of an intervention to a person's mobility, but rather its contribution to a person's possibilities for activity participation. Indeed, the proposed approach to transportation planning underscores that the main benefit of transportation interventions lies in the *accessibility gains* generated through an improvement in potential mobility (Martens 2006). The replacement of travel time savings with accessibility gains within the framework of cost–benefit analysis is not a simple matter, because it implies that accessibility will have to be monetized. While some progress has been made in this direction (Nahmias-Biran and Shiftan 2015), this is certainly still a major challenge (Martens 2006).

The fifth, and perhaps most important, concern relates to the weighing of benefits and costs in standard cost–benefit analysis. Typically, the weighing of benefits and costs, if applied at all, is not related to the characteristics of the person receiving a particular cost or benefit. Thus one unit of benefit typically has an identical weight, irrespective of the recipient of that unit of benefit. This approach is at odds with the fundamentals of transportation planning based on principles of justice, which stress the importance of accessibility benefits accruing to persons below the sufficiency threshold and thus suggest that the value of accessibility benefits should be based on the characteristics of the person receiving them. While the literature on cost–benefit analysis abounds with discussions on the possibilities for incorporating weights based on normative considerations, it has been shown that such weighing is highly problematic within the context of cost–benefit analysis (Harberger 1978).

These concerns question the suitability of cost–benefit analysis as an evaluation methodology within the context of transportation planning based on principles of justice. Clearly, each of the concerns could be accommodated within the cost–benefit framework. For instance, the weighing of benefits and costs could be based on normative considerations, while the results of a cost–benefit analysis could be presented per population group as well as per benefit or cost. Such adjustments, however, would practically mean the abandoning of cost–benefit analysis as an evaluation methodology. It would not only imply an end to the integrative framework of cost–benefit analysis, but would also fundamentally violate the theoretical underpinnings of the approach.

An alternative approach to evaluation, which better matches the fundamentals of transportation planning based on principles of justice, is cost-effectiveness analysis. Cost-effectiveness analysis is a form of analysis that compares the relative costs and (positive) effects of two or more possible interventions. Unlike cost–benefit analysis, cost-effectiveness analysis does not rely on monetary valuation of the effects of these interventions. Typically, the cost-effectiveness of an intervention is expressed as a ratio, where the denominator is a measure of the positive effects and the numerator is the cost associated with the intervention. Cost-effectiveness analysis has been used extensively in the domain of health care, as it is often deemed inappropriate to monetize health effects. In this domain, the positive effects of an intervention are expressed in terms such as years of life, premature births averted, or an integrated measure like quality-adjusted life years (see, for instance, Black 1990).

Some of the concerns related to cost–benefit analysis do not apply to cost-effectiveness analysis. First, cost-effectiveness analysis is typically used to assess a particular type of benefit or group of related benefits that can be captured by an integrated measure. Thus the approach does not lump together a range of benefits and costs of an intervention. Second, and related, cost-effectiveness analysis does not necessitate ascribing monetary values to benefits or costs, thereby avoiding the implicit preference for higher income groups in cost–benefit analysis. Finally, cost-effectiveness analysis can accommodate normative weighing of benefits without violating the theoretical underpinnings of the approach, even though such a form of weighing is by no means standard practice.

The normative weighing of benefits is of special importance for transportation planning based on principles of justice. The reasons for this have already been outlined above. Merely applying cost-effectiveness analysis instead of cost–benefit analysis does not avoid the risk that interventions are selected that hardly mitigate the hardships of persons below the accessibility sufficiency threshold. Indeed, the application of cost-effectiveness analysis may well lead to the prioritization of interventions that generate more benefits for advantaged than for disadvantaged groups. This risk is especially prominent in the domain of transportation, because many interventions tend to serve a range of persons, due to the network effect and the public character of these interventions.

Thus the application of cost-effectiveness analysis does not erase the need to apply normative weighing of benefits. This raises the question of how, exactly, the benefits should be weighed. While the previous arguments, especially those developed in Chapter 7, provide some directions, it is worthwhile to briefly discuss two philosophical approaches that explicitly address the issue of weighing: sufficientarianism and prioritarianism. Drawing on Meyer and Roser (2006) and Casal (2007), amongst others, I will briefly discuss these lines of thought, before exploring their relevance for evaluation within the context of transportation planning based on principles of justice.

A key starting point for sufficientarianism, as developed by e.g. Crisp (2003), is the observation that justice requires first and foremost the avoidance of misery: "What is important from the point of view of morality is not that everyone should have the same, but that each should have enough. If everyone had enough, it would be of no moral consequence whether one had more than others" (Frankfurt 1987, p. 21). Casal (2007) distinguishes between the positive and negative theses embodied by the notion of sufficientarianism. The positive thesis "stresses the importance of people living above a certain threshold, free from deprivation" (Casal 2007, pp. 297–298). The negative thesis underscores the irrelevance of additional benefits for persons already above the threshold. Casal argues that pure sufficientarianism embodies both claims. In line with both theses, Crisp, the most prominent representative of sufficientarianism, thus argues that "absolute priority is to be given to benefits below the threshold" (Crisp 2003, p. 758). The distinctive feature of sufficientarianism, then, is the view that there is a threshold and that persons below the threshold have absolute priority over persons above the threshold.

On a first reading, the accessibility sufficiency threshold can be seen as a special case of the threshold discussed in sufficientarianism. Basing transport project evaluation on sufficientarianism would thus imply a rigid way of weighing the benefits reaped by different population groups. Only benefits reaped by groups below the accessibility threshold would be given weight, with no value being ascribed to benefits accruing to population groups with already sufficient levels of accessibility.

Sufficientarianism has been criticized on a number of grounds. The most important criticism centers on the understanding that it seems practically impossible to justify a strict sufficiency threshold. First, it is difficult to uphold a sharp dividing line between persons who do and who do not deserve consideration. Why are persons just below the threshold entitled to moral priority over persons that are just above that threshold? Both Casal (2007) and Meyer and Roser (2006) point to a second, related problem. They point out that, if the threshold is so important, "it better be set in some very principled way with strong reasons supporting exactly this or that point" (Meyer and Roser 2006, p. 236). A third criticism concerns the lack of "additional distributive requirements" (Casal 2007, p. 300). By this, Casal refers to the costs to society that may be implied by the absolute priority for sufficiency.

Strictly following sufficientarianism's rules might imply granting small benefits to someone below the threshold even if it would come at the expense of bringing many more persons down to that threshold. That, obviously, goes strongly against widely held intuitions about fairness (and efficiency) (Di Ciommo and Lucas 2014).

These arguments suggest that it is difficult to defend the absolute priority for persons below the sufficiency threshold. Prioritarianism offers a way out. Prioritarianism is based on the view that benefits matter more the more worse-off the person to whom the benefits accrue. Proponents of prioritarianism argue that the moral value of a benefit, or the disvalue of a burden, diminishes as its recipient becomes better off (Casal 2007). Meyer and Roser argue that prioritarianism is a very attractive theory: "It explains our intuitions about the importance of equality ... about the importance of giving priority to the badly off and, in addition, explains why equality among the very well off has little importance. It does all this without a strict threshold or without ascribing intrinsic value to equality" (Meyer and Roser 2006, p. 238).

Like sufficientarianism, prioritarianism can be applied to the evaluation of transport interventions. The approach underscores the extreme difficulty in determining a sufficiency threshold for accessibility, as was already discussed at length in Chapter 7. Rather than focusing on that threshold value, prioritarianism proposes a weighing of benefits depending on the position of a person in the distributive spectrum. For the transport domain, this implies a ranking of population groups in terms of their accessibility levels. The higher the current levels of accessibility of a group, the lower the value ascribed to the accessibility benefits reaped by that group.

Following Meyer and Roser (2006), the difference between the approaches described above can be captured in a graphical representation (Figure 8.4). The horizontal axis depicts the initial (current) accessibility level experienced by a particular population group. The vertical axis represents the moral value that should be ascribed to the benefits accruing to a population group. In traditional cost–benefit analysis, all benefits (and costs) are ascribed an identical value, (implicitly) based on the theory of utilitarianism (Figure 8.4a). In contrast, in sufficientarianism, no value is attached to benefits accruing to persons positioned above the sufficiency threshold. Below that threshold, various ways of valuing or weighing benefits is possible. For instance, higher weights could be ascribed to population groups with accessibility levels farther below the sufficiency threshold, or all benefits could be given equal value. The latter case is depicted in Figure 8.4b. Figure 8.4c represents the case of prioritarianism. Benefits accrued by all recipients are valued, but the normative value ascribed to these benefits decreases with rising initial accessibility levels. Clearly, the resulting 'priority curve' could take various shapes and the figure represents only one possible option.

The analysis presented in Chapter 7 suggests that the priority approach could be further refined. In that chapter, it was found that real-life agents engaged in democratic deliberation may be able to distinguish three domains of the accessibility spectrum: a domain of clearly insufficient accessibility, a domain of clearly sufficient accessibility, and a domain of disagreement. The normative valuation of benefits may be determined in relation to these three domains. Figure 8.4d provides an example, showing how the value of benefits decreases with increasing strength as the initial level of accessibility goes up from low to high. The figure serves only as an illustration of a possible approach. Real-life agents could agree on any particular 'depreciation slope' of the value of accessibility gains. Clearly, reaching such an agreement will not be a simple matter and may well be very contentious. That does not imply, however, that the agents should revert to equal weighing of benefits, as that would certainly be at odds with the approach developed here.

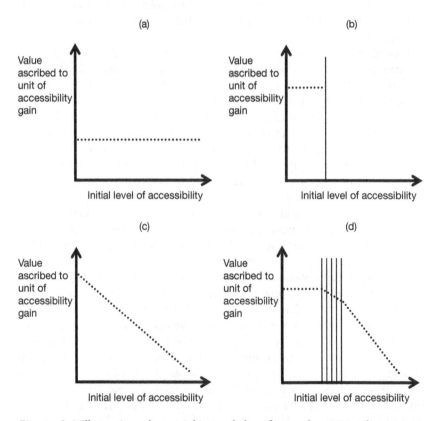

Figure 8.4 Illustrating the weighing of benefits under (a) utilitarianism, (b) sufficientarianism, (c) prioritarianism, and (d) a refined application of prioritarianism in line with the fundamentals of transportation planning based on principles of justice. The vertical lines represent accessibility sufficiency thresholds. Source: Figures a, b and c based on Meyer and Roser 2006.

The rules of transportation planning based on principles of justice

Based on the previous discussions, it is now possible to present a general approach to transportation planning based on principles of justice. Below, I will describe the steps or informal rules of this approach to transportation planning (Figure 8.5). Note that the rules are based on the assumption that the approach is applied in the context of a region or metropolitan area, as this is in many respects the most relevant scale at which persons organize their daily life. However, applications of the approach at lower and higher spatial scales are certainly possible.

The rules below give a description of the largely technical part of transportation planning. As mentioned in several instances, transportation planning can never be an exclusively technical exercise. Indeed, as mentioned throughout this chapter, a top-down, technical, approach will have to be complemented by a bottom-up, participatory, approach. I will not elaborate on this latter approach, as it would require a discussion of the extensive literature on, and practices with, forms of participatory decision-making. Suffice to say that efforts can build on the expertise in the domain of transportation planning (among which are 'best practices' in accessibility planning in the UK; see Lucas 2012), as well as on the vast and still increasing number of experiments with bottom-up, participative, modes of decision-making in a range of policy domains (for a discussion of the difficulties of such approaches in the domain of transportation see: Hajer and Kesselring 1999; Bickerstaff, Tolley *et al.* 2002; Bickerstaff and Walker 2005).

The aim of the first step of transportation planning based on principles of justice is to break up the overall population of a region into groups that may be expected to experience distinctly different accessibility levels. Given the often pervasive impact on accessibility levels, a distinction of population groups based on residential location, mode availability (broadly conceived), and income may be called for. The division of groups may be further refined based on additional characteristics of persons, such as travel-related abilities, gender or ethnicity, certainly if these attributes shape accessibility levels in a systematic way. This may be the case, for instance, if concerns about personal safety limit women's or minorities' use of parts of the transportation system, perhaps during part of the day, or if (public) transport systems exclude a substantial group of persons experiencing a particular spectrum of travel-related abilities. Clearly, it is of special importance to explicitly identify groups who are most likely to experience low levels of accessibility under the prevailing circumstances.

The second step encompasses the measurement, for each group, of levels of accessibility and potential mobility. The word level is used in the plural, because both accessibility and potential mobility have multiple dimensions, as has been discussed before. This implies that accessibility especially has to be measured in various ways, in order to capture its multi-dimensional character. This may include, for instance,

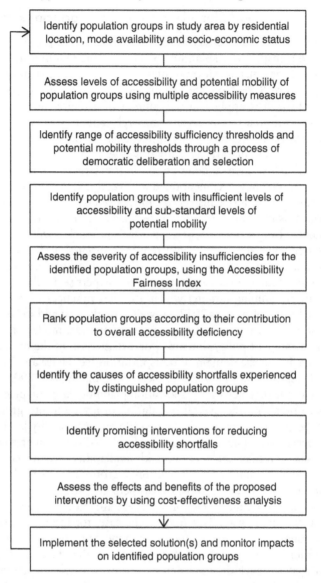

Figure 8.5 The rules of transportation planning based on principles of justice.

the measurement of accessibility to employment as well as services, and the measurement of 'local' accessibility as well as 'regional' accessibility (as reflected in e.g. travel time thresholds or the specifications of a gravity function). The measurement of potential mobility should be adjusted accordingly. Based on these measurements, it is then possible to position all population groups, as distinguished in the first step, vis-à-vis the coordinate system of accessibility and potential mobility.

This exercise will have to be repeated for the different ways in which accessibility is measured.

The measurement of accessibility and potential mobility levels across a population serves as the basis for the establishment of sufficiency thresholds in the third step. This is clearly the most political step of transportation planning based on principles of justice. The reasoning described in Chapter 7 provides the basis for the process of democratic deliberation and decision-making to determine the accessibility sufficiency threshold. Even if supported by this process, real-life agents may find it difficult to demarcate a precise sufficiency threshold and may prefer to identify a range of possible sufficiency thresholds. Such an approach would be in line with the critique of sufficientarianism briefly summarized in the previous section. That critique is especially relevant for the domain of accessibility, as the assessment will always be based on a 'general' notion of accessibility, thereby providing only partial insight into the particular accessibility problems experienced by persons belonging to each population group. The demarcation of one, single, accessibility threshold may thus be undesirable. In addition to delineating a (set of) threshold(s) of sufficient accessibility, it will be necessary to determine a sufficient level(s) of potential mobility. It may be argued that any population group with a level of potential mobility above the average in a particular study area is relatively well-served by the transportation system and thus not entitled to improvements in that system. Yet real-life agents may well agree to accept a somewhat less strict standard, i.e. to also include groups with a potential mobility level somewhat above the average. It may, after all, still be possible to raise the accessibility levels of these groups above the sufficiency threshold by further improvements in the transportation system.

Based on the second and third step, it is possible in the fourth step to identify the population groups that experience insufficient accessibility due to a sub-standard transportation system. These groups have an accessibility level below (one of) the accessibility sufficiency threshold(s) and experience a sub-standard level of potential mobility. Clearly, multiple sets of groups will be identified, as each way of measuring accessibility (in the second step) may lead to different groups falling below the accessibility and potential mobility thresholds. This, however, should not be perceived as a problem, but rather as a strength of the analysis: population groups that are identified again and again, irrespective of the particular accessibility measure being used, are clearly more likely to experience accessibility shortfalls than groups falling below a threshold in only one or two analyses. Note furthermore that the use of multiple sufficiency thresholds will lead to a yet wider variation in the set of groups singled out as being entitled to accessibility improvements. The results of the analyses in this step, as in any other step, should therefore be seen as the input for democratic deliberation, rather than as an end result.

The fifth step encompasses the measurement and assessment of the severity of accessibility insufficiencies experienced by the population groups identified in the fourth step. In this step both the prevalence and the intensity of accessibility shortfalls are assessed, based on the Accessibility Fairness Index developed in this chapter. As discussed above, the Accessibility Fairness Index makes it possible to determine the contribution of a population group to the accessibility deficiency in a region. The analysis will result in the identification of population groups experiencing the most severe level of accessibility insufficiencies, because of an extremely low level of accessibility, or a very large size of the population group, or both. The contribution of a population group to overall accessibility deficiency will obviously depend on the way accessibility is being measured and on the sufficiency threshold being used. Clearly, again, the latter is of special importance, as a group's contribution to accessibility deficiency in a region or city will strongly depend on the sufficiency threshold. The lower the threshold, the fewer groups will experience an insufficient level of accessibility, and the higher the contribution of the remaining groups to overall accessibility deficiency. The selection of a particular accessibility measure is obviously also relevant, as the selected measure will determine the size of a group's accessibility shortfall. For this reason, multiple analyses, invoking several accessibility measures, are to be preferred above a single 'best' accessibility measure.

In the sixth step, the outcomes of the previous step are integrated into overarching indicators as much as possible in order to set priorities and identify population groups that should be served first. The aim here is to bring together, separately for each accessibility sufficiency standard, the results of the analyses carried out using various types of accessibility measurements. This can be done based on the results of the fifth step by adding up, for each population group, the contribution to overall accessibility deficiency for each way of measuring accessibility. This will result in a measure of 'overall' contribution to accessibility deficiency per group, which will enable the identification (and perhaps ranking) of population groups which are most entitled to improvements in accessibility. Since the accessibility sufficiency threshold may strongly shape the outcomes of these analyses, it is preferable to carry out the analyses for each threshold separately and to assess how the contribution to accessibility deficiency of each group changes for different sufficiency thresholds. This may result in the identification of population groups that show a substantial contribution to overall accessibility deficiency across all thresholds. Certainly if real-life agents agree to employ multiple sufficiency thresholds, the results of the analyses in this sixth step should be seen, once again, as an input for democratic deliberation.

The seventh step consists of a top-down and bottom-up analysis of the causes of accessibility shortfalls experienced by the identified population groups. The top-down approach is largely technical in nature, encompassing detailed analyses of the weakness in the existing transportation systems. The bottom-up approach would tap into the local knowledge of persons affected by accessibility shortfalls. Clearly, the eventual analysis of causes should be based on both sources of knowledge.

The top-down and bottom-up assessment of the causes of accessibility deficiencies provides the basis for the process of generating alternatives. This eighth step is both creative and technical in nature, as it will require a bouncing back and forth between generating ideas and estimating their potential contribution to the reduction in the accessibility deficiency in a region or city. As discussed in this chapter, the identification of possible solutions is no simple matter, because there is no direct relationship between the identification of population groups entitled to accessibility improvements and the interventions in the transportation system that can most effectively and efficiently contribute to such an improvement.

The ninth step of transportation planning based on principles of justice consists of the assessment and comparison of the solutions generated in the previous step. This ninth step entails a systematic application of cost-effectiveness analysis. The effects are limited to the accessibility increases generated by the various alternative solutions; the costs encompass at least the investment and operation costs of a solution. It may be clear that it is by no means a simple matter to determine the accessibility effects of alternatives, if only because these effects can and have to be measured in multiple ways. Here, again, the multi-dimensional nature of accessibility poses substantial challenges. While the abstract notion of accessibility gains can be helpful, as I have argued elsewhere (Martens 2006), it is less clear how the gains captured by different ways of measuring accessibility can or cannot be added up to form an overall estimate of the accessibility gains generated by a particular solution (see the brief discussion of my earlier work in Berechman 2009). The exercise is also no simple matter, because the proposed approach to cost-effectiveness analysis requires the normative valuation of accessibility gains in relation to the initial accessibility level experienced by a population group. These complexities may well prove to be less pressing in actual practice, if the assessment generates consistent results irrespective of a particular accessibility measure or normative valuation of accessibility gains, i.e. if the assessment consistently points in the direction of a particular solution. Preliminary analyses which I have carried out with colleagues show, however, that this is unlikely to be the case, even in a highly simplified environment (Martens, Di Ciommo *et al.* 2014). The step is thus, again, more than a merely technical exercise; it requires the explicit judgment of decision-makers and stakeholders.

The final, tenth, step of transportation planning based on principles of justice consists of the implementation of the selected solution(s) and monitoring of the impacts. Even the latter is no simple matter, as multiple accessibility measures should be used and applied in the monitoring exercise. Furthermore, proper monitoring will also require, at least in a tentative way, examination of the changes in the composition of the population, their residential locations, and their abilities to make use of particular transportation modes. The monitoring is thus a fundamentally more complex exercise than the tracking of congestion levels, which has been at the heart of traditional transportation planning.

It should be clear to the reader that the rules outlined above can only give general guidance on how to conduct 'proper' transportation planning based on principles of justice. This is so, for at least two reasons.

First, it is hopefully apparent throughout this entire chapter that transportation planning based on principles of justice cannot be, and should not be, a merely technical exercise, as traditional transportation planning has often been perceived and practiced. Virtually all steps of transportation planning based on principles of justice are empirical and normative in nature at the same time. They require explicit judgment, which cannot be left to the transportation expert however defined. Indeed, while transportation planning remains in part a technical exercise, requiring an in-depth understanding of the relationship between transportation systems, accessibility, land use patterns, and activity participation, as well as often highly technical skills to analyze and scrutinize accessibility patterns, it is also a fundamentally democratic exercise involving both deliberation and selection. This should clearly not be seen as a disadvantage of the approach proposed here, but as an inevitable part of any form of planning in a democratic society.

Second, the rules presented here hardly provide a comprehensive 'cookbook' for transportation planning, as virtually all steps need to be developed further through research and practical experimentation in a variety of contexts, in a range of institutional settings, and by a variety of stakeholders. I thus leave much of the work to professionals and advocates seeking to change the existing practices of transportation planning. This may be disappointing for practitioners looking for such 'ready-to-implement' approaches. Yet I trust that the rules provided here, and the first application presented in the following chapter, can serve as a source of inspiration for all who are seeking transportation justice.

References

Berechman, J. (2009). *The Evaluation of Transportation Investment Projects*. New York/Oxon, Routledge.

Bickerstaff, K. and G. Walker (2005). Shared visions, unholy alliances: power, governance and deliberative processes in local transport planning. *Urban Studies*, 42(12): 2123–2144.

Bickerstaff, K., R. Tolley and G. Walker (2002). Transport planning and participation: rhetoric and realities of public involvement. *Journal of Transport Geography*, 10: 61–73.

Black, W.C. (1990). The CE plane: a graphic representation of cost-effectiveness. *Medical Decision Making*, 10: 212–214.

Casal, P. (2007). Why sufficiency is not enough. *Ethics*, 117(2): 296–326.

Crisp, R. (2003). Equality, priority, and compassion. *Ethics*, 113(4): 745–763.

Daniels, N. (1985). *Just Health Care*. Cambridge, Cambridge University Press.

Daniels, N. (2008). *Just Health : meeting health needs fairly*. Cambridge, Cambridge University Press.

Di Ciommo, F. and K. Lucas (2014). Evaluating the equity effects of road-pricing in the European urban context – the Madrid Metropolitan Area. *Applied Geography*, 54: 74–82.

Foster, J. and A.K. Sen (2008 [1997]). On economic inequality after a quarter century. In: A. Sen (ed.), *On Economic Equality*. Oxford, Clarendon Press.

Foster, J., J. Greer and E. Thorbecke (1984). A class of decomposable poverty measures. *Econometrica: Journal of the Econometric Society*: 761–766.

Frankfurt, H. (1987). Equality as a moral ideal. *Ethics*, 98: 21–43.

Geurs, K.T. and B. van Wee (2004). Accessibility evaluation of land-use and transport strategies: review and research directions. *Journal of Transport Geography*, 12(2): 127–140.

Grengs, J. (2015). Nonwork accessibility as a social equity indicator. *International Journal of Sustainable Transportation*, 9(1): 1–14.

Gutierrez, J., A. Monzon and J.M. Pinero (1998). Accessibility, network efficiency, and transport infrastructure planning. *Environment and Planning A*, 30: 1337–1350.

Hägerstrand, T. (1970). *What about people in regional science?* Paper presented at the Ninth European Congress of the Regional Science Association.

Hajer, M.A. and S. Kesselring (1999). Democracy in the risk society? Learning from the new politics of mobility in Munich. *Environmental Politics*, 8(3): 1–13.

Harberger, A.C. (1978). On the use of distributional weights in social cost–benefit analysis. *The Journal of Political Economy*, 86(2, Part 2): S87–S120.

Helm, D. (2013). British infrastructure policy and the gradual return of the state. *Oxford Review of Economic Policy*, 29(2): 287–306.

Levinson, D.M. and K.J. Krizek (2008). *Planning for Place and Plexus: metropolitan land use and transport*. New York/London, Taylor & Francis.

Lucas, K. (2012). A critical assessment of accessibility planning for social inclusion. In: K.T. Geurs, K.J. Krizek and A. Reggiani (eds), *Accessibility Analysis and Transport Planning: challenges for Europe and North America*. Cheltenham, Edward Elgar, p. 228.

Martens, K. (2006). Basing transport planning on principles of social justice. *Berkeley Planning Journal*, 19: 1–17.

Martens, K. (2007). Integrating equity considerations into the Israeli cost–benefit analysis: guidelines for practice. Tel Aviv/Nijmegen, Israeli Ministry of Transport.

Martens, K. (2011). Substance precedes methodology: on cost–benefit analysis and equity. *Transportation*, 38(6): 959–974.

Martens, K. and J. Bastiaanssen (2015). *An index to measure accessibility poverty risk*. Paper presented at the 14th IATBR Conference, 19–23 July 2015, Windsor.

Martens, K., F. Di Ciommo and A. Papanikolaou (2014). *Incorporating equity into transport planning: utility, priority and sufficiency approaches*. Paper presented at the PANAM, 11–13 June 2014, Santander, Spain.

Mees, P. (2010). *Transport for Suburbia: beyond the automobile age*. London/Washington DC, Earthscan.

Metz, D. (2008). The myth of travel time saving. *Transport Reviews*, 28(3): 321–336.

Meyer, L. and D. Roser (2006). Distributive justice and climate change: the allocation of emission rights. *Analyse und Kritik-Zeitschrift fur Sozialwissenschaften*, 28(2): 223–249.

Nahmias-Biran, B.-h. and Y. Shiftan (2015). *Using activity-based models and the capability approach to evaluate equity considerations in transportation projects.* Paper presented at the 14th International Conference on Travel Behaviour Research, July 2015, London.

Needham, B. (2006). *Planning, Law and Economics: an investigation of the rules we make for using land.* London/New York, Routledge.

Neutens, T., S. Daniels, J. Minnen, *et al.* (2014). Spatial and temporal fluctuations in individual accessibility: a comparative analysis among subgroups of the population. *Geografisk Tidsskrift*, 114(2): 119–131.

Ravallion, M. (1992). Poverty comparisons. *Living Standard Measurement Study Working Paper*, 88.

Ravallion, M. (1994). *Poverty Comparisons.* Taylor & Francis US.

Rawls, J. (1971). *A Theory of Justice.* Cambridge, MA, Harvard University Press.

Rofe, Y., I. Benenson, K. Martens, *et al.* (2015). Accessibility and social equity in Tel-Aviv Metropolitan Area: examination of the current conditions and development scenarios. Beer Sheva/Tel Aviv, Report for the Israeli Ministry of Transport.

Sen, A.K. (1992). *Inequality Reexamined.* Cambridge, MA, Harvard University Press.

van der Kloof, A., J. Bastiaanssen and K. Martens (2014). Bicycle lessons, activity participation and empowerment. *Case Studies on Transport Policy*, 2(2): 89–95

9 Case Study

The Fairness of Amsterdam's Transportation System

Introduction

In *The Just City*, Fainstein explores the extent of justice in three world cities: New York, London and Amsterdam. She ends her critical study by concluding that "Amsterdam remains the strongest of the three cities ... in terms of diversity, democracy, and equity" (Fainstein 2010, p. 162). She continues: "Amsterdam may not be the ideal city, and it is less egalitarian than in the past, but it still represents a model to which others may aspire" (ibid., p. 164). This conclusion relates to the fairness of Amsterdam's policies regarding housing, urban planning, and economic development. Fainstein, however, did not explicitly scrutinize the city's approach to transportation planning in her study.

In this chapter, I will explore the fairness of the transport-land use system in Fainstein's 'exemplary city'. I will extend the analysis beyond the boundaries of the city itself to encompass the entire area governed by the City Region of Amsterdam, a cooperation of sixteen municipalities. I focus on the region for two reasons. First, since Amsterdam is a major economic center, it provides employment and services to a much larger region. This in itself warrants an analysis of the fairness of the transport-land use system at the regional level. Second, for many years the city region has held important responsibilities regarding the planning of the transportation system in the entire area. The region would thus be an appropriate governmental organization to take up transportation planning based on principles of justice. This chapter, so to say, takes some of the work out of the hands of the regional authority: it presents the technical part of the analyses the region would need to carry out if it were to adopt the approach developed in this book.

This chapter does not cover the entire process of transportation planning based on principles of justice. For one thing, it is limited to the technical part of the analyses and excludes the key processes of democratic deliberation and selection. But even the coverage of the technical analyses is still modest in scope, because it does not encompass all the steps of transportation planning based on principles of justice. The reasons for this are twofold. First, as mentioned in the previous chapter, not all the steps of the approach have been sufficiently developed so that they can be directly applied. But second, and more importantly, a full-fledged execution of all the steps would require the identification and ex ante assessment of transportation interventions seeking to address accessibility shortfalls in the Amsterdam region. The identification of solutions would require an in-depth analysis of the causes of accessibility shortfalls, which cannot be done without the involvement of the persons affected by these shortfalls. The assessment of these interventions, in turn, would require a major analytical effort, including the employment (and possible modification) of advanced transportation models. This was beyond the scope of the work presented here. Thus the aim of this chapter is to illustrate how the technical part of the early steps of transportation planning based on principles of justice could proceed.

Data

The data requirements of transportation planning based on principles of justice are relatively modest in scope. They are limited to data sets available in an increasing number of cities and regions around the world. The necessary sets include data on total population, population by income class, travel times to all surrounding zones, aerial distances between all zones, and accessibility levels for a range of travel time thresholds, all at a zonal or other level of spatial aggregation. Most of these data sets are readily available in most developed and developing contexts; only the latter data set may require some effort of data compilation or collection. There are thus no data limitations to prevent transportation planning agencies from carrying out the analyses necessary for transportation planning based on principles of justice.

The analyses for the Amsterdam region have been carried out at the level of four-digit postal code areas. The Amsterdam region encompasses a total of 190 four-digit postal code areas. For each postal code area, data is available on the total population, population by income quintile, urbanization level, travel times to all surrounding postal code areas, and the number of jobs accessible by car or public transport within a 20-, 30- and 45-minute travel time threshold. Data on population and urbanization levels were obtained from the Dutch Bureau of Statistics (CBS, 2013). Data on travel times and accessibility by car and public transport were provided by the Dutch consultancy Goudappel Coffeng. For car-based travel, data are available for both morning peak hours and off-peak hours, while for public transport only data on morning peak hours were provided. Based on the travel time data and aerial distance from a regular GIS package, potential mobility levels have been calculated for all 190 zones in the region.

Obviously, the Amsterdam data have been collected for other purposes and so the findings presented in this chapter should be interpreted with some care. Still, I am confident that the analyses provide fundamental insights into the fairness of the transport-land use system in the Amsterdam region.

In what follows, I will carry out step one through step six of transportation planning based on principles of justice (see Figure 8.5). Since the steps have only been described briefly in the previous chapter, I will start each step with a brief conceptual discussion about the proper way to conduct the proposed step. The chapter thus provides additional guidance on how to conduct proper transportation planning. Taken together, the six steps will lead to the identification of the population groups experiencing accessibility shortfalls. In other words, the analyses presented here result in the delineation of the transportation problem to be addressed through interventions in the transportation (and land use) system. I will refrain from giving a general judgment regarding the fairness of the transport-land use system in the Amsterdam region, as such an assessment is meaningless without a comparison with other regions or without an analysis of the changes over time in the Amsterdam region. I leave this challenge for another occasion (for a first exercise in this direction, see the report with my colleagues Rofe, Benenson *et al.* 2015).

Step 1: Population groups

The aim of the first step is to break up the overall population of a region into groups that may be expected to experience distinctly different accessibility levels. The distinction of different population groups is of key importance and should be based on theoretical and practical considerations.

The theoretical considerations relate first of all to the influence of personal characteristics on accessibility levels. Given their often pervasive impact on accessibility levels, a person's residential location, mode availability, and income should surely be taken into account when distinguishing population groups, as was suggested in the previous chapter. The division of groups may be further refined based on additional characteristics of persons, such as travel-related abilities, household composition, gender or ethnicity, particularly if these attributes shape accessibility levels in a systematic way that goes beyond what can be explained by residential location, mode availability, and income. This broad set of factors shaping accessibility suggests that, ideally, a substantial range of groups should be distinguished as the starting point for transportation planning based on principles of justice.

Yet the theoretical considerations do not only relate to the relationship between personal characteristics and accessibility levels. They also relate to the moral limits of the measurement of differences between persons. Following Rawls' argument, public policy should be based on information that is publicly available to all. As discussed in the previous chapter, the measurement of accessibility that takes into account the entire variety in persons' abilities and circumstances would violate this condition. The division of groups will thus have to be based on data that is typically collected for a range of administrative purposes (such as taxation) or through population censuses and other surveys, as well as on the restrictions that are typically imposed by these data sources because of privacy considerations.

This implies, first, that a certain level of aggregation will always be necessary, ruling out the detailed accessibility analysis that takes into account a person's particular time–space setting. It also implies that the division of the population will necessarily have to be relatively 'rough', as statistical data typically do not allow linking a range of data to a particular person. Thus data may be available on income levels, household composition, or car ownership, even at a detailed spatial scale like a block or a census tract, but it is typically an entirely different matter to determine the size of each population group based on these three (or additional) characteristics simultaneously. Such a specification of population groups clearly becomes more problematic the more detailed the spatial scale of analysis, because of concerns over privacy as well as data availability. At the same time, analysis at a detailed spatial scale is important, not only because of the so-called modifiable area unit problem (e.g. Murray 2005; Stępniak and Rosik 2015), but equally as much because of its relationship with the measurement of accessibility. The assessment of accessibility levels provided by non-motorized modes and public transport services can especially benefit from a fine-grained spatial analysis (Benenson, Martens *et al.* 2011).

These theoretical considerations thus pull in opposite directions, toward and away from a fine-grained division of population groups. As a consequence, there is no ideal or perfect division of a population into distinctive groups. It will always require local judgment to navigate these conflicting considerations and develop tailor-made solutions, while keeping in mind the ultimate goal of delivering information on accessibility patterns across a population that can feed into the decision-making process in a meaningful way.

In addition to the theoretical considerations, practical considerations will obviously also have to play a role in the distinction of population groups. Data availability is the most important concern here. This not only concerns data about the characteristics of population groups, but equally as much data on accessibility levels. Clearly, the spatial scale of population characteristics and accessibility measurement should be in line with each other. The measurement of accessibility is in the lead here: the division of population groups does not have to be more fine-grained than the spatial scale at which accessibility measurement can be conducted.

These theoretical and practical considerations have played a major role in the distinction of population groups in the Amsterdam case study presented here. The availability of data on accessibility in the Amsterdam region, in terms of both spatial scale and transportation modes, has especially played a decisive role. As mentioned above, data are only available at the level of rather large zones (based on postal codes) and only for car-based and public transport-based accessibility. No data is available on accessibility by bicycle or by the combination of bicycle and public transport, both of which are important in the overall mode split in the Dutch context (Martens 2004; Martens 2007). This clearly limits the division of population groups.

Data availability has thus strongly determined the distinction of population groups. This may be seen as a limitation, but at the same time it should be noted that such limitations may be the rule rather than the exception in many regions across the world. Transportation planning based on principles of justice will have to work within these limitations, certainly in the short-term, so that the case study presented here may actually be more representative of what can be done in other contexts than an idealized example based on near-complete data availability.

Let me then outline how the population groups have been distinguished for the Amsterdam case study. Groups have been distinguished based on three characteristics: persons' residential location, mode availability, and income level. Population groups have first of all been distinguished based on the zones for which data on accessibility by car and public transport is available.

The second distinction is based on mode availability. Clearly, the Amsterdam region shows a considerable diversity in the set of transportation modes available to persons. Yet, given the available accessibility data, in the analysis that follows only two groups will be distinguished: persons with access to a car and persons with access to public transport services. For reasons of simplicity, it is assumed that the accessibility levels experienced by the former group is determined entirely by the road system. The underlying reasoning here is that the car provides superior accessibility in virtually all cases and that adding other transportation modes adds relatively little to the accessibility levels experienced by persons with continuous access to a car. This assumption is supported by a study comparing travel times by car and public transport for the Netherlands (Bakker, Zwaneveld *et al.* 2009), but may warrant additional exploration regarding the bicycle and multi-modal forms of travel, certainly for persons living in the urban core of the Amsterdam region. Likewise, it is assumed that the accessibility of the latter group is shaped solely by the available regular public transport services. More precisely, it is assumed that price does not play a role in the use of the public transport system (i.e. persons belonging to this group are expected to be able to use both cheap bus services and relatively expensive train services in the Amsterdam region), that persons can use all services (i.e. it is assumed that persons have knowledge about all available services and do not experience travel barriers due to a particular set of travel-related abilities), and that persons do not make use of subsidized on-demand taxi services which are also available in the Amsterdam region for particular groups. These are clearly strongly simplifying assumptions. The distinction captures only a small part of the wide variety observed in the Amsterdam region. It neither captures the absolute top of the spectrum of accessibility (as this will include persons with access to all transportation modes, including bicycle and multi-modal transportation options) nor the bottom of the spectrum (as this will include, for instance, persons who have no access to a car and can only access parts of the public transport system). Yet I argue that the distinction captures the most pervasive differences in accessibility in the region. That is, I assume that relying only on the measurement of car-based accessibility does not lead to a substantial underestimation of the accessibility levels experienced by the majority of car-owning persons, while I also assume that the accessibility levels experienced by most car-less households depends mostly on the quality of the public transportation system (and much less so on the bicycle or the occasional reliance on friends or relatives to receive a ride by car).

This distinction of population groups by transportation mode does not yet specify which persons actually belong to each group. A logical way forward here would be to rely on car ownership data and to assume that car ownership determines mode availability. This approach is certainly feasible, as the available data on the Amsterdam region do provide insight into the share of car ownership in each neighborhood and this data could be used to extract car ownership estimates at the level of postal zones. Yet the reliance on car ownership data as the basis for assigning persons to one of the two population groups based on transportation mode is problematic, for two reasons. First, there may be a certain degree of forced car ownership among low income persons, especially in more suburban and rural areas (Mattioli 2014). Car ownership is 'forced' when a person or household has limited capacity to afford the high costs of car ownership and use, yet can hardly avoid these costs because of a lack of alternative means of transportation in combination with the spatial dispersion of out-of-home activities (Currie and Delbosc 2011). These persons may de facto be exchanging accessibility shortfalls for income poverty by purchasing a car. The literature on transport-related social exclusion also suggests that some low income car-owning households make little use of the car in everyday life due to the relatively high costs of car use. This group is thus de facto living a virtually car-less life. Ignoring both groups of persons would lead to an underestimation of the number of people who (would prefer to) rely on (subsidized) public transportation services. Second, some persons may have sufficient income to purchase a car, but may have a pattern of activity participation that enables them to live without actual ownership of a car, relying on walking, cycling, public transport, car sharing services and perhaps an occasional ride from friends or family members. Some of these persons may well live in an area with a general accessibility level by public transport below the sufficiency threshold. They may only experience this sub-standard level of accessibility if circumstances change, e.g. if they need to find a new job, if they have to rely on health care services for a period of time, or if friends or family members move to places poorly accessible without a car. Such persons could face accessibility shortfalls if such changes occur, but since they have sufficient income it is more likely that they will solve their accessibility problems by purchasing a car or more regularly relying on car sharing services, certainly if the unwanted situation persists. Thus including voluntarily car-less persons in the population group relying on public transport services might lead to an over-estimation of the accessibility deficiencies in a region.

In light of the above, I argue that the level of income is a more appropriate indicator for a person's mode availability, since it strongly correlates with access to a car. In what follows, I assume that low income households are dependent on the cheaper mode of transport (i.e. public transport), while all other households are assumed to be able to secure access to car-based mobility (which may be obtained through car sharing services or through the purchase of a car only when circumstances require). Obviously, this is a gross simplification of the situation, as some low income households may well have sufficient income to own and operate a car (e.g. because of low residential costs), while some higher income groups may lack the means to purchase a car for every adult (e.g. because of household size or high non-transport expenses) or may not be able to drive (e.g. due to impairments). I maintain, however, that a distinction of population groups by income provides a better proxy for identifying the population at risk of accessibility shortfalls in the subsequent steps of transportation planning based on principles of justice than a differentiation of households based on car ownership, for the reasons given above.

Based on the lengthy argumentation above, it is now possible to distinguish the relevant population groups for the case study. Groups will be distinguished based on residential location and mode availability. The former division will be based on postal zones, the latter on data on income quintiles at the level of postal zones. Persons belonging to the lowest income quintile (as determined for the Netherlands as a whole) are assumed to rely solely on public transport services, while all other persons are assumed to be able to take advantage of car-based accessibility. The Amsterdam region consists of 190 postal zones, so 380 population groups are distinguished in the analyses that follow. Figure 9.1 shows the spatial distribution of the lowest income quintile groups over the Amsterdam region. In total 204,740 residents, or 14.8% of the total population of 1,387,640 residents, belong to the lowest income quintile and are thus assumed to rely on public transport in order to participate in out-of-home activities (CBS, 2013).

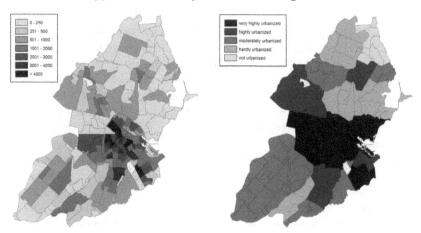

Figure 9.1 Number of persons belonging to the bottom income quintile in each zone (i.e. the number of persons in each zone assumed to rely solely on available public transport services for their accessibility); and the urbanization grade of each zone.
Source: Based on Dutch Central Bureau of Statistics.

It is expected that the low-income population groups will be more prone to experience accessibility shortfalls than population groups who can benefit from car-based accessibility. At the same time, accessibility shortfalls among the latter groups cannot be ruled out altogether. The assessment of the fairness of a transport-land use system should be open to such possibilities and should not start from predisposed positions regarding the pattern of accessibility deficiency.

Step 2: Measuring potential mobility and accessibility

The second step of transportation planning based on principles of justice consists of the measurement of the potential mobility and accessibility levels experienced by the population groups distinguished in the first step. Since accessibility is a multi-dimensional phenomenon, it is not desirable to employ only one measurement. Ideally, the measurement of accessibility will be conducted for a range of activities and a range of spatial scales, as persons have an interest in protecting their range of possibilities. Thus, in order to gain a rich understanding of the accessibility levels experienced by the groups distinguished in the first step, it is desirable to measure accessibility to key destinations such as employment, shops, and health care services. The measurement of accessibility should preferably also be conducted at various spatial scales. For instance, analyses could be conducted for travel time thresholds of 15, 30 or 45 minutes, reflecting the various spatial scales at which persons may engage in out-of-home activities (which may also differ between activities) and the limitations persons may have on spending time or monetary resources for traveling (e.g. because of dependent children and related care tasks or because of a low income). Clearly, also, accessibility should be measured for different periods of the day and week, as it typically varies across time due to congestion and variations in service provision.

The measurement of potential mobility and accessibility can be based in part on data generated by travel demand models typically applied within the context of traditional transportation planning, and in part on land use data that is increasingly available around the world. Travel demand models, or more advanced activity-based travel models, generate data on travel times, typically separately for car and public transport, and typically between relatively large transport activity zones. Based on these travel time data and easily obtainable data on the aerial distance between centroids of these zones, it is possible to calculate mode-based PMI-scores for each zone. In combination with data on land use, which can often be derived from geographical information systems, the data on travel times can be used to calculate accessibility levels for population groups. Travel demand models typically generate data at a relatively high level of spatial aggregation and often also generate relatively unreliable estimates of zone-to-zone travel times, because these models are calibrated based on traffic volumes rather than traffic speeds. Big data approaches offer another possibility to determine current travel speeds and travel times, by various transportation modes, and across different times of the day and week. These big data approaches are likely to deliver more reliable estimates of travel times than transport models and thus a more solid basis for measuring potential mobility and accessibility levels.

For the Amsterdam case study, the measurement of potential mobility and accessibility has been based on a travel demand model. Clearly, lacking big data on travel times, this data is to be preferred over no data at all. And while the travel time data may be somewhat unreliable, the analyses are still expected to deliver highly relevant insights about the patterns of potential mobility and accessibility in the Amsterdam region. These insights can at least serve as the basis for additional analyses, which may make use of big data-style estimates of travel times.

The analyses presented here are also relatively limited in terms of the measurement of the multi-dimensional nature of accessibility, as it will only address accessibility to employment. The assessment will take into account, however, various ways of capturing employment accessibility. More precisely, accessibility analyses have been conducted for three travel time thresholds (20, 30 and 45 minutes), for two periods of the day (peak and off-peak), and for two types of accessibility measures (a cumulative opportunity measure and a gravity-based measure). Taken together, this results in twelve different analyses for car-based accessibility and six different analyses for public transport-based accessibility. The lower number of analyses for public transport is due to a lack of data on public transport travel times in off-peak hours (Table 9.1).

Table 9.1 Overview of the accessibility measurements carried out for population groups with access to a car and groups dependent on public transport services.

Travel time threshold	Period of day	Type of measure	Population groups	
			With access to a car	Dependent on public transport
20 minutes	Peak	Cumulative opportunity	✓	✓
		Gravity-based (linear)	✓	✓
	Off-peak	Cumulative opportunity	✓	
		Gravity-based (linear)	✓	
30 minutes	Peak	Cumulative opportunity	✓	✓
		Gravity-based (linear)	✓	✓
	Off-peak	Cumulative opportunity	✓	
		Gravity-based (linear)	✓	
45 minutes	Peak	Cumulative opportunity	✓	✓
		Gravity-based (linear)	✓	✓
	Off-peak	Cumulative opportunity	✓	
		Gravity-based (linear)	✓	

The results of one of these analyses are presented in the coordinate system of potential mobility and accessibility (Figure 9.2). The average potential mobility and accessibility level enabled by the car system during peak hours, weighed by the population size of the zones, is used to establish the origin of the coordinate system. This is based on the assumption that land use patterns adjust to the speed allowed by the dominant mode of transportation under worst-off conditions. That is, it is assumed that households and firms will seek to adjust their location choices over time to the speeds allowed by road travel under congested conditions. Note that this assumption neither implies that accessibility by public transport or—in the Dutch circumstances —the bicycle do not play a role in location decisions of firms and households, nor that all households or firms can freely choose a location.

The diagram depicted in Figure 9.2 presents the pattern of potential mobility and accessibility for a 30-minute travel time threshold and a cumulative accessibility measure (i.e., adding up all jobs that can be reached within a 30-minute total travel time). The dots in the diagram represent the 380 population groups distinguished above, based on residential location (by postal zone) and mode availability (based on

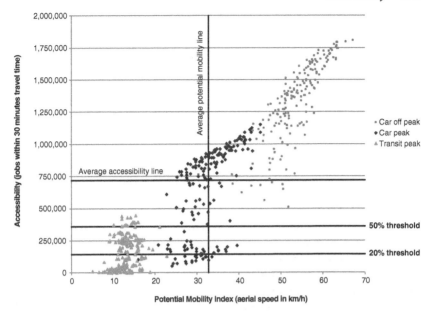

Figure 9.2 Visual representation of the levels of potential mobility and accessibility as experienced by different population groups, for peak hours and off-peak hours, for employment accessibility, a 30-minute travel time threshold and a cumulative opportunity measure.

income quintiles, with a distinction between the lowest and the four highest income quintiles). The population groups with access to a car (the four highest income quintiles) are depicted twice in the diagram, reflecting their situation in peak and off-peak hours respectively. The population groups who only have access to the public transport system are depicted only once, for the peak hour situation, as no data were available on their situation in off-peak hours (so the total number of dots in the diagram is 3 × 190 = 570). While public transport services may also suffer from (in-vehicle) congestion during peak hours, these services typically provide higher frequencies and a more dense network structure in peak hours, so it is assumed that the position of the low-income groups during off-peak hours will be roughly comparable to their position in peak hours.

The diagram shows the vast disparities in potential mobility and accessibility in the Amsterdam region, in spite of its relatively well-developed public transport system. The weighted average potential mobility level (i.e. the aerial speed provided by the transportation system weighed by the size of the population in each zone) for the public transport-dependent groups is about 40% of the average car-based potential mobility level in peak hours and only 24% of the level during off-peak hours (13.1 km/h versus 32.8 km/h versus 54.4 km/h). The differences are also substantial in terms of accessibility level: the weighted average accessibility level experienced by public transport-dependent groups is 28% of the weighted average car-based accessibility level in peak hours and a mere 14% of the car average in off-peak hours (199,784 jobs versus 717,894 jobs versus 1,397,232 jobs).

These differences are clearly reflected in the position of the population groups in the diagram: all groups assumed to be dependent on public transport fall into the left-bottom quadrant of the diagram (Quadrant 1). That means that the transport-land use system delivers all these groups a below-average potential mobility and accessibility level. The situation is entirely different for the population groups who are assumed to have access to a car, even under congested conditions. More than 60% of the persons belonging to these groups experience an above-average potential mobility and accessibility level during peak hours (i.e. they are positioned in Quadrant 3). However, since the position of the axes in the diagram is based on the average potential mobility and accessibility level experienced by the groups with access to a car in peak hours, by definition a substantial share of these groups experience a below-average level of accessibility. This holds for 42% of these groups, with 34% of the groups positioned in the bottom-left quadrant and 8% in the bottom-right quadrant (Table 9.2). The situation for these groups is fundamentally different in off-peak hours, when 99% of all persons with access to a car have an above-average level of potential mobility and accessibility. The patterns are largely comparable for a 20- and a 45-minute travel time threshold.

The graphical representation of the patterns of potential mobility and accessibility in Figure 9.2 provides a powerful portrayal of the disparities between groups with and without access to a car. Clearly, even this preliminary assessment gives important pointers for transportation planning, suggesting that interventions in the transportation system should first and foremost address the plight of population groups without access to a car. At the same time, the case study illustrates the open-ended nature of the measurement of potential mobility and accessibility if this is done *by population group*. That is, the approach proposed here does not ex ante suggest that transportation planning should focus on particular population groups (or transportation modes), but rather aims to assist in identifying the groups that warrant attention. Indeed, one of the findings in the Amsterdam case study is that population groups with access to a car may also experience a below-average accessibility level, even in off-peak hours. It requires additional steps to determine whether interventions would also be in place for these groups. These steps are elaborated below.

Table 9.2 Number and share of zones and population in each of the four quadrants of Figure 9.2, for employment accessibility, a travel time threshold of 30 minutes and a cumulative opportunity measure.

	Persons with access to a car								Persons dependent on public transport services			
	Peak hours				Off-peak hours				Peak hours			
	Groups		Population		Groups		Population		Groups		Population	
	#	%	#	%	#	%	#	%	#	%	#	%
Quadrant 1	64	34%	350,703	30%	0	0%	0	0%	190	100%	204,498	100%
Quadrant 2	40	21%	288,353	24%	1	1%	477	0%	0	0%	0	0%
Quadrant 3	71	37%	470,383	40%	180	95%	1,168,256	99%	0	0%	0	0%
Quadrant 4	15	8%	73,714	6%	9	5%	14,419	1%	0	0%	0	0%
Total	190	100%	1,183,152	100%	190	100%	1,183,152	100%	190	100%	204,498	100%

Step 3: Sufficiency thresholds

The third step of transportation planning based on principles of justice encompasses the delineation of a sufficiency threshold for accessibility and potential mobility. As discussed in Chapter 7, the delineation of the sufficiency thresholds should ultimately be the subject of democratic deliberation and selection. The analysis presented here does not draw on such a process, but merely describes an approach that could be used to determine a set of sufficiency thresholds.

In Chapter 7, I presented two approaches to setting the accessibility sufficiency threshold: an approach based on an analysis of the interrelationship between accessibility levels and activity participation, and a pragmatic approach in which the sufficiency threshold is defined as a percentage of the average or median level of accessibility (cf. Ravallion 1992). In what follows, I have adopted the pragmatic approach. This approach obviously has its limitations. First, it results in an arbitrary determination of the sufficiency threshold. In order to avoid this pitfall, I will use a range of sufficiency thresholds and will compare the pattern of accessibility deficiencies across the thresholds. Second, since this pragmatic approach will make the sufficiency threshold dependent on the particular regional situation, it may well result in an under-estimation of accessibility shortfalls if accessibility levels are relatively poor across the board, e.g. due to extreme forms of congestion resulting from a rapid population growth outpacing investments in transportation infrastructure and services. Yet it could also be argued that this cross-regional variation in sufficiency thresholds is an advantage of this approach, as it is in line with the century-old observation that sufficiency is not an absolute, but a relative phenomenon: basic needs tend to expand with increasing affluence in a society, shifting the sufficiency threshold upwards (see e.g. Sen 1983). Furthermore, since accessibility is measured in a relatively straightforward way, notably without taking into account competition effects over jobs or services, it is all the more appropriate to employ a regionally specific average accessibility level to set sufficiency thresholds. Differentiation in the sufficiency threshold across cities or regions is thus acceptable, although it may call for additional analysis, and scrutiny of the underlying datasets, for different localities.

In what follows, I will present the results for five accessibility sufficiency thresholds: 10%, 20%, 30%, 40%, and 50% of the average level of car-based accessibility during peak hours. For purposes of illustration only, two of the sufficiency thresholds of this set are depicted in Figure 9.2.

The third step of transportation planning based on principles of justice requires an additional decision before it is possible to continue with the next step. Transportation planning, whether based on principles of justice or not, focuses on interventions in the transportation system. It is therefore of key importance to delineate in which cases interventions in the transportation system are warranted and in which cases not. The potential mobility index has been specifically designed to support this decision-making process. The potential mobility index indicates when a population group receives an above-average or below-average service from the transportation system. The index helps to delineate the role of transportation planning in two important ways. First, the index helps to determine to what extent the plight of population groups receiving an accessibility level below the sufficiency threshold is actually caused, at least in part, by a sub-standard transportation system. The lower the potential mobility level, the larger the contribution of the transportation system to a sub-standard level of accessibility, and the more warranted the claims for interventions in the transportation system. Second, the index can play an important role in delineating when further interventions in the transportation system are likely to deliver accessibility increments. The higher the existing level of potential mobility, the less likely that additional interventions in the transportation system will significantly improve potential mobility and thereby accessibility. At very high levels of potential mobility such interventions are only likely to have any impact if they introduce a transportation service of a fundamentally different quality than provided by the existing transportation system(s), which often implies extremely high costs (e.g. the introduction of high speed rail infrastructure and services). Both lines of reasoning thus suggest that the lower the level of potential mobility, the more warranted claims for improvements in the transportation system.

These two considerations obviously do not lead to a clear demarcation point or threshold regarding potential mobility. For reasons of simplicity, in what follows I will use the average level of car-based potential mobility in peak hours as the threshold for distinguishing groups entitled to improvements in the transportation system from groups that can claim no such entitlement. Graphically, this threshold is represented by the vertical axis in Figure 9.2. Clearly, as in the case of the accessibility sufficiency threshold, this is a decision that should be subject to democratic deliberation and selection. Here, I can only propose a possible demarcation level.

Step 4: Population groups entitled to accessibility improvements

The aim of the fourth step of transportation planning based on principles of justice is to identify population groups that are, at least in principle, entitled to accessibility improvements. This analysis can now be carried out with relative ease, based on the boundaries determined in the previous step. Clearly, all population groups falling below the accessibility sufficiency threshold and experiencing a below-average level of potential mobility belong to the set of groups potentially entitled to interventions in the transportation system.

Yet again, the analysis is less straightforward than it may seem at first. This is so because of the multi-dimensional nature of accessibility and the use of multiple accessibility sufficiency thresholds. Because of the former, multiple accessibility analyses will have to be conducted to gain an understanding of the size and scope of accessibility shortfalls experienced by different population groups. Because of the latter, the assessment of the situation of a population group will depend on the exact threshold that is selected. The use of twelve measurements of accessibility (Table 9.1) and five accessibility thresholds (10%-20%-30%-40%-50% of average car-based accessibility in peak hours) leads to a total of 60 assessments. This underlines, once again, that transportation planning based on principles of justice cannot be a simple 'cookbook' approach to identify and address transportation problems.

Figure 9.3 presents one set of results for the Amsterdam region. The case presented relates, again, to employment accessibility in peak hours for a 30-minute travel time threshold using a cumulative opportunity measure of accessibility. The data presents the situation for all sufficiency thresholds, from the most 'compassionate' threshold of 50% of average car-based accessibility in the region up to the 'harsh' threshold of only 10%. The figure shows that a high share of persons relying on public transport experience accessibility shortfalls for the highest sufficiency threshold, but also that this share is rapidly dropping with a decrease in the sufficiency threshold, from an initial 78% to 13% of the transit-dependent population for the lowest sufficiency threshold. The figure clearly shows that the share of the population is dropping more rapidly than the share of the zones with sub-standard accessibility levels by public transport, underscoring that low income groups are relatively over-represented in areas with comparatively high public transport accessibility. This may be the result of various processes, such as the residential choice behavior of low income groups, affordable housing policies, or public transport investment priorities, or all of these together. The situation is different for the high income groups, all of whom are assumed to have access to a car. Less than one-fifth of this population experiences accessibility shortfalls for the highest sufficiency threshold in peak hours, a number that drops gradually to less than 1% of the high-income population if the harshest threshold is applied.

This pattern roughly repeats itself for the peak hour period for other travel time thresholds and for a gravity-based measurement of accessibility. The situation is quite different, however, for accessibility to employment during off-peak hours. Indeed, during off-peak hours virtually none of the population groups with access to a car experiences a sub-standard level of accessibility. Even for the highest sufficiency threshold of 50%, only 2% of the population groups with access to a car (9 zones) experience a sub-standard accessibility level. All these groups, however, have an above-average level of potential mobility and are thus relatively well-served by the transportation system.

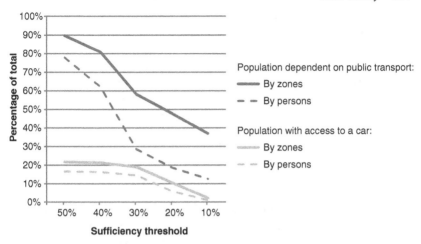

Figure 9.3 Share of the population with an accessibility level below the respective sufficiency thresholds, for accessibility to employment, a 30 minutes travel time threshold, a cumulative opportunity measure, and during peak hours.

These results for off-peak accessibility underscore that persons with access to a car typically experience reasonably high levels of accessibility. It is to be expected that this pattern will largely repeat itself for accessibility to other types of destinations, such as health care services and retail, and for other time slots, such as weekends and evening and night hours. Indeed, as Figure 9.2 powerfully depicts, the car provides a high level of accessibility in the Amsterdam context, even for persons living on the periphery of the region, throughout most of the day and the week, when (nearly) uncongested travel is typically possible. The situation is clearly fundamentally different for persons relying on public transport as their main mode to access places. A substantial share of this population experiences low levels of accessibility throughout most of the day and the week, because it is to be expected that the accessibility levels provided by the public transport system during off-peak hours is at best comparable to the levels during peak hours. The situation of these population groups is likely to be even worse during the evening and night hours, as well as at weekends, when public transport services are reduced or not available at all.

Step 5: Assessing the severity of accessibility deficiency

The results of the previous step of transportation planning based on principles of justice show that especially transit-dependent population groups are prone to experience accessibility shortfalls, but they also reveal that shortfalls occur among population groups with access to a car, at least during peak hours. The aim of the fifth step of the analysis is to assess the fairness of the transportation system in the Amsterdam region.

This assessment takes into account the prevalence and intensity of accessibility shortfalls, i.e. both the number of persons with an accessibility level below the sufficiency threshold and the size of their accessibility shortfalls, using the approach described in Chapter 8.

The analysis is first of all carried out separately for the transit-dependent population groups and the groups with access to a car. Subsequently, the pattern of accessibility deficiency will be analyzed for both types of population groups together. Since the assessment of the fairness of the transportation system depends on the accessibility threshold and the way of measuring accessibility, it is again necessary to carry out these analyses multiple times. In what follows, I will only present the results of the case described above: accessibility to employment in peak hours for a 30-minute travel time threshold using a cumulative opportunity measure of accessibility, for all five accessibility sufficiency thresholds (50% to 10% of average car-based accessibility in peak hours).

Accessibility deficiency among transit-dependent population groups

The analysis is conducted first for population groups assumed to rely solely on public transport for their travel. Nearly 90% of all 190 population groups (170 groups) contribute to overall accessibility deficiency when applying the most compassionate sufficiency threshold of 50% of car-based accessibility in peak hours. The vast majority of these 170 groups contribute less than 1% to total accessibility deficiency, while only ten groups show a contribution of more than 2% (Figure 9.4). The contribution of these latter groups is determined by both their population size (with an average population of 2,094 persons versus 1,076 persons for all 190 population groups) and their accessibility shortfall (the distance between the measured accessibility level and the sufficiency threshold). The situation obviously changes for lower sufficiency thresholds. As the number of population groups experiencing accessibility shortfalls drops, the contribution of these population groups to overall accessibility deficiency obviously goes up. For instance, for the 20% threshold, 'only' 90 population groups experience a sub-standard accessibility level. Of this set, 21 groups contribute more than 2% to total accessibility deficiency.

The spatial pattern of accessibility deficiency changes fundamentally with a decrease in the sufficiency threshold. For the 50% threshold, only the transit-dependent population groups residing directly in and around the city center of Amsterdam have a sufficient level of accessibility (20 zones, i.e. 11% of all zones in the region). These population groups obviously benefit from the high quality of the public transport system in the urban core, as well as from the proximity to jobs in both the city center and the concentration of offices in the south of the city. The small core of postal zones enjoying a sufficient level of public transport

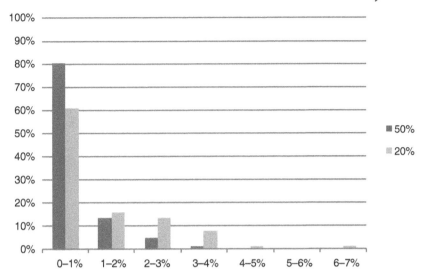

Figure 9.4 Share of transit-dependent population groups by their contribution to overall accessibility deficiency, for a 50% (n = 170) and 20% (n = 90) sufficiency threshold, for a 30-minute travel time threshold, a cumulative opportunity measure, and during peak hours.

accessibility expands, in a nearly exemplary way, outward with each drop in the sufficiency threshold (Figure 9.5). Note that this pattern emerges in spite of the fact that all jobs around a zone, whether located within or outside the Amsterdam region, are taken into account in measuring accessibility. That is, the zones on the outskirts of the Amsterdam region do not have a low level of accessibility because of their peripheral location vis-à-vis the concentration of jobs in the city of Amsterdam. Actually, the zones in the south of the Amsterdam region are located relatively close to the city of Utrecht as well as to the international airport of Amsterdam, both of which are concentrations of employment. Apparently, the relative proximity to these centers does not translate into substantial job accessibility by public transport, probably at least in part because of the historic structure of the public transport system and its orientation towards the city center of Amsterdam.

The analysis of the spatial pattern suggests that accessibility deficiency retreats to rural areas with a decrease in the sufficiency threshold. This impression is misleading, however. An additional analysis by urbanization level shows that accessibility deficiency remains a primarily (sub)urban phenomenon in the Amsterdam region. To see this, all zones have been arranged by urbanization level and the contribution of each type of zone to overall accessibility deficiency in the region has been analyzed. This analysis results in the percentage that each type of zone is contributing to overall accessibility deficiency, with the total adding up to 100%. As

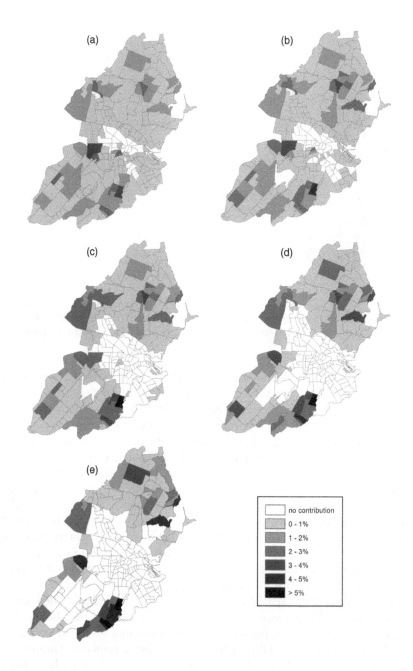

Figure 9.5 Spatial pattern of accessibility deficiency among transit-dependent population groups in the Amsterdam region, for sufficiency thresholds of (a) 50%, (b) 40%, (c) 30%, (d) 20% and (e) 10%, for accessibility to employment, for a 30-minute travel time threshold, a cumulative opportunity measure, and during peak hours.

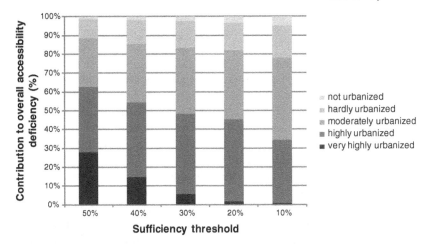

Figure 9.6 Contribution of transit-dependent population groups to overall accessibility deficiency, by level of urbanization and as dependent on the sufficiency threshold, for accessibility to employment, a 30-minute travel time threshold, a cumulative opportunity measure, and during peak hours.

discussed in the previous chapter, the Accessibility Fairness Index enables this analysis, which is one reason for adopting this measure. The results are shown in Figure 9.6. This figure shows that the contribution of the 'very highly urbanized' zones drops rapidly with a decrease in the sufficiency threshold, but the overall contribution of the 'highly urbanized' zones actually increases with a drop in the threshold. Only for the lowest thresholds of 20% and 10% does the relative share of the 'highly urbanized' zones decrease in favor of the 'moderately urbanized' zones. The contribution of the 'hardly urbanized' and 'not urbanized' zones remains low, irrespective of the sufficiency threshold. This is obviously the consequence of the small size of the population groups residing in these two types of zone. Thus, while the accessibility shortfalls are most substantial in these zones, the number of people affected by these extremely low levels of accessibility is limited.

Accessibility deficiency among groups benefitting from car-based accessibility

The situation of the population groups benefiting from car-based accessibility is substantially different from the conditions experienced by the transit-dependent groups. In this case, 41 population groups (22% of 190 groups) contribute to overall accessibility deficiency when applying the sufficiency threshold of 50%, and this number drops to 4 groups for the lowest threshold of 10%. Since a relatively small number of population groups experience accessibility shortfalls, their contribution to overall accessibility deficiency is relatively high. For the 50% threshold, the average contribution of a population group to overall accessibility deficiency, if weighed by population size, is 4%. The figure obviously goes up with a drop in the sufficiency threshold. Note that these results relate to the situation for peak hours and that the accessibility sufficiency thresholds are derived from the average car-based accessibility under peak conditions. Under off-peak conditions, no person with access to a car experiences an accessibility level below the accessibility sufficiency threshold due to a poorly functioning transportation system. This holds irrespective of the threshold that is applied.

The spatial pattern of accessibility deficiency for the groups benefiting from car-based accessibility is quite distinct from the pattern observed for the transit-dependent population groups. Virtually all groups with access to a car and experiencing accessibility shortfalls are located in the north of the Amsterdam region. This may come as no surprise, as the area to the north of Amsterdam offers relatively few jobs and is also bordered by the North Sea to the west and Lake IJssel to the east, substantially reducing the benefits of the higher speeds afforded by the car-road system. Furthermore, the North Sea Canal and River IJ create a barrier to accessing employment in the south of the region, in particular during rush hours. In contrast, the population groups residing to the south of Amsterdam benefit substantially from their proximity to the employment in and around the cities of The Hague, Utrecht and Rotterdam and the excellent road network connecting these cities to Amsterdam.

As is the case for public transport-based accessibility deficiency, car-based accessibility deficiency is hardly a rural phenomenon (Figure 9.8). The highest levels of urbanization account for the vast majority of the accessibility deficiency, for all sufficiency thresholds except the lowest one. For the lowest threshold, the moderately and hardly urbanized areas have a comparable contribution to overall accessibility deficiency. Interestingly, the areas with the highest and lowest urbanization level hardly contribute to overall accessibility deficiency, irrespective of the sufficiency threshold.

Accessibility deficiency across the entire population

The final analysis in this step of transportation planning based on principles of justice provides an assessment of accessibility deficiency across all population groups, i.e. jointly for population groups with and without access to a car. This results in an understanding of the overall patterns of accessibility deficiency across the region, as well as in the relative contribution of each of these population groups.

The analysis is carried out first for the case of employment accessibility, for a 30-minute travel time threshold, a cumulative accessibility measure, and during peak hours. Perhaps against expectations, population groups

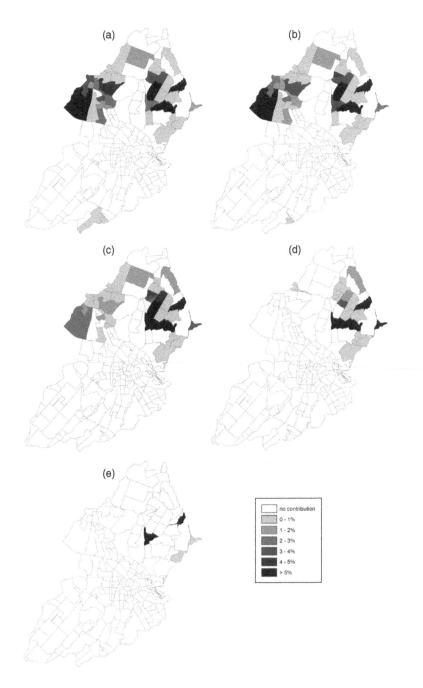

Figure 9.7 Spatial pattern of accessibility deficiency among population groups with access to a car, for sufficiency thresholds (a) 50%, (b) 40%, (c) 30%, (d) 20% and (e) 10%, for accessibility to employment, for a 30-minute travel time threshold, a cumulative opportunity measure, and during peak hours.

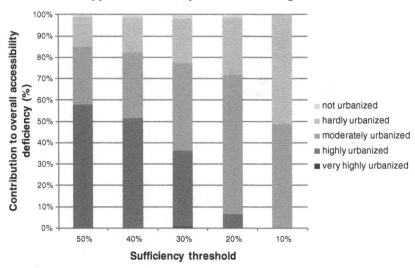

Figure 9.8 Contribution of population groups with access to a car to overall accessibility deficiency, by level of urbanization and as dependent on the sufficiency threshold, for accessibility to employment, a 30-minute travel time threshold, a cumulative opportunity measure, and during peak hours.

with access to a car show a larger contribution to overall accessibility deficiency than transit-dependent groups. Indeed, the former groups account for 61% of overall accessibility deficiency for the highest sufficiency threshold, a share that drops gradually to 13% for the harshest threshold. Only for the two lowest sufficiency thresholds do transit-dependent groups account for a higher share of overall accessibility deficiency than groups with access to a car (Figure 9.9).

There are a number of reasons that can explain this counter-intuitive result. First, these results are the consequence of the way in which population groups have been distinguished in Step 1, above. The assumption that all persons, except for those in the lowest income quintile, have access to a car directly determines the size of both types of population groups. The four highest income quintiles account for 85% of the total population of the Amsterdam region, meaning that it is assumed that 85% of all adults in the region have access to a car or have the (financial) means to secure access to a car if necessary. Clearly, this assumption can be criticized on a number of grounds (in spite of the reasons for adopting it, as outlined above).

Second, and just as important, is the fact that the analysis conducted here relates to the particular case of employment accessibility, for a 30-minute travel time threshold and a cumulative accessibility measure, during peak hours. Since accessibility is a multi-dimensional concept, as discussed in Chapter 8, the assessment of accessibility deficiency should be based on multiple ways of measuring accessibility and should take into account the situation of persons as it changes throughout the day and the

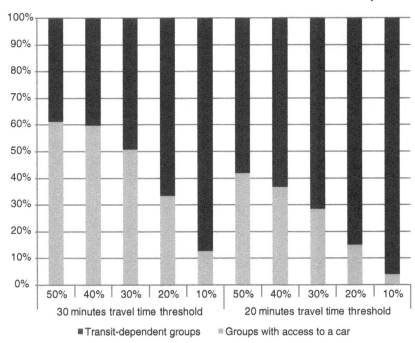

Figure 9.9 Contribution to overall accessibility deficiency of groups with access to a car and transit-dependent groups, for a 30- and a 20-minute travel time threshold, a cumulative accessibility measure, and during peak hours.

week. For instance, it may be expected that the relative contribution to overall accessibility deficiency of population groups with and without access to a car will differ fundamentally between peak and off-peak hours.

To show how the contribution of all population groups to overall accessibility deficiency changes under different circumstances, the analysis has been repeated for a 20-minute travel time threshold (Figure 9.9). As before, the analysis was carried out for employment accessibility, for peak hours, using a cumulative opportunity measure of accessibility. Note that the sufficiency thresholds for accessibility have been defined as a percentage of the average level of car-based accessibility for a 20-minute travel time threshold under peak travel conditions. That is, the sufficiency thresholds are adjusted to the way of measuring accessibility. Based on these starting points, the contribution of the population groups to overall accessibility deficiency changes radically. The population groups with access to a car only account for 42% of overall accessibility deficiency for the highest sufficiency threshold. This contribution decreases gradually as harsher sufficiency thresholds are employed, to a mere 4% for the harshest sufficiency threshold.

Due to a lack of data it is not possible to carry out a comparable analysis for off-peak hours. Yet, even lacking data on public transport accessibility during these hours, it may be clear that population groups dependent on public transport will account for the bulk of the accessibility deficiency in the region during off-peak hours. This clearly holds for the case used throughout this entire chapter: accessibility to employment, for a cumulative accessibility measure, and a 30-minute travel time threshold. For these parameters, none of the population groups with access to a car experiences an accessibility level below any of the sufficiency thresholds. This implies that for this case the entire burden of accessibility deficiency is carried by the population groups without access to a car.

These findings suggest that the results of the accessibility analyses, for various travel time thresholds and various accessibility measures, should be considered jointly in order to determine which population groups are most entitled to interventions in the transportation system. This challenge will be taken up in the sixth step of transportation planning based on principles of justice.

Step 6: Prioritizing population groups

The sixth step of transportation planning based on principles of justice, and the last step to be illustrated in this book, consists of the prioritization of population groups entitled to accessibility improvements. The results of the analyses so far have generated a rich understanding of the patterns of accessibility deficiency in the Amsterdam region, based on different measurements of accessibility and different sufficiency thresholds. Each of these analyses generates a different pattern of accessibility deficiency and suggests that a different set of groups are experiencing the impacts of accessibility deficiency in the region. The aim of the sixth step is to bring these analyses together in order to identify the groups that are most entitled to interventions in the transportation system.

The approach proposed in the previous chapter consisted of adding up, by population group, the contribution to accessibility deficiency for each way of measuring accessibility. By doing so, a measure of the total contribution of a population group to 'overall' accessibility deficiency is created, which enables the identification (and perhaps ranking) of population groups most entitled to improvements in accessibility. It was also suggested in the previous chapter that these analyses should be carried out separately for each accessibility sufficiency threshold, because the threshold strongly determines the pattern of accessibility deficiencies. In line with these suggestions, the analysis has been carried out for the entire set of sufficiency thresholds distinguished above.

The analyses are based on twelve different ways of measuring car-based accessibility (including peak and off-peak measurement) and six different ways of measuring transit-based accessibility (excluding off-peak measurement) (see Table 9.1). The average contribution to accessibility deficiency by population group has been calculated by adding up the contribution by group to each type of accessibility measurement, divided by the number of accessibility measurements (so divided by 12 for car-based accessibility and divided by 6 for transit-based accessibility). This approach is in many ways arbitrary, but it does give a grasp of the extent to which a particular population group may be affected by the accessibility deficiency in a region under various circumstances.

Clearly, each way of measuring accessibility will result in a distinct pattern of contributions to overall accessibility deficiency. The variation in these patterns is not only the direct result of the differences in the measurement of accessibility, but also the indirect consequence of accessibility measurement on the composition of the population below and above the sufficiency thresholds. For instance, if a gravity-based accessibility measure implies that a relatively large number of groups falls below the sufficiency threshold, then each of these groups will clearly show a relatively small contribution to overall accessibility deficiency. Likewise, if fewer groups fall below the sufficiency threshold when measuring accessibility for off-peak hours, then each group falling below the threshold will clearly show a relatively high contribution to overall accessibility deficiency for this way of measuring accessibility.

Let me now turn to the analysis of the pattern of accessibility deficiencies, in order to provide direction for the identification of population groups particularly entitled to improvements in accessibility. Before presenting the results, it is important to underscore that the Accessibility Fairness Index combines the size of the accessibility shortfall and the size of the population group into one composite index. This implies that the high ranking of a population group is shaped by both factors. The definition of the population groups thus directly impacts the results of the analyses. This is important for two reasons. First, population groups have been distinguished based solely on income levels and without taking into account the variety of (im)possibilities across these population groups for using a range of transportation modes. As discussed above, this raises some concerns about the size of the population groups with and without access to a car. A more fine-grained distinction of population groups may well be called for (see Currie 2010 for one possibility). Second, the size of each population group is at least in part an artifact of the way in which the Amsterdam region is divided up into smaller and larger zones. The use of zones as the unit of analysis and the arbitrary delineation of the zones also directly impact on the measurement of accessibility and thus have consequences for the 'observed' levels of accessibility for each population group. In light of these concerns, it may be clear that the application of the Accessibility Fairness Index within the context of transportation planning based on principles of justice would benefit substantially from a more systematic way of distinguishing population groups and a more detailed measurement of accessibility (see Martens and Plomp 2014 and Rofe, Benenson *et al.* 2015 for some steps in this direction). Clearly, the moral significance of the way in which population groups are distinguished and accessibility is measured becomes increasingly apparent the more the analysis proceeds towards feeding the democratic decision-making process with information directly relevant to priority setting. In spite of these concerns, an analysis has been conducted of the average contribution of each population group to total accessibility deficiency based on the data at hand: population groups as defined by income levels; accessibility as measured at the zonal level; the full range of accessibility measurements; and the entire set of sufficiency thresholds.

The results of this analysis are quite complex in nature. For each sufficiency threshold, a different ranking of population groups emerges. This is the result of the fact that a group's contribution to overall accessibility deficiency is dependent on the composition of the entire set of groups below the sufficiency threshold, as mentioned above. Thus a group may go up in the ranking when moving from the 50% to the 40% sufficiency threshold, while going down when moving from the 40% to the 30% sufficiency threshold, and so on. Likewise, some groups may rank high for the most compassionate sufficiency threshold due to their population size, while disappearing from the ranking altogether with a decrease in the sufficiency threshold because of a relatively low accessibility shortfall.

This complex pattern is clearly visible when analyzing the ranking of the population groups dependent on public transport across the range of sufficiency thresholds. Of all transit-dependent population groups, only three end up in the 'top ten' for each sufficiency threshold. This suggests that these population groups are particularly entitled to improvements in their accessibility level. Interestingly, all three population groups are located in parts of three relatively large suburbs of Amsterdam: Volendam, Uithoorn, and Amstelveen. The ranking of other transit-dependent population groups varies more strongly in relation to the sufficiency threshold and is therefore less clear-cut.

A complex pattern also emerges if a ranking is created for both sets of population groups jointly, i.e. for groups with and without access to a car. For the 50% sufficiency threshold, the ranking is 'headed' by a transit-dependent population group (located, against expectations, within the city of Amsterdam), but the second and third 'place' are taken by population groups with access to a car (both zones are located in the suburb of Volendam). The average accessibility shortfall of these latter groups is relatively modest (46% and 60% respectively of the accessibility shortfall experienced by the first-ranked transit-dependent population group), but their contribution to overall accessibility deficiency is still very high due to the population size of each group (nearly three and two times the size of the first-ranked transit dependent population group). As may be expected, the number of population groups with access to a car ending up relatively high in the ranking decreases with a drop in the sufficiency threshold. This is the result of the fact that the average accessibility shortfall is relatively limited for most groups with access to a car. For the harshest sufficiency threshold, only one group with access to a car ends up relatively high in the ranking of all population groups (the group in the small town of Ilpendam). The contribution of the population groups with car access located in the two zones in the suburb of Volendam remains high, also vis-à-vis all transit-dependent population groups in the region, for all sufficiency thresholds except the harshest threshold of 10% (see Figure 9.10).

The latter finding is highly relevant from a policy perspective. It suggests that a large part of the population of the suburb of Volendam is experiencing sub-standard levels of accessibility, irrespective of whether they have access to a car or not. It also suggests that interventions in the transportation system should be inclusive in nature, at least potentially serving all population groups, i.e. groups with and without access to a car, at the same time. Interestingly enough, and perhaps resonating Fainstein's positive assessment of the fairness of planning in Amsterdam, since the mid-1990s the suburb of Volendam has already been connected to Amsterdam through a free bus lane running along a relatively long stretch of the N247 connector road between the town and the city (Figure 9.10). The results of the analyses suggest that this investment has been more than warranted to guarantee at least some level of accessibility for this part of the region; but the results also underscore that more is needed to bring the accessibility levels of population groups with and without access to a car above the sufficiency threshold (however defined). This may well imply a further improvement of the bus lane, a higher priority for buses at intersections, or a higher frequency of buses throughout a larger part of the day and week. The metro line currently under construction in Amsterdam may well boost accessibility to employment for residents of Volendam, provided transfers between bus and metro are smooth and high frequencies are offered on both transportation modes so as to reduce transfer times.

The analyses furthermore seem to suggest that public transport connections to Uithoorn and Amstelveen are in need of substantial improvement, but without further analyses it is unclear whether connections should be improved with the city of Amsterdam or with Schiphol airport or other centers of employment in the Amsterdam region or beyond (notably, Utrecht). In the case of Uithoorn, improvements are also warranted to address the situation of persons with car access, as they, too, experience a sub-standard accessibility level for all sufficiency thresholds, although the accessibility shortfall is much less severe than for the transit-dependent population. The southern part of Amstelveen does provide a sufficient level of accessibility for persons with access to a car, so improvements are solely required to address the accessibility shortfall experienced by persons dependent on public transport. This does not imply, of course, that persons with access to a car cannot benefit from improvements in the public transport system.

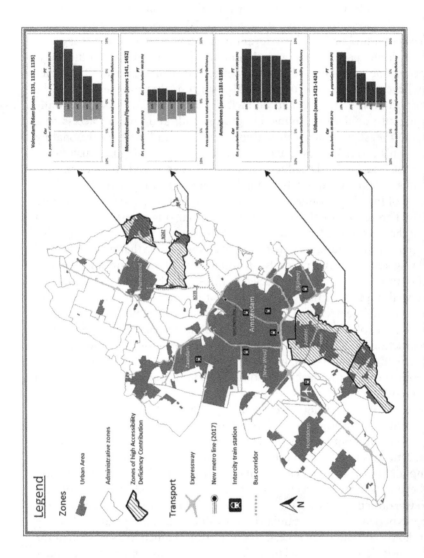

Figure 9.10 The location of the population groups with the highest contribution to overall accessibility deficiency in the Amsterdam region; the size of the contribution for groups with and without access to a car; and the location of key transportation infrastructures. Map produced by Sonam Plomp.

In addition to these three zones, transit-dependent population groups in a number of other zones contribute a relatively large share to overall accessibility deficiency across all five sufficiency thresholds. These zones include Monnickendam and Edam, both located in close proximity to Volendam, as well as the zones belonging to the 'growth town' of Purmerend and the smaller town of Middenbeemster. Furthermore, groups with access to a car located in Ilpendam and Monnickendam also bear a substantial share of the burden of overall accessibility deficiency (Figure 9.10). All these zones are located to the north of Amsterdam, an area with a relatively low job density and small size due to its location between the North Sea in the west and Lake IJssel in the east. The employment located in and around Amsterdam is thus of vital importance for the residents of these towns.

These findings suggest that interventions in the transportation system may well serve multiple population groups experiencing accessibility shortfalls at the same time. The zones in and around the suburb of Volendam will all be served by an improvement in the public transport service to the core of the Amsterdam region along the existing N247 connector road. Likewise, the zones in Purmerend and the towns of Middenbeemster and Ilpendam can benefit from an improved bus service along the existing N235 connector road. Furthermore, both parts of the region may well benefit from the new metro line which is currently under construction, as this line may substantially improve the accessibility to employment located in and on the (southern) edges of the city of Amsterdam, provided the bus–metro combination outperforms the existing direct bus lines between the towns and the center of Amsterdam. As mentioned before, this will require high speeds and frequencies of the bus and metro services, as well as easy transfers between both transportation modes. Because of the network effect, the importance of the new metro line thus reaches well beyond Amsterdam and may well be crucial to push the Amsterdam region towards a fair transport-land use system.

The above observations are based on a preliminary analysis of the pattern of accessibility deficiency and should therefore be interpreted with care. For one, the analyses cover only a limited set of accessibility measurements and do not include, for instance, an assessment of accessibility during evening and night hours and during weekends, nor an explicit assessment of accessibility to key destinations like hospitals or other vital services. Expanding the range of accessibility measurements is likely to change the pattern of accessibility deficiency, probably showing an increasing contribution of transit-dependent population groups to overall accessibility deficiency. Just as important is the fact that the analyses have been carried out without further delineating the accessibility sufficiency threshold. While some zones emerge irrespective of the exact sufficiency threshold, the plight of persons living in other zones is only visible for some of the sufficiency thresholds. This suggests that further democratic deliberation and decision-making is necessary to set a sufficiency threshold or at least to reduce the range of relevant sufficiency thresholds. Furthermore, the insights of the top-down analyses need to be complemented with a bottom-up understanding of accessibility problems. Clearly, the analyses presented here are only the beginning of the priority setting exercise.

Conclusion

In this chapter, I have shown how the 'rules' of transportation planning based on principles of justice can be applied to a practical case. The application has shown, perhaps first and foremost, that transportation planning is inevitably a political exercise. It requires a range of decisions that are partly technical and partly political in nature. It concerns decisions regarding the type of accessibility to be measured (to employment, services, or other land uses), the way to measure accessibility (cumulative versus gravity-based, but also ways of measuring waiting and transfer times, etc.), the way to distinguish population groups (by income, by access to transportation means, by ability, by education level), the types of transportation modes to be included (cycling, on-demand public transport), and so on. It also includes the key decisions about the thresholds for potential mobility and accessibility, which are a prerequisite for setting priorities. The setting of these thresholds may have to go beyond the fairly straightforward approach presented in the chapter. After all, it may be expected that Dworkin's imaginary immigrants as well as real-life persons will not only be concerned about the number of destinations (jobs, services, and so on) they can reach within a certain travel time threshold during peak and off-peak hours, but also about their level of accessibility during weekends and during evening and night hours, as well as about possible barriers that may lead to disparities between measured and experienced levels of accessibility. A proper measurement of the fairness of transport-land use systems is thus likely to be more complex than the exercise presented here. Some of these decisions can remain within the realm of technical experts, provided the consequences of such 'technical' decisions are systematically explored, assessed and, where necessary, presented to, and discussed with, multiple stakeholders. Other decisions, most notably the decision regarding the sufficiency thresholds, must be subject to explicit, transparent and well-structured democratic deliberation and selection. Transportation planning cannot move forward without being fed, from the initial stages onwards, by a democratic process of decision-making.

In the case study presented in this chapter, all of these decisions have been made by an 'expert', without a process of democratic deliberation. As a result, many arbitrary choices have been made. The key decision regarding the accessibility sufficiency threshold has been avoided by employing a range of thresholds. This has complicated the analyses, but has also provided a rich perspective on the pattern of accessibility deficiency in the Amsterdam region, among persons with and without access to a car. The application of transportation planning based on principles of justice to the Amsterdam region, while limited to the first six steps of the transportation planning process, has resulted in a preliminary identification of population groups entitled to improvements in accessibility through interventions in the transportation system. The application has not included the identification of possible interventions nor the assessment of these interventions, which is the subject of the final steps of transportation planning based on principles of justice. Yet, taken together, the results do provide an indication of possible interventions that could address the plight of the population groups affected by severe accessibility shortfalls, as well as a preliminary assessment of the possible benefits of the metro line that is currently under construction in the city of Amsterdam. While heavily criticized for its cost overruns and extensive delays in construction (see e.g. de Jong 2010), the line does seem to address accessibility shortfalls of population groups to the north of Amsterdam, thereby potentially improving the fairness of the transport-land use system in the entire region (albeit in a perhaps very expensive way). Clearly, it would require a full assessment of the impacts of the metro line in order to judge whether this major infrastructure investment reduces accessibility shortfalls in a cost-effective way or whether other interventions could achieve such a goal more effectively and efficiently. But while the national government has invested, and continues to invest, heavily in the expansion of the road network in the Amsterdam region, thus failing to address the plight of the population groups experiencing the most severe accessibility shortfalls, it could be argued that Amsterdam's firm political commitment to finish constructing the metro line supports Fainstein's claim that "Amsterdam may not be the ideal city ... but it still represents a model to which others may aspire" (Fainstein 2010, p. 164).

References

Bakker, P., P. Zwaneveld, J. Berveling, *et al.* (2009). Het belang van openbaar vervoer: de maatschappelijke effecten op een rij. Den Haag, Kennisinstituut voor Mobiliteit/Centraal Planbureau.

Benenson, I., K. Martens, Y. Rofé, *et al.* (2011). Public transport versus private car: GIS-based estimation of accessibility applied to the Tel Aviv metropolitan area. *The Annals of Regional Science*, 47(3): 499–515.

Currie, G. (2010). Quantifying spatial gaps in public transport supply based on social needs. *Journal of Transport Geography*, 18(1): 31–41.

Currie, G. and A. Delbosc (2011). Mobility versus affordability as motivations for car-ownership choice in urban fringe, low-income Australia. In: K. Lucas, E. Blumenberg and R. Weinberger (eds), *Auto Motives: understanding car use behaviours*. Bingley, Emerald, pp. 193–208.

de Jong, M. (2010). *The North-South line: explaining cost overruns and traffic shortfalls.* Paper presented at the 12th WCTR Conference, 11–15 July 2010, Lisbon, Portugal.

Fainstein, S.S. (2010). *The Just City.* Ithaca/London, Cornell University Press.

Martens, K. (2004). The bicycle as a feedering mode: experiences from three European countries. *Transportation Research Part D: Transport and Environment,* 9(4): 281–294.

Martens, K. (2007). Promoting bike-and-ride: the Dutch experience. *Transportation Research Part A: Policy and Practice,* 41(4): 326–338.

Martens, K. and S. Plomp (2014). Openbaar vervoer-bereikbaarheid in de Regio Utrecht: de kwaliteit van het dragende OV-netwerk. Nijmegen, Report for Bestuur Regio Utrecht.

Mattioli, G. (2014). Where sustainable transport and social exclusion meet: households without cars and car dependence in Great Britain. *Journal of Environmental Policy & Planning,* 16(3): 379–400.

Murray, A.T. (2005). Geography in coverage modeling: exploiting spatial structure to address complementary partial service of areas. *Annals of the Association of American Geographers,* 95(4): 761–772.

Ravallion, M. (1992). Poverty comparisons. *Living Standard Measurement Study Working Paper,* 88.

Rofe, Y., I. Benenson, K. Martens, *et al.* (2015). Accessibility and social equity in Tel-Aviv Metropolitan Area: examination of the current conditions and development scenarios. Beer Sheva/Tel Aviv, Report for the Israeli Ministry of Transport.

Sen, A. (1983). Poor, relatively speaking. *Oxford Economic Papers,* 35(2): 153–169.

Stępniak, M. and P. Rosik (2015). *The impact of data aggregation on potential accessibility values.* Springer International Publishing (Lecture Notes in Geoinformation and Cartography).

10 Seeking Transportation Justice

Radical consequences

I have nearly come to the end of my explorations of fairness in the domain of transportation. It has taken a lengthy argument to draw a conclusion that perhaps seems obvious to the reader: a transportation system is fair if, and only if, it provides a sufficient level of accessibility to all under most circumstances. This strong correspondence between the outcome of a lengthy philosophical exploration and what are perhaps readers' intuitions should not be seen as a failure of systematic argumentation. The goal of the entire effort has not been to prove wrong particular intuitions regarding justice in the domain of transportation. Its aim was rather to employ systematic reasoning to delineate a set of principles that could be defended on rational grounds. If this has led to a more solid footing for the often intuitive appeals to justice in transportation, all the better. In line with Rawls' notion of reflective equilibrium, the strong correspondence between reasoned argumentation and considered intuitions suggests that the principles developed in the book may well be widely shared and robust in character (Rawls 1971; see also Daniels 1996).

While the definition of a fair transportation system as a system that provides a sufficient level of accessibility to all under most circumstances may not seem radical in character, its consequences for transportation planning could not be more radical.

First, this definition of a fair transportation system has fundamental consequences for the obligations of persons vis-à-vis each other, and thus for governments as the practical vehicle to honor and implement these obligations. The definition goes hand in hand with the demarcation of a domain of insufficiency and a domain of sufficiency. As argued in the previous chapters, members of society only have obligations vis-à-vis each other in the domain of insufficiency. More precisely: persons experiencing insufficient levels of accessibility are entitled to improvements in their situation. They can rightfully make a claim on the wealth that is being generated by all members of society jointly for the improvement of their situation. In contrast, no such obligation exists in the domain of sufficiency. That is, persons experiencing a sufficient level of accessibility, as defined through the processes of democratic deliberation and selection, are in no way entitled to improvements in accessibility based on considerations of justice. In other words, the delineation of a fair transportation system sets strict boundaries around the role of governments in the domain of transportation.

Second, and related, the obligation to provide sufficient accessibility to all under most circumstances implies a radically different practice of transportation planning. While transportation planning is practiced in different ways in different places, the practice often represents some of the elements of the approach to transportation planning outlined in Chapter 2. Indeed, in many localities, the problems of congestion and environmental externalities take center stage in transportation planning. The former directs the attention to the functioning of the transportation system, rather than to the users of that system. The latter draws the focus towards car use and car users, rather than to all (potential) users of the transportation system (Martens 2015). Transportation planning based on principles of justice implies a radically different focus. It takes a person-centered approach. It starts from an analysis of the accessibility levels experienced by persons, explicitly and systematically taking into account their diversity in terms of available means of transportation, residential location, income levels, travel-related abilities, and so on. The pattern of accessibility levels, in turn, serves as the lens through which the functioning of the transportation system is analyzed. The focus thus radically shifts towards persons and towards the contribution of the transportation system to a person's ability to participate in out-of-home activities.

Third, the requirement on governments to provide sufficient accessibility to all under most circumstances has fundamental consequences for the financing of (interventions in) the transportation system. Given the importance of the financing scheme for transportation planning in general, and particularly for transportation planning based on principles of justice, I will take up this issue in the next section.

Fair financing of transportation

Our explorations so far have resulted in the delineation of the contours of a fair transportation system. That system should provide a sufficient level of accessibility to all under most, but not all, circumstances. The provision of such a fair transportation system will clearly be a costly matter. I therefore now turn to a brief exposition of the way in which a fair transportation system could and should be financed, as such a financing scheme is a crucial component of a fair transportation system.

Before doing so, let me first briefly describe the way in which transportation systems are currently being financed. Typically, transportation infrastructures and services are financed through a wide variety of sources. In both developed and developing countries, these sources include various types of user fees (e.g. fuel taxes, parking fees, public transport fares), infrastructure-related payments (such as road taxes, transport-related property taxes, and transport-related sales taxes), and general taxes (e.g. income, property and general sales taxation) (see Martens 2013 for a more elaborate discussion). Countries show considerable differences in the mixture of sources to finance the costs of operating, maintaining and expanding their transportation system. For instance, European countries typically rely heavily on fuel taxes and road taxes, while transport-related property taxes and transport-related sales taxes are increasingly used in the USA to finance maintenance and expansion of the transportation system (Goldman and Wachs 2003).

The use of the collected funds tends to be subject to sometimes heated societal debates. Since many of the resources are collected in relation to car ownership and car use, the debates often revolve around the appropriate use of these resources. Some perceive the various forms of taxation on car ownership and use (fuel tax, road tax, sales tax, parking levies, etc.) as imperfect proxies of a user fee paid to consume the infrastructures and services catering for the car. As a result, they argue that car-related taxes should only be used for operating, maintaining and investing in roads and other car-related facilities. Others argue in favor of various forms of cross-subsidy between car and other modes of transportation, most notably public transport services and bicycle infrastructures, often drawing on arguments about the environmental externalities and health benefits of different modes of transportation (Taylor and Norton 2009).

Transportation planning based on principles of justice proposes an entirely different financing scheme for the transportation domain, thereby shedding a new light on these societal debates. The financing scheme encompasses two distinct components. The first component consists entirely of user fees and applies to, but also defines, the domain of sufficiency. The second component applies to the domain of insufficiency and consists of a fair taxation scheme that generates the resources to guarantee a sufficient level of accessibility to persons struck by various forms of brute bad luck. Let me briefly elaborate both components.

User fees

The first component of the financing scheme for the transportation domain consists entirely of user fees. The case for financing transportation infrastructure and services based on user fees follows directly from the argument developed in Chapter 6. There, I argued that prudent immigrants would only seek insurance against forms of brute bad luck that might leave them stranded in the future. One of the insurance schemes sought by immigrants would protect them against the risk of disproportionately high transportation costs in relation to their level of income. But this argument also holds the other way around: prudent immigrants have no reason to purchase an insurance scheme to reduce their transportation costs if they have a sufficient level of income. Translated to the real world: prudent persons have no reason to agree to an inevitably coercive taxation scheme if they can afford the costs of transportation from their regular income. For persons with a sufficient income, transportation costs are an expense like any other good. By definition, a sufficient level of income enables them to purchase a sufficient level of travel and thus to obtain a sufficient level of 'consumption' of accessibility under (competitive) market conditions. Clearly, in any society a (substantial) part of the population will enjoy a sufficiently high income. The design of the basic scheme for financing the transportation system should be based on this understanding. That implies that the financing of all transportation infrastructures and services should be based, as much as practically possible, on user fees.

In line with mainstream economic theory, the level of the user fees should be set according to the principle of marginal cost pricing (Verhoef and Mohring 2009). This notion has important implications for the costs covered by the user fees. These fees are to pay for the costs of the initial capital investment and for the costs of operating and maintaining the available transportation infrastructures and services over time. The user fees can only include the costs of the initial capital investment until the initial investment is recouped. The moment the investment costs are redeemed, the user fees should be reduced to cover *only* operating and maintenance costs. Any user fee above this marginal cost level would imply a cost for users beyond what is necessary for the continued operation of the transportation facility and would thus de facto constitute a coercive form of taxation. Such an excessive user fee would be a form of taxation (or of excess profits where a transportation facility is offered by a for-profit organization), because the fees lie beyond the socially optimal marginal costs. The excess fees would be coercive because persons have no possibility of avoiding paying the excessive user fee whenever they want to 'consume' accessibility to participate in out-of-home activities. While the excessive user fees may be funneled back into the transportation system in the form of new expansions of the system, these expansions will inevitably only serve a limited number of persons and not necessarily the persons shouldering the cost of the excessive user fees. An excess charge would thus turn user fees into a coercive taxation scheme to be used for purposes beyond the direct interest of a large share of users themselves. In sum, fairness requires that the financing of the transportation system should be based, at least in the first instance, on the principle of marginal cost pricing.

This proposal for user fees differs fundamentally from real-world taxation schemes. Many countries use fuel taxes and road taxes as proxies for user fees on road travel. In countries with high levels of car-related taxation, the total sum of resources collected through these schemes often exceeds the costs of operating and maintaining the road system and for recouping the initial capital investments, certainly if external costs are excluded from the equation. These schemes are thus not mere proxies for a proper user fee, but actually include a form of (coercive) taxation that goes beyond that user fee. The approach underlying transportation planning based on principles of justice suggests that these taxation schemes should be replaced by a proper, limited, user fee and a different form of taxation explicitly directed towards the domain of insufficiency, as I will discuss below. In other countries, notably the USA, fuel taxes are an inadequate proxy for user fees for opposite reasons, as they fail to generate the funds necessary to maintain the infrastructure (Kirk and Mallett 2013). In this case, transportation planning based on principles of justice would result in the perhaps unpopular, but fair, proposition to replace fuel taxes by a proper and more expensive user fee.

Below, I will develop an argument based on the insurance schemes developed in Chapter 6 to deviate from user fees based on marginal cost pricing. Here, it is important to stress that other arguments may be put forward to deviate from applying user fees across the board for the entire transportation system. For instance, concerns regarding freedom of movement as a basic right may be a reason to refrain from applying user fees to walking, while environmental considerations may provide convincing arguments to refrain from a user fee for cycling, or high transaction costs may make a scheme of user fees based on marginal cost pricing highly inefficient. It is beyond the scope of the book to develop the entire argument to defend such deviations. What the argumentation developed here underlines is that deviations from a user fee principle should not be introduced too lightly.

Five final remarks are in place regarding financing based on user fees. First, new technologies make it increasingly possible to introduce pay-as-you-go schemes that are largely in line with the principle of user fees outlined here (Eliasson 2014). Second, the requirement that user fees only cover the costs of operation, maintenance and initial capital investment does not imply that improvements in the transportation system are impossible in the domain of sufficiency. It only implies that these improvements should be self-financing, as discussed in Chapter 7 (see also Verhoef and Mohring 2009). Third, it is an open question whether user fees should include external costs, such as traffic accidents, health costs or environmental pollution. It would require a full-fledged argument, but it seems reasonable to suggest that transportation should be treated in the same way as other activities: external costs should only be included in transportation user fees if such external costs are also included in the prices of other activities. Without any additional argument, there seems no particular reason to single out transportation for its external effects. I will return to some of these considerations below. Fourth, it is important to note that collective action, often facilitated through governments, remains essential even for investments fully financed through user fees, in order to obtain or retain the right-of-way typically necessary for transportation infrastructures and services. The requirement of self-finance thus does not imply that governments do not have a role in the domain of sufficiency, but it does severely limit that role. Fifth, and last, the development of a financing scheme based on user fees will require a major research effort, for instance to obtain detailed information on fixed costs, long-run marginal costs and short-run marginal costs, preferably at the level of individual links (see Eliasson 2014). Lacking such information, it will be necessary to revert to rough proxies, like fuel taxes or kilometer-based pricing, to implement the notion of user fees, in spite of the problems of the former approach in light of the rapidly changing fuel efficiency and composition of the car fleet.

Fair taxation

Let me now turn to the second component of a fair financing scheme for the transportation domain. This second component applies to the domain of insufficiency and consists of a fair taxation scheme that generates the resources to guarantee a sufficient level of accessibility for persons struck by various forms of brute bad luck. Let me briefly highlight the various forms of brute bad luck that may befall real-life persons, as they were discussed in Chapter 6.

First, a person may lack the financial resources required to purchase a sufficient level of accessibility. The share of persons experiencing this situation will depend not only on the income distribution in a society (and whether that distribution is shaped by the principles outlined by Rawls or Dworkin), but also on the pattern of transportation user fees that follows from the first component of the fair financing scheme. The user fees, in turn, will depend on the circumstances, such as urban densities, topological conditions, technological development, economies of scale in infrastructure provision, and so on. It is the height of the transportation user fees (in combination with the costs of all other goods) that determines what is a sufficient level of income in a particular situation. Persons with insufficient income either experience consumption poverty (in which case they use their insufficient income to maintain a sufficient level of accessibility) or accessibility poverty (in which case they use their insufficient income to consume other goods than accessibility) (see Chapter 6). The aim of the fair taxation scheme is to mitigate this form of brute bad luck caused by too high transportation user fees. Thus in this case, the resources generated through the fair taxation scheme will be used to reduce the transportation user fees for persons with an insufficient level of income. This can be done in various ways, such as in-cash payments or earmarked vouchers for the purchase of public transport tickets or fuel for transportation (see for an interesting parallel, subsidies on fuel for home heating in the UK; Walker 2008). Clearly, schemes that directly target the population affected by this form of brute bad luck are to be preferred over general schemes aimed at lowering the costs of travel across the board for the entire population, unless the latter type of schemes are more cost-effective because of, for instance, transactions costs involved in earmarked schemes.

Note that a strict application of marginal cost pricing may well result in fairly high user fees during hours in which many people seek to use the transportation system. Thus, since persons often have little choice regarding their time of travel, especially during peak hours, a strict application of marginal cost pricing may well push a substantial number of persons into a situation of insufficient income to maintain a sufficient level of accessibility. Clearly, prudent and well-informed immigrants would seek protection against such a form of brute bad luck (i.e. the bad luck that societal arrangements leave the immigrants little choice but to travel during peak hours). The argument developed here could thus also support a reduction in the user fees during peak hours for a large segment of the population, well below the level of user fees based on marginal cost pricing. The explorations thus provide support for the arguments of opponents of the introduction of congestion pricing schemes based on the principle marginal cost pricing, certainly if such schemes are applied to all available transportation services (i.e. for road and public transport) and do not include any exemptions for particular (low income) groups.

The extent to which persons experience a lack of financial resources to purchase a sufficient level of accessibility will obviously depend on the residential location of the person. The costs of maintaining a sufficient level of accessibility will go up as a person moves away from a central location towards a more peripheral location, as the person will have to travel over larger distances and will thus incur higher total user fees. Since residential location is certainly not always a matter of choice, as was discussed in Chapter 6, these differences in the costs of maintaining a sufficient level of accessibility should be taken into account in the subsidies provided to persons. As discussed before, these subsidies could take different forms, such as in-cash payments or earmarked vouchers. What is important to underline here is that the level of these payments or vouchers should be differentiated according to the residential area of the persons, taking into account their income levels as well as housing costs (which are likely to be lower in the periphery) (in line with the findings of e.g. Mattingly and Morrissey 2014).

The second form of brute bad luck that may adversely affect a person's accessibility levels relates to the quality, rather than the pricing, of the transportation system. In particular, persons who cannot make use of the dominant transportation system in a society, for reasons of physical or mental abilities or for legal reasons, may be subject to this form of brute bad luck, as alternative transportation services may be non-existent or provide a sub-standard level of service (see Chapter 6 on 'Insuring for travel-related impairments'). Yet persons with access to the dominant transportation system may also face this risk whenever the dominant system provides a sub-standard level of service resulting in an insufficient level of accessibility. Such sub-standard levels of service may have various causes, such as long access and egress times, low in-vehicle speeds, multiple transfers, or even concerns regarding personal risk and safety. Each of these components can de facto reduce the level of accessibility as experienced by persons. What is important here is that the resulting lack of accessibility cannot simply be solved through some form of monetary subsidy that reduces the costs of obtaining a sufficient level of accessibility. The only way to avoid this form of brute bad luck is by improving the transportation system so that a sufficient level of accessibility is restored. In this case, the aim of the fair taxation scheme is to generate financial resources that can be used for improving the transportation system so as to increase the accessibility level of persons below the sufficiency threshold. In other words, the purpose of the fair taxation system is to generate the funds to expand the existing (alternative) transportation system. Clearly, no taxation scheme will be able to generate sufficient funds to finance improvements that bring all persons above the accessibility sufficiency threshold in one sweeping move. Building a just transportation system will take years of sustained effort. The fair taxation scheme should enable such a sustained effort: it should generate sufficient funds for the gradual improvement of the (alternative) system for the benefit of persons below the sufficiency threshold. Note that improvements in the alternative system may not only solve the accessibility deficiencies of persons excluded from the dominant transportation system because of travel-related impairments. If the price of using the alternative system is lower than the price of the dominant transportation system, it may also provide an efficient way to improve the accessibility of persons excluded from the dominant transportation system for reasons of cost.

What would a fair taxation scheme in the domain of transportation look like? Following the argument developed in Chapter 6, there is no reason to link the taxation scheme to the use of the transportation system, as is currently the case in many countries around the world (typically in the form of road taxes and fuel taxes). In contrast to these forms of taxation, which are often at least in part a proxy for a user fee which has historically been difficult to implement and administer, the fair transportation tax is a form of insurance that protects all persons against various forms of accessibility risk. It follows that the taxation is thus also to be paid by all (adult) persons in a society to protect them against these risks. Since the taxation is not a user fee 'in disguise', there is no reason to link the level of the taxation to the actual use of the transportation system. Indeed, following Dworkin's argument in support of a progressive taxation scheme, it seems most reasonable to link the level of taxation to a person's income level.

Clearly, it is beyond the scope of any theoretical exploration to determine in even an approximate way the total size of the fair taxation scheme. The only indication that can be derived from the brief argument above is that the total size of the resources generated through the fair taxation scheme should be able to cover the costs of the monetary subsidies on the user fees and still leave sufficient funds to gradually upgrade the transportation system wherever it still provides insufficient levels of accessibility. Only if significant resources are generated will it be possible to finance interventions that will gradually move the transportation system towards the domain of sufficiency.

Let me summarize the fair financing scheme for the transportation domain. The core of the scheme consists of user fees based on the principle of marginal cost pricing. The user fees are to cover the costs of operation, maintenance and the initial capital investment of transportation infrastructures or services. The proceeds from the user fees are to be complemented by funds raised through a fair taxation scheme. The resources generated through this scheme serve two purposes. First, they may be used to allow for deviations from marginal cost pricing whenever persons are pushed into the domain of insufficiency because of the high costs of transportation. In this case, the proceeds of the taxation scheme may be used to provide subsidies on user fees (for the use of the dominant or alternative transportation systems) in order to bring persons back into the realm of sufficiency. Second, the proceeds of the taxation scheme may be used for improvements in the (dominant or alternative) transportation system wherever a sub-standard quality leads to insufficient levels of accessibility. The funds collected through the fair taxation scheme may only be used for these two purposes and not for any other goals. Expansions of the existing transportation system(s) that are not warranted based on considerations of justice should be self-financing based on user fees or financed through a separate taxation scheme justified on other grounds than considerations of justice.

The search for transportation justice thus requires a radical overhaul of current financing schemes in the domain of transportation. Indeed, justice in transportation cannot be pursued without a fair financing scheme. It is the prerequisite for a transformation of the transportation system towards a system that provides a sufficient level of service to (virtually) all persons.

Justly solving congestion

Over the past decades, the bulk of the intellectual energy, societal debates, and public resources have been dedicated to solving congestion (Goodwin 1997). This may come as no surprise, as traditional transportation planning has emerged first and foremost as an approach to addressing (road) congestion (see Chapter 2). The argumentation put forward in this book suggests that this attention has at best been misplaced. Indeed, following transportation planning based on principles of justice, congestion seems to be hardly a transportation problem at all. More precisely, from the justice perspective developed in this book, congestion is only a transportation problem if it leads to an insufficient level of accessibility. This is clearly a far-reaching statement which is in need of further support and specification. Let me do this separately for the domains of insufficiency and sufficiency.

The domain of insufficiency relates to all cases in which persons experience an insufficient level of accessibility. Clearly, such a situation can be caused by (severe levels of) congestion. Indeed, as illustrated in the Amsterdam case study, a small share of the population with access to a car experiences an insufficient level of accessibility which is in part caused by a sub-standard functioning of the transportation system. Most of these population groups face insufficient levels of accessibility only during a small part of the day, and typically experience relatively high levels of accessibility during off-peak hours. Yet it would be fundamentally mistaken to assume at the outset that access to a car always delivers sufficient accessibility or that congestion will never lead to insufficient levels of accessibility for persons with access to a car. Transportation planning based on principles of justice is and should be open-ended in this sense. It takes the situation of *all* persons as its starting point and is fundamentally open to the wide diversity in persons' abilities and circumstances. The accessibility level experienced by persons with (continuous) access to a car should be subject to assessment just as much as the accessibility level of persons who rely on public transport or other modes of transportation.

The approach developed throughout this book clearly suggests that all persons experiencing an accessibility level below the sufficiency threshold due to a sub-standard transportation system are, at least in principle, entitled to interventions in the transportation system. This basic principle also applies to persons with access to a car who fall below the sufficiency threshold, irrespective of the exact cause of the accessibility shortfall. Clearly, in cases where the shortfall is at least in part caused by (severe) congestion on the road network, interventions are warranted to address this cause of injustice. At the same time, the identification of congestion as a cause for accessibility poverty does not translate directly into a specific type of intervention in the transportation system. As has been argued in Chapter 8, the search for solutions should be guided by the understanding that interventions should address accessibility shortfalls of as many groups simultaneously as possible. The search for solutions should thus start by identifying other groups, in particular in and around the same locality, who also experience accessibility shortfalls. It may be expected that neighborhoods with an insufficient level of car-based accessibility will often (although not necessarily always) also provide an insufficient level of accessibility to persons dependent on public transport.

Indeed, in the Amsterdam case study, each zone with an insufficient car-based accessibility provides an even lower level of accessibility to persons who rely on public transport to engage in out-of-home activities. In such cases, inclusive solutions that improve the situation of as many persons as possible simultaneously are highly preferred over more exclusionary forms of interventions for only a segment of the population, certainly if the costs of the former stay within reasonable proportions in comparison to less-inclusive solutions. In practical terms, this may imply giving preference to improvements in the public transport system over upgrades of the road network as a means of addressing the plight of persons with an insufficient level of car-based accessibility.

To summarize the argument, accessibility shortfalls caused by congestion are as much an injustice as accessibility shortfalls caused by inadequate public transport services or any other cause. But justice considerations also suggest that whenever inclusive solutions are available that can address the plight of as many persons as possible simultaneously, these solutions are strongly preferred over more exclusionary forms of interventions such as road widening or traffic management schemes.

Let me now turn to congestion in the domain of sufficiency. Following the principles of justice laid out in the previous chapters, interventions in the transportation system financed through a fair taxation scheme are not warranted within the domain of sufficiency. This also implies that if congestion does not lead to insufficient levels of accessibility, no interventions in the transportation system are justified based on considerations of justice. It would, however, be too quick to conclude that no interventions are acceptable whatsoever to reduce congestion in the domain of sufficiency. Two types of interventions to alleviate congestion can be distinguished.

The first type encompasses all interventions that are self-financing and can be realized without an, inevitably coercive, scheme of taxation. This type of interventions are only legitimate if they do not aggravate existing injustices in the domain of transportation. That is, these interventions are acceptable only if they do not increase the level of accessibility deficiency, i.e. as long as the accessibility improvements for persons above the sufficiency threshold do not lead to transport or land use dynamics with detrimental impacts on the accessibility levels experienced by persons with already poor accessibility levels, or as long as these detrimental effects are compensated through measures improving the accessibility levels for persons below the sufficiency threshold. A second condition could be added, although it does not flow directly from the argumentation developed in this book. This condition states that interventions in the transportation system that improve the situation of persons who already experience an accessibility level above the sufficiency threshold are only acceptable if they do not lead to an increase in the environmental impacts of the transportation system. The argument here would be that interventions that affect the environment as a resource shared by all members of society are only acceptable if there are strong reasons for them. Clearly, if interventions only improve the accessibility provided to persons who already have sufficient accessibility (and do not generate other benefits, notably in terms of economic growth, health or road safety), then strong reasons for such interventions are lacking. This is a strong condition, which obviously requires further support, but I will leave this to another occasion.

The second type encompasses interventions in the domain of sufficiency that cannot be entirely self-financing. If this is the case, i.e. if it is not possible to generate enough funds through user fees or through third-party beneficiaries such as landowners to finance a particular intervention, then such interventions can only be financed through some scheme of taxation that is different from the fair taxation scheme outlined above. Such a (inevitably coercive) scheme of taxation obviously requires a strong justification. Yet there may be valid reasons to reduce congestion apart from its detrimental impact on persons' ability to participate in out-of-home activities. The arguments most often alluded to in societal debates and the academic literature address economic growth and environmental quality (see also Martens 2016). That is, it is (implicitly) argued that the promotion of economic growth or the protection of environmental quality is a sufficient justification for a taxation scheme to finance interventions to alleviate congestion. It is beyond the scope of this book to provide a full account of possible justifications for such interventions, but some observations are in order.

First, it is important to underscore again that all interventions that fall into the domain of sufficiency and are not fully self-financing cannot be financed through the fair taxation scheme outlined in the previous section. Indeed, the funds collected through the fair taxation scheme are solely intended to address the plight of persons experiencing an accessibility level below the sufficiency threshold. The financing of interventions that seek to reduce congestion for other reasons than fairness, thus needs to be based on a separate taxation scheme. The funds collected through the fair taxation scheme should be earmarked for interventions in the domain of insufficiency only.

Second, interventions in the transportation system that seek to alleviate congestion in order to promote economic growth or environmental quality are only warranted if these interventions outperform other types of interventions that may stimulate economic growth or improve environmental quality (such as subsidies for research and development in case of economic development or environmental regulations in case of environmental quality). After all, transport interventions are only one possible means to promote economic growth or environmental quality and should therefore be systematically compared to other types of interventions with the same goals (Hill 1973). Given the high costs of typical congestion alleviation measures, such as road widening or road construction, this suggests that interventions to reduce congestion may be less warranted than is often suggested.

Third, as in the case of self-financing facilities or services, interventions that are not fully self-financing should live up to the condition mentioned above: that these interventions are only legitimate as long as they have no detrimental impact on the accessibility levels experienced by persons with already poor accessibility levels. This is so because the argument developed in this book has established, as strongly as possible, that sufficient accessibility should be seen as a right or entitlement of members in a fair society. This implies that actions that impinge on these rights are not acceptable, at least in principle. Following this claim, congestion-reducing interventions that would negatively affect the accessibility of persons below the sufficiency threshold are only acceptable if these interventions are compensated by adequate measures. This requirement has two possible consequences. First, it will substantially increase the costs of traditional measures to mitigate congestion because they may have to be combined with other measures improving accessibility for persons without access to a car, suggesting again that these traditional interventions to reduce congestion may be less desirable than often presented in political debates. Second, it suggests that it may well be preferable to solve congestion through interventions that directly benefit persons below the sufficiency threshold, because only in this case would it be possible to co-finance congestion alleviation interventions through the funds collected with the fair taxation scheme. This, in turn, would increase the attractiveness of alternative measures to alleviate congestion, such as employer-provided transportation or priority lanes for public transport services.

These observations are not intended to rule out any improvements in the transportation system for other reasons than considerations of justice alone. Clearly, interventions in the transportation system may generate substantial benefits in terms of economic growth, particularly in (rapidly) developing countries, benefits that may well go beyond the benefits of interventions in other domains of society. If this is the case, improvements in the transportation system can be easily justified and based on a (regular income) taxation scheme that is distinct from the fair taxation scheme outlined above. Yet in these cases too, it is of crucial importance to continuously track and assess the consequences of such investments for accessibility patterns across population groups and to give preference where possible to inclusive interventions serving a wide range of persons over investments catering for a limited group of persons. Such inclusive interventions may obviously consist of a package of measures that, taken together, serve the entire range of population groups. It should also be acknowledged that the situation will be quite different for highly-developed societies. The argument developed above suggests that in such societies it will be much harder to justify interventions in the transportation system based on the expected economic benefits alone. Indeed, advanced economies typically have highly developed transportation systems that have largely exhausted the network effect to generate productivity gains (Preston 2001). Under such conditions, economic growth may be more effectively stimulated through other means.

If the above lines of argumentation are accepted, one cannot dispute the claim that most interventions in the transportation system over the past decades in highly-developed countries, which have usually been justified on grounds of economic development and sometimes on grounds of environmental quality, have in fact been cases of transportation injustice. These interventions have typically enhanced the accessibility of persons above the sufficiency threshold (however defined), more often than not to the detriment of persons falling below the sufficiency threshold. The fact that these interventions have usually been financed through imperfect user fees (fuel taxes) and other proxies of user fees (road taxes) does not make them more justified. Even more, as argued above, such taxes are unjustified if they are higher than strictly necessary for covering the costs of capital investments in the existing infrastructures and the costs of operating and maintaining the existing transportation facilities and services. Indeed, the argument developed here suggests that these traditional taxes, to the extent that they have generated more funds than necessary to cover the costs related to the existing transportation system, should be perceived as an imperfect proxy of the fair taxation scheme outlined above. These excess funds should thus be used, first and foremost, for improving the situation of persons with accessibility levels below the sufficiency threshold, so that the transportation system can move towards a state of fairness over time.

Returning to Los Angeles

I started my journey at the beginning of this book with a brief account of the struggle for transportation justice in Los Angeles. It has taken a long journey to delineate an intuitively appealing principle of justice for the transportation domain: all members of society should be guaranteed a sufficient level of accessibility under most, but not all, circumstances. This principle has far-reaching consequences for the moral obligations persons have vis-à-vis each other, and thus for governments as the elected and democratically controlled vehicle for realizing these obligations. It obliges governments to enact a coercive taxation scheme to collect the funds necessary to guarantee all persons, under virtually all circumstances, a sufficient level of accessibility. This set of principles sheds a more radical light on the plight of the Bus Riders Union and the related court decision with which I opened the book.

First, the application of the principles to the Los Angeles case reveals that the justice of the court decision does not lie so much in the fact that it implied "the transfer of billions of dollars from a plan that disproportionately favored the wealthy to a plan that worked more to the benefit of the poor" (Soja 2010, p. viii). Justice in the domain of transportation is not about guaranteeing that funds are distributed in a proportional way over population groups, nor about a proper distribution of those funds over income groups. As argued in this book, justice in transportation is about providing sufficient accessibility to all under most circumstances, *irrespective* of income, ethnicity, gender, abilities, and so on. The justice of the court decision lies in the fact that it moved funds from car-owning population groups with typically high levels of accessibility provided through an extensive road system, to population groups with low levels of accessibility delivered by a crumbling bus service. Lacking the appropriate data on accessibility patterns across the Los Angeles metropolis, this is clearly a somewhat speculative statement, but given the extensive body of evidence on accessibility disparities collected in the spatial mismatch literature and other strands of research, it is probably not far off the mark.

Second, the principles developed in this book suggest that even the radical redistribution of the funds of the Los Angeles Metropolitan Transit Agency (MTA), from middle class suburbanites most probably enjoying sufficient levels of accessibility to low income minorities most likely suffering from insufficient accessibility, does not go far enough. While the Bus Riders Union and other members of the grass roots coalition were legally confined to the discriminatory practices of the MTA, morally their claim should have also addressed the (implicit and perhaps unintended) discriminatory practices of the Southern California Association of Governments (SCAG), the metropolitan planning organization giving direction to the investments in the entire transportation system in the Los Angeles region, affecting bus, rail, and roadway levels of service. Following the principles of justice laid down in this book, much of the investment in roads and commuter rail proposed by SCAG in its subsequent regional plans should be fully self-financing, perhaps through tolling schemes and public transport fares, while the investment funds collected through other tax schemes, such as sales taxes, should be dedicated to developing and operating a (public) transport system serving population groups now suffering sub-standard levels of accessibility and to subsidizing transportation expenses of persons lacking the income to purchase a sufficient level of accessibility. As progressive as the Los Angeles court decision may have been, the decision still fell short of the radical overhaul that would follow from the fundamentals of transportation planning based on principles of justice.

At the same time it could be argued that the principles of justice laid down in this book are not radical enough, because they do not rule out inequalities in other domains being reproduced in the domain of transportation. Following Young's influential analysis (Young 1990), it could be argued that transportation planning based on principles of justice ignores the powerful processes of domination and oppression that systematically disadvantage particular groups in society, such as ethnic minorities, women, and lesbian, gay, bisexual and transgender persons. By only requiring the provision of a sufficient level of accessibility to all members of society, and thus allowing for substantial disparities in accessibility levels, transportation planning based on principles of justice is highly likely to deliver only minimal, albeit sufficient, levels of accessibility to persons already disadvantaged in other dimensions. In other words, it could be argued that the principles propagated in this book are not radical enough, as they only codify existing injustices in the domain of transportation.

I have two responses to this criticism. First, the systematic implementation of the proposed principles in the practice of transportation planning will at least reduce the existing disparities in the domain of transportation, with possible positive benefits in terms of employment, better health, and stronger social relationships for persons thus affected. Second, and more importantly, justice clearly does not only require a fair transportation system. It demands fairness across the entire range of domains or 'spheres' that shape a person's life opportunities. It would be mistaken to assume that injustices in one domain can simply be undone or compensated for through interventions in another domain. Such forms of compensation would misunderstand the social meaning of goods whose distribution is at stake (cf. Walzer 1983). Precisely because goods have distinct social meanings, and persons thus have reasons to value these goods, compensation between spheres should only be accepted if it enables a person to obtain a fair 'amount' of the socially valued good. Translated to transportation, and as argued in Chapter 6, financial transfers are acceptable if they provide persons with the additional means to purchase a sufficient level of accessibility. They do not promote justice if they merely constitute a financial compensation for a level of accessibility that cannot be brought up to the sufficiency level in any way. Likewise, a level of accessibility far above the sufficiency threshold cannot compensate for an unfair level of income or for discrimination on the job market. Thus the fact that transportation planning based on principles of justice may reproduce existing injustices in other domains does not imply that the principles underlying the approach are flawed, but only underlines that the search for transportation justice is but a small part of the struggle for a just society.

The struggle for transportation justice, so heroically fought in Los Angeles, has a long challenge ahead. It is probably not an overstatement to claim that most cities and regions around the world, perhaps with the exception of cities with an extremely well-developed and fairly priced public transport service, currently lack a fair transportation system. As Soja rightfully points out, the emergence of these unfair transportation systems over the past decades is not necessarily the result of "evil people intentionally making ... biased decisions" (Soja 2010, p. xvi). As Soja argues, all it required were "well-trained experts following conventional procedures" to generate decisions and plans that almost inevitably favored already highly-mobile persons (ibid.).

The ambition of this book has been to develop an alternative approach to these conventional procedures, an approach firmly rooted in well-founded principles of justice, so that well-trained experts following these alternative procedures can contribute to a fair transportation system. If governments take the constitutive interests of every person seriously, as arguably they should, then transportation planning has to be based on such principles of justice. Justice cannot be an add-on to the regular transportation planning process, nor a 'niche' on the research agenda. It can only be, and should be, a foundational component of transportation planning and thus a guiding force for both education and research in the transport domain.

It is my conviction that the systematic application of the 'rules' of transportation planning based on principles of justice over time will lead to the emergence of fair transportation systems in cities and regions across the world.

References

Daniels, N. (1996). *Justice and Justification*. Cambridge, Cambridge University Press.

Eliasson, J. (2014). Opportunities for transport financing through new technologies. In: Elliott D. Sclar, Måns Lönnroth and Christian Wolmar (eds), *Urban Access for the 21st Century: finance and governance models for transport infrastructure*. Oxon/NewYork, Routledge, pp. 118–145.

Goldman, T. and M. Wachs (2003). A quiet revolution in transportation finance: the rise of local option transportation taxes. *Transportation Quarterly*, 57: 19–32.

Goodwin, P.B. (1997). Solving congestion (when we must not build roads, increase spending, lose votes, damage the economy or harm the environment, and will never find equilibrium). Inaugural Lecture for the Professorship of Transport Policy, ESRC Transport Studies Unit, University College London.

Hill, M. (1973). *Planning for Multiple Objectives: an approach to the evaluation of transportation plans*. Philadelphia, PA, Regional Science Research Institute.

Kirk, R.S. and W.J. Mallett (2013). *Funding and Financing Highways and Public Transportation*. Washington, Congressional Research Service.

Martens, K. (2013). *On fair financing in the transport domain*. Paper presented at the RGS-IBG Annual International Conference, 28–30 August 2013, London, UK.

Martens, K. (2015). *Traditional transportation planning and its alternatives*. Paper presented at the 94th Annual Meeting of the Transportation Research Board, 10–15 January 2015, Washington DC.

Martens, K. (2016). Why accessibility measurement is not merely an option, but an absolute necessity. In: C. Silva, L. Bertolini and N. Pinto (eds) *Designing accessibility instruments: lessons on their usability for integrated land use and transport planning practices*. New York/Oxford, Routledge.

Mattingly, K. and J. Morrissey (2014). Housing and transport expenditure: socio-spatial indicators of affordability in Auckland. *Cities*, 38(0): 69–83.

Preston, J. (2001). Integrating transport with socio-economic activity – a research agenda for the new millennium. *Journal of Transport Geography*, 9(1): 13–24.

Rawls, J. (1971). *A Theory of Justice.* Cambridge, MA, Harvard University Press.

Soja, E.W. (2010). *Seeking Spatial Justice.* Minneapolis, University of Minnesota Press.

Taylor, B.D. and A.T. Norton (2009). Paying for transportation: what's a fair price? *Journal of Planning Literature*, 24(1): 22–36.

Verhoef, E.T. and H. Mohring (2009). Self-financing roads. *International Journal of Sustainable Transportation*, 3(5-6): 293–311.

Walker, G. (2008). Decentralised systems and fuel poverty: are there any links or risks? *Energy Policy*, 36(12): 4514–4517.

Walzer, M. (1983). *Spheres of Justice: a defense of pluralism and equality*, New York, Basic Books.

Young, I.M. (1990). *Justice and the Politics of Difference.* Princeton, NJ, Princeton University Press.

Index